East Asian Economic Integration: A China-ASEAN Perspective

WANG Liqin

Paths International Ltd

社会科学文献出版社
SOCIAL SCIENCES ACADEMIC PRESS (CHINA)

To my mother and mother-in-law

About the Author

Liqin, WANG, joined the lecturing staff at the School of Political Science and International Relations, Tongji University in 2012. Previously, she got her Ph.D. from the Department of Politics and International Studies, University of Hull, the United Kingdom (2008/09-2012/01). Her main research interests are in the field of international political economy (IPE) with a special interest in trade and investment in East Asia (with a particular focus on China and ASEAN) and the economic integration in East Asia. Her main theoretical and analytical interests lie in (neo) liberal institutionalism, policy analysis of China (with a special focus on economic diplomacy) and varieties of regionalism/regionalization in East Asia. She can be reached at wangliqin@tongji.edu.cn.

Abstract

East Asian regionalism substantially intensified after the 1997-8 Asian Financial Crisis (AFC), which was a significant research case and an increasingly emerging issue of new regionalism after the Cold War ended in the early 1990s. In contrast with business-led regionalization, government-led regionalism was the key way leading to East Asian economic integration, of which bilateral governmental economic cooperation between China and ASEAN was the substance.

The book explores China's shifting role in economic cooperation with ASEAN before and after its WTO accession in 2001 within a theoretical framework of complex interdependence. In the bilateral interdependent economic relations, China became a mutual complementary partner of ASEAN from a natural competitor; and became a foreign direct investment (FDI) source of ASEAN from a net recipient after the WTO accession. This laid a sound basis for China to be well placed as the leader in East Asian economic integration.

The book investigates the motives that prompted China to shift its attitude towards economic cooperation with ASEAN (clearly illustrated by China's initiative of the China-ASEAN Free Trade Area (CAFTA) proposal in 2001) from a Chinese perspective. China's grand strategy, which highlighted the neighbours' stability and prosperity in political sense and exploration of regional markets in neighbour countries in economic sense, was the radical motives. In addition, Beijing desired to diminish the two domestic problems: the disparity between East and West China and the gap between the urban and rural areas by enhancing economic cooperation with ASEAN. This, as the key motive, induced China's shifting attitude towards economic cooperation with ASEAN and towards economic integration in East Asia.

This book contributed to the second wave of regionalism studies after the 1997-8 AFC by examining the implications of China's domestic politics on regionalism in East Asian case from a Chinese inward-looking perspective.

Liqin, WANG

July, 2014

Acknowledgement

The book is based on my doctoral thesis, which I did during my PhD period from September 2008 to November 2011 at the Department of Politics and International Studies, University of Hull, the United Kingdom. I would like to express my cordial gratitude to people who supported me academically, spiritually and financially.

First of all, I am grateful to my first doctoral supervisor Dr. Mahrukh Doctor and my second supervisor, Dr. Xiudian Dai. Dr. Doctor instructed me to do this thesis from scratches. She helped me raise the main research questions, reviewed the thesis word by word and gave me constructive comments and suggestions for revision. Dr. Dai helped me to find an appropriate research method to deal with the special case of China, based on his wealth of research experience on China and his familiarity with the academic environment in China. In a word, while my mother gave me the physical life, Dr. Doctor and Dr. Dai gave me the academic life.

I owe special thanks to Prof. Lu Minghua, Prof. Hong Yousheng, Prof. Ji Qiufeng and Prof. Zhu Yingquan at Nanjing University in China for their steadfast encouragement and support. Their spiritual encouragement and practical support made me brave enough to complete this PhD studies alone, abroad.

I would like to extend my thanks to the University of Hull and China Scholarship Council, from which I obtained a scholarship. Their financial support for my PhD studies relieved me from financial worries, which was important in enabling me to finish my studies on time. Moreover, I would like to thank Tongji University with the project of '2013 High Level Publication of Humanities and Social Sciences' and Shanghai Planning Office of Philosophy and Social Science (Sh-POPSS) with the 'Translation Project of the Shanghai Chinese Humanities and Social Sciences Academic Boutique' for their financial support publishing of the book. In addition, I appreciate the help from Ms. Liang Yanling and Ms. Liang Ke at the Social Science Academic Press (China) and people at the Path International Ltd. (UK), who made the dream of publishing the book come true.

Last but the most important, I owe deep and sincere thanks to my family. My husband, Xiaochun, took all the responsibility/burden of my family after I left. My mother and mother-in-law took good care of my son (who was only 14 months old when I left) in such a harmony that I was so moved during the three years of my stay in the UK. Their unconditional love for me is what I could never pay back to them!

All cordial thanks,

Liqin, WANG

24 July, 2014

Abbreviation

AATC	Agreement on Accelerated Tariff Elimination
ACBC	ASEAN-China Business Council
ACC	ASEAN Chamber of Commerce
ACIA	ASEAN Comprehensive Investment Agreement
ADBI	Asian Development Bank Institute
ADSM	Agreement on Dispute Settlement Mechanism
AEC	ASEAN Economic Community
AEM	ASEAN Economic Ministerial Meeting
AFC	Asian financial crisis
AFTA	ASEAN Free Trade Area
AIA	ASEAN Investment Area
AJCEP	ASEAN-Japan Comprehensive Economic Partnership Agreement
AMM	ASEAN Ministerial Meeting
APEC	Asia-Pacific Economic Cooperation organization
ARATS	Association for Relations across the Taiwan Strait
ARF	ASEAN Regional Forum
ASC	ASEAN Standing Committee
ASEAN	The Association of Southeast Asian Nations
ASEAN+1	ASEAN plus China/Japan/South Korea
ASEAN+3	ASEAN plus China, Japan and South Korea
ASEAN+6	ASEAN plus China, Japan, South Korea and Australia, New Zealand and India
ASEAN-5	Indonesia, Malaysia, the Philippines, Singapore, Thailand
ASEAN-6	six old ASEAN members (Brunei, Indonesia, Malaysia, the Philippines, Singapore, Thailand)
ASEAN-CCI	ASEAN Federation of Commerce and Industry
ATG	Agreement on Trade in Goods
ATS	Agreement on Trade in Service
BCLMV	Brunei, Cambodia, Laos, Myanmar and Vietnam
BNCCI	Brunei National Chamber of Commerce & Industry
BRIC	Brazil, Russia, India and China

CABIS	China-ASEAN Business and Investment Summit
CAExpo	China-ASEAN Expo
CAFTA	China-ASEAN Free Trade Area
CASAS	China Association of Southeast Asian Studies
CCC	Cambodia Chamber of Commerce
CCPIT	China Council for Promotion of International Trade
CEPA	Closer Economic Partnership Agreement
CEPEA	Comprehensive Economic Partnership in East Asia
CEPT	Common Effective Preferential Tariff
CIT	Complex Interdependence Theory
CICIR	China Institute of Contemporary International Relations
CLMV	four newer ASEAN members (Cambodia, Laos, Myanmar and VietNam)
CMI	Chiang Mai Initiative
COTT	Committee on Trade & Tourism
CPC	Communist Party of China
DPP	Democratic Progressive Party
EAC	East Asian Community
EAEC	East Asia Economic Caucus
EAEG	East Asia Economic Group
EAFTA	East Asian Free Trade Area
EAS	East Asia Summit
EASG	East Asian Studies Group
EAVG	East Asian Vision Group
ECFA	Economic Cooperation Framework Agreement
ECSC	European Coal and Steel Community
EEC	European Economic Community
EGEC	Expert Group on Economic Cooperation
EHP	Early Harvest Plan
EL	Exclusive List
EPG	Eminent Persons Group
EURATOM	European Atomic Energy Community
EVSL	Early Voluntary Sectoral Liberalization

FDI	foreign direct investment
Framework Agreement/CA-FACEC	Framework Agreement on Comprehensive Economic Cooperation between China and ASEAN
FTA	free trade area
FTI	the Federation of Thai Industries
GATT	General Agreement on Tariff and Trade
GDP	gross domestic product
GMS	Greater Mekong Sub-region
GMT	Grounded Theory Method
GNP	gross national product
GWD	greater Western development
HS	Harmonized Commodity Description and Coding System
IA	Investment Agreement
ICCI	Indonesia Chamber of Commerce and Industry
IL	Inclusive List
JACEP	Japan-ASEAN Comprehensive Economic Partnership
JAPIT	Association for the Promotion of International Trade, Japan
JCC	Joint Cooperation Committee
JCETC	Joint Committee on Economic Trade Cooperation
JCST	Joint Committee on Science and Technology
KA-FACEC	Framework Agreement on Comprehensive Economic Cooperation between South Korea and ASEAN
KAFTA	South Korea-ASEAN Free Trade Area
KOTRA	Trade-Investment Promotion Agency
LNCCI	Laos National Chamber of Commerce & Industry
MFA	Ministry of Foreign Affairs
MFN	Most Favoured Nation
MNCs	multi-national corporations
MOA	Ministry of Agriculture
MOC	Ministry of Commerce
MOFTEC	Ministry of Foreign Trade and Economic Cooperation
MOP	Margin of Preference

MOU	Memorandum of Understanding
MTNs	Multilateral Trade Negotiations
NAFTA	North America Free Trade Area
NCCE	Nanning (China-ASEAN) Commodity Exchange
NCCIM	National Chamber of Commerce and Industry, Malaysia
NDRC	National Development and Reforms Commission
NEAT	Network of the East Asian Think Tank
NGO	non-governmental organization
NIEs	newly industrializing economies
NSC	New Security Concept
NTBs	non-tariff barriers
PBG	Pan-Beibu Gulf
PCCI	Philippine Chamber of Commerce and Industry
PLA	People's Liberation Army
PPI	Promotion and Protection of Investment
PRC	People's Republic of China
PTA	preferential trade agreement
RCA	revealed comparative advantage
REITI	Research Institute of Economy, Trade and Industry
RMB	Ren Min Bi
ROC	Republic of China
SASAC	State-Owned Assets Supervision and Administration Commission
SAR	Special Administrative Region
SBF	Singapore Business Federation
SEF	the Strait Exchange Foundation
SEZ	Special economic zone
SITC	Standard International Trade Code
SMEs	small-and-medium enterprises
SOEs	State-owned Enterprises
TAC	Treaty of Amity and Cooperation
TNCs	transnational corporations
TNC-WGI	Trade Negotiations Committee Working Group on Investment

TPP	Trans-Pacific Partnership
UMFCCI	The Union of Myanmar Federation of Chambers of Commerce and Industry
VCCI	Vietnam Chamber of Commerce and Industry
WTO	World Trade Organization

List of Tables and Figures

List of Tables

Figures

1 Introduction

The end of the Cold War in the early 1990s and the Asian financial crisis in the late 1990s had significant impact on the evolution of regionalism in East Asia. First and foremost, the end of the Cold War disentangled countries in East Asia from the political tensions of the two camps and made it possible for them to cooperate on economic issues. Besides, the 1997-1998 Asian Financial Crisis (1997-8 AFC) highlighted the need for joint cooperation among countries in East Asia in order to address any future crisis. It was during the 1997-8 AFC that East Asian countries built the cooperative frameworks of ASEAN[1]+1 (China/Japan/South Korea) and ASEAN+3 (China, Japan and South Korea), where they first worked to overcome the crisis and later to promote economic integration in East Asia. The past decade witnessed the progress of economic integration in East Asia. Bilateral free trade areas were set up or in the process of cooperation respectively between ASEAN and China, ASEAN and South Korea and ASEAN and Japan. However, an all inclusive East Asian free trade area was still a vision and a future mission.

The book considers the following two main research questions. The first question is: why did China change its attitude towards economic cooperation with ASEAN at the turn of the century? The second question is: what kinds of features of regional economic integration in East Asia are illustrated by the specific economic cooperation between China and ASEAN, given the latter was the substance of the former? To answer the first question, there are three sub questions: 1. what role did China play in trade cooperation with ASEAN before and after 2001? 2. What role did China play in investment cooperation with ASEAN before and after 2001? And 3.What motives prompted China to change its attitude towards economic cooperation with ASEAN?

As far as the first research question is concerned, the book analyses it by comparing China's trade and investment policy, Sino-ASEAN trade and investment relations and China's role in trade and investment cooperation with ASEAN before and after 2001. Beijing shifted its trade policy focus from the international level to the regional level after its accession to the WTO in 2001; it enhanced trade cooperation with ASEAN by establishing the China-ASEAN Free Trade Area (CAFTA) and it became a trade complementary partner of ASEAN. Beijing stressed attracting foreign investment from ASEAN by

---

[1] The Association of Southeast Asian Nations (ASEAN) was set up in August 1967, in Bangkok, Thailand, with the signing of the ASEAN Declaration (Bangkok Declaration) by five founding members-the Republic of Indonesia (Indonesia), Malaysia, the Republic of the Philippines (the Philippines), the Republic of Singapore (Singapore)and the Kingdom of Thailand (Thailand). Later Brunei Darussalam (Brunei) then joined on 7 January 1984, the Socialist Republic of Vietnam (Vietnam) on 28 July 1995, the Lao People's Democratic Republic (Lao) and the Union of Myanmar (Myanmar) on 23 July 1997, and the Kingdom of Cambodia (Cambodia) on 30 April 1999, making up what is today the ten Member States of ASEAN.

implementing the 'bringing in' policy during the 1990s, and then shifted to encourage Chinese enterprises to invest overseas by implementing the 'going out' policy during the 2000s. It promoted investment cooperation with ASEAN and turned from a net Foreign Direct Investment (FDI) recipient from ASEAN during the 1990s to be one of the key sources of FDI in ASEAN during the 2000s.

Comparing China's role in economic cooperation with ASEAN laid a sound basis for exploring China's motives for shifting its attitude towards economic cooperation with ASEAN at the turn of the century. The book, from a Chinese perspective, argues that three factors were instrumental in prompting China to shift its attitude towards economic cooperation with ASEAN. The radical motive derived from China's grand political and economic strategy. The former, in form of regional diplomacy, underlined the significance of ASEAN on China's political stability and economic stability and development at home; the latter highlighted the weakness of the WTO framework and attempted to explore regional markets in East Asia as the second step after China's entry into the WTO. In addition, Beijing dwelt on two domestic problems caused by the intensified economic reform at home: the increasing disparity between the east and west part of China and the growing gap between the urban and rural areas. Beijing hoped to eliminate the two imbalances with resort to the enhanced economic cooperation with ASEAN in consideration of the geographical proximity of ASEAN and Southwest China and the complementarity on agriculture between China and ASEAN.

As to the second research question, the book argues that China was a *de facto* non-hegemonic leader in economic integration in East Asia. However, China had no intention of playing such a leading role in it. This led to the lack of a leader in regional economic integration in East Asia. ASEAN acted as the engine for regional economic integration in East Asia by diverting its inward-looking economic policy to an outward-looking one after the 1997-8 AFC. However, ASEAN preferred to promote regional economic integration in an incremental way and prioritized the economic integration in Southeast Asia over that in East Asia. This made ASEAN a weak engine for regional economic integration in East Asia. Comparison between regionalism and regionalization in East Asia illustrates that state-led regionalism was the key factor in economic integration in East Asia; business-led regionalization was the supplementary way even if the pragmatic direction of East Asian integration. Contrast between bilateralism and multilateralism in East Asia indicates that bilateralism was the essential substructure of the regional order and the key inter-state interaction at the current stage of East Asian economic integration, although multilateralism was emerging and burgeoning.

Next, it is important to clarify what is meant by East Asia. Sometimes it was asserted that Asia-Pacific (Lloyd, 2002) (Rajan, 2005) (Wanadi, 2004) or Asia (Hamilton-Hart, 2003) (Frost, 2008) (Katzenstein, Hamilton-Hart, Kato, & Yue, 2000) (Zhang, 2009), instead of East Asia, was where regionalism sprang up after the Cold War ended. Sometimes when East Asia (Liu & Régnier, 2003) (Lincoln, 2004) (Dent, 2008) was defined as the geographical scope where regionalism emerged in the east of the world, it was argued that East Asia should refer to all the national/regional/sub-regional actors who are located geographically in East Asia. Whatever the terminology used- East Asia, Asia or Asia-Pacific-they all are knots on the string of regionalism in the east of the world. For the purpose of this book, given the fact that three bilateral free trade areas were negotiated and established between Southeast Asia and Northeast Asia during the 2000s, East Asia makes more sense than Asia or Asia-Pacific. However, this does not exclude the possibility that integration will expand and reach Asia/Asia-Pacific in the future. This book uses the term East Asia to refer to the actors at the governmental or sub-regional level of People's Republic of China (hereafter China), Japan and the Republic of Korea (hereafter South Korea) in Northeast Asia, as well as the members of ASEAN in Southeast Asia, which actually constitute the elements of the cooperative framework of ASEAN plus Three (ASEAN+3). This has a more political sense than a geographical sense because it is these four actors who were the key participants in East Asian regionalism during the past decade.

East Asian regionalism includes a variety of contents such as trade cooperation, investment cooperation, financial cooperation, sub regional cooperation, etc. Among them, finance was the first area on which East Asian cooperation focused. This was because of the urgent needs within the general context of the 1997-8 AFC. After the crisis, East Asian countries found that the financial area was not a workable starting area for regional cooperation. They shifted their cooperation to trade and investment areas, often the traditional start of regional integration. Meanwhile, sub regional integration also developed. It covered two great programmes, which were the Greater Mekong Sub-regional (GMS) Programme, initiated by the Asian Development Bank (ADB) in 1992, and the Pan-Beibu Gulf (PBG) programme, initiated by China in 2007. After development over a decade, East Asian regionalism made great progress in various areas. This helped East Asian countries to survive the crisis, increase the economic interdependence among them, and reinforce East Asia's status in the world. However, trade and investment cooperation remained the key areas where regional economic integration proliferated. Therefore, trade and investment cooperation is the focus of this research.

The driving force for East Asian regionalism came from both the increasing economic interdependence of countries in East Asia, the impetus provided by the great powers in East Asia and ASEAN's coordination and cooperation. After the 1997-8 AFC, East Asian countries enhanced their financial, trade and investment cooperation, which increased their mutual interdependence among them; great powers such as China, South Korea and Japan took the initiatives to set up bilateral FTA with ASEAN, which supplied driving force for East Asian regionalism; and ASEAN diverted its focus of economic policy to cooperation with partners in East Asia, which, acted in concert with three economic partners in Northeast Asia. Therefore, the driving force of East Asian regionalism derives not only from the mutual interdependence at the regional level but also from the economic and political motivations of actors at the national/sub regional level.

Nevertheless, essentially, bilateral economic cooperation between China and ASEAN comprised the substance of East Asian regionalism. Firstly, China created the economic and political domino effect (Ravenhill, 2010, p. 11) of proliferating free trade agreements in East Asia by acting as the first one who proposed to set up the CAFTA with ASEAN. This exerted pressure for Japan and South Korea to enhance their economic cooperation with ASEAN. Shortly after China's proposal of the CAFTA, Japan and South Korea also put forth their proposals to set up FTAs with ASEAN and finally, after China endorsed the Framework Agreement with ASEAN in November 2002, they also signed free trade agreements with ASEAN in December 2005 and April 2008 respectively. Secondly, among the three, China was the only one who aimed at 'strengthening cooperation and supporting economic stability in East Asia', besides 'creating a partnership between parties.' (Framework Agreement on Comprehensive Economic Cooperation between ASEAN and China, 2002) China's focus was not limited to improving the bilateral relationship between China and ASEAN by establishing the CAFTA; it also took into consideration the overall economic stability in East Asia, which Japan and South Korea ignored to some extent. Thirdly, China, Japan and South Korea each promised to give special treatment and flexibility to the newer ASEAN members (Cambodia, Laos, Myanmar and Vietnam) in their free trade agreements with ASEAN; however, only China actually managed it. China applied most favoured nation (MFN) treatment to the four newer ASEAN members, who were not World Trade Organization (WTO) members at the time. Finally, in regard to the agricultural cooperation on which ASEAN placed much emphasis, only China gave it relatively high priority. Among China's five priority cooperation areas with ASEAN, agricultural cooperation ranked first; it ranked tenth (Agreement on Comprehensive Economic Partnership among Japan and Member States of ASEAN, 2008) of thirteen priority cooperation areas between Japan and ASEAN and finally it narrowly focused on information exchange, capacity building, joint research and technical assistance (Framework Agreement on Comprehensive Economic Cooperation between Korea and ASEAN, 2005) instead of tariff reduction in the agreement between South Korea and ASEAN. Thus, the bilateral economic cooperation between China and ASEAN became the substance of East Asian regionalism, given the aforementioned four reasons. It is the Sino-ASEAN bilateral economic cooperation and China's role in it that are the focus of the book.

China and ASEAN enhanced their bilateral economic cooperation on trade and investment at the turn of the century. After the 1997-8 AFC, ASEAN placed much emphasis on mutual cooperation with external partners outside of Southeast Asia to fight against any future crisis. China stood at the gate of the WTO after finishing key negotiations with the United States and European Union in 2000. The coming accession of China to the WTO triggered ASEAN's worries. On the one hand, ASEAN was very worried that once China joined the WTO, abundant and cheap Chinese exports would have freer access to the Western markets and compete with ASEAN's exports there; on the other hand, ASEAN was afraid that China would crowd out ASEAN's FDI flows from the developed economies because China was a much more attractive investment destination in comparison with ASEAN. In order to diminish ASEAN's worries, China put forth the proposal to set up the CAFTA and enhance bilateral economic cooperation between China and ASEAN in a hope of sharing the bonus of WTO-accession together with ASEAN.

Usually, the year 2000 or 2001 has been applied as the key watershed for studies of China's economic policy towards ASEAN. Some scholars picked 2000 (Wang, 2005, p. 56) (Zhao, 2002, p. 28) (Wang Y. , 2003, p. 59) because Zhu Rongji, China's premier at the time, proposed 'in the long term, China and the ASEAN countries can also further explore the establishment of a free trade relationship' (Zhu, 2000) at the 4th ASEAN-China Leaders Summit in Singapore in November 2000. This was seen as a signal of China's economic policy's shift from the international level to the regional level. Others applied 2001 (Sheng, 2003) (Lloyd, 2002) because Zhu Rongji clearly stated China's desire 'to promote the establishment of the CAFTA' (Zhu, 2001) at the 5th ASEAN-China Leaders Summit in Brunei in November 2001. At this summit, ASEAN also agreed on the establishment of the CAFTA within ten years (that is by 2010). This book applies 2001 as the critical time moment with two justifications. First, China entered the WTO in 2001, which was a prerequisite to establish the CAFTA with ASEAN. China's entry into the WTO was a new start for China's economic liberalization and privatization at home. It constructed a platform where China and ASEAN could negotiate to set up the FTA with the guidance of rules and regulations within the framework of the WTO. Secondly, ASEAN and China agreed to set up the CAFTA in 2001; thereafter both sides dedicated ten years to the establishment of the CAFTA. This changed China's role in economic cooperation with ASEAN and its role in economic integration in East Asia as well.

The book has seven main chapters to analyze the two main research questions. Chapter One provides an extensive literature review about the origin, driving forces, norms and key concepts of new regionalism, the theoretical frameworks of economic integration and their relevance to new regionalism in East Asia and China's role in bilateral economic cooperation with ASEAN. Chapter Two consists of a theoretical part and a methodological part. The former addresses the evolution, key concepts and main assumptions of the complex interdependence theory and its relevance to Sino-ASEAN economic relationship and to China. The latter presents why and how the grounded theory method was applied in this book to collect and analyse data.

Chapter Three presents the changes of general context and the subsequent changes of ASEAN's economic policy in order to assess the background for economic cooperation between China and ASEAN. The chapter finds that the end of the Cold War, the 1997-8 AFC and China's accession to the WTO played significant roles in stimulating ASEAN and China to shift their economic policy towards each other. ASEAN's economic policy diverted from an inward-looking focus to an outward-looking one after the 1997-8 AFC, which highlighted the significance of economic cooperation with external partners. China's entry into the WTO caused ASEAN's worries about its possible negative impacts. In order to eliminate ASEAN's worries, China took the initiative to set up the CAFTA, which was accepted by ASEAN in 2001.

Chapters Four and Five explore China's role in trade cooperation and investment cooperation with ASEAN before and after 2001, following a similar structure. Chapter Four explores China's trade policy, Sino-ASEAN trade relations before and after 2001 and specifically discusses the issue whether China and ASEAN were competitive on markets in western countries. Chapter Five explores China's investment policy, Sino-ASEAN investment relations before and after 2001 and specifically analyzes whether China crowded out ASEAN's FDI flows from the developed economies after its accession to the WTO in 2001. Each chapter addresses one of ASEAN's two worries about the potential implications of China's accession to the WTO for ASEAN's trade and investment status.

Chapter Six looks in-depth into the motives that caused China to shift its attitude towards economic cooperation with ASEAN before and after 2001 from a Chinese perspective. Two domestic problems in China are taken into consideration. One is the increasing development gap between Eastern and Western part of China; the other is the growing disparity between the urban and rural areas. These two daunting problems, resulting from the intense domestic reforms, had prevailed for decades after the 'open door' policy was implemented in the late 1970s. These problems had to be appropriately addressed; otherwise there was a risk of deterioration in the future. Part of West China is located adjacent to ASEAN, most members of which are mainly agricultural economies. This encouraged China to cooperate with ASEAN on economic issues as a measure to further boost China's opening up and help solve domestic problems resulting from reforms.

While all the previous chapters are studies at the national level, the last chapter provides an analysis of East Asian regionalism at the regional level. The studies on bilateral economic cooperation between China and ASEAN in the previous chapters lay a solid basis for further research on East Asian regionalism, in that the former is the substance of the latter. On the basis of analysis of bilateral economic cooperation between China and ASEAN, the last chapter summarizes the features of East Asian regionalism during the past decade, supplemented by other two sets of bilateral economic cooperation respectively between Japan and ASEAN, and South Korea and ASEAN. In Chapter Seven, China and ASEAN's role are further clarified based on their positions in East Asian regionalism. In addition, regionalism versus regionalization and bilateralism versus multilateralism in East Asia are described in detail and future prospects for East Asian economic integration are considered.

2 Literature Review

2.1 Introduction

Western Europe, North America and East Asia are three major regional integration processes developing in parallel in today's world. In the wake of the economic miracle in East Asia in the early 1990s, the fulcrum of the world economy gradually diverted from the west to the east. East Asia, as a rising region, attracted scholars' attention. A vast body of literature reflected their interest on the new regionalism in East Asia, which emerged shortly after the Cold War ended, was driven by the 1997-8 AFC and was accelerated by China's proposal for the CAFTA in 2001. Among factors that promoted East Asian regionalism, China's shifting attitude towards regional economic cooperation was the most important. Before China initiated the proposal to set up the CAFTA in 2001, China played an inactive role in regional economic cooperation in East Asia. After the proposal, China took active participation in promoting regional economic integration in the region. The year 2001 was not the watershed for China's attitude toward regional cooperation in East Asia. However, on 6th November 2001, China's former premier, Zhu Rongji, officially proposed to set up the CAFTA at the 5th ASEAN-China Leaders Summit in Brunei. This more or less sent a signal of China's policy shift. China's proactive participation in regional economic integration in East Asia constituted the most effective factor for economic cooperation in the region.

In order to explore a.) China's role in economic cooperation with ASEAN in particular and in regional economic integration in East Asia in general; b.) China's motives for shifting its attitude towards regional economic cooperation in East Asian and c.) the features of East Asian regionalism embodied through bilateral economic cooperation between China and ASEAN during the first decade of the 2000s, the author collected relevant Chinese-language and English-language sources. As far as Chinese-language sources are concerned, the author searched fifteen kinds of the most relevant periodicals from 1991 to 2010, including the *World Economics and Politics, Contemporary International Relations, Southeast Asia Studies* and so on. As far as English-language sources are concerned, the author found after the 1997-8 AFC, many academic periodicals, based variously in Australia, Canada, South Korea, Singapore, the United Kingdom, the United States and Hong Kong, opened specific columns to discuss the newly emerging regionalism in East Asia. Based on the number of citations, the author listed sixteen periodicals on international politics/international economy/area studies in this region and six countries, whose databases were available and searched them to collect English-language sources from 1991 to 2010. English-language sources included *Review of International Political Economy, International Relations of Asia-Pacific, Contemporary Southeast Asia* and so forth. In addition, the author also collected related monographs, newspapers and official websites to search for sources for studies on regionalism in East Asia.

Both Chinese-language and English-language publications showed scholars' studies on East Asian regionalism focused on four broad fields as follows:

● The origins, driving forces and norms of the new regionalism and several key concepts

● Theoretical studies on new regionalism in East Asia

● China-ASEAN relations in particular and China's role in economic integration in East Asia in general

The author, in this chapter, summarizes what is known about East Asian regionalism, finds out what we do not know and identifies a gap which this book tries to fill.

2.2 The Origin, Driving Forces, Norms and Key Concepts of New Regionalism in East Asia

The 1990s witnessed the emergence and flourishing of the first wave[2] of academic studies on regionalism. English-language publications showed that Western scholars launched second wave in the late 1990s, based on the new topics in the wake of the 1997-8 AFC attracting much of their attention. Chinese-language publications showed that Chinese scholars followed in the early 2000s. They summarized the findings from the first wave of studies in terms of their theoretical and empirical backgrounds, main topics, research methods, representative researchers, benefits and weaknesses and so on. Then they turned to the new regional topics brought by the 1997-8 AFC and developed the second wave of research after the AFC. During the second wave, they investigated the origin, driving forces, and norms of the new regionalism and tried to define several key concepts for it.

2.2.1   The Origin, Driving Forces and Norms of the New Regionalism

Based on English-language publications, the evolution of regionalism occurred in four waves[3], in a historic sequence. The initial episode occurred during the second half of the nineteenth century and was largely a European phenomenon. The second wave of regionalism began soon after the First World War ended. The third wave rose when national states began to organize on a regional basis after the Second World War. The latest wave of regionalism, namely, the new regionalism, emerged in the wake of the Cold War's conclusion and the attendant changes in interstate power and security relations (Mansfield & Milner, 1999, pp. 596-599). In contrast, Chinese scholars had a different view on when new regionalism emerged. Some

---

[2] The word 'wave' in this paragraph refers to the empirical research wave in academia.

[3] The word 'wave' in this paragraph refers to the practical evolution of regionalism, differentiating from that in the last paragraph.

Chinese scholars agreed to their Western counterparts that new regionalism started after the Cold War ended, while others insisted that it started after the Second World War (Li, 1999, p. 11). However, not all China's scholars thought the new regionalism existed. Lu Guangsheng criticized the so-called new regionalism as nothing different from the old one (Lu, 2005, p. 25). His reasons for this conclusion were as follows:

- *In terms of the theoretical paradigm, the 'new regionalism' has not formed a relatively independent, systematic theoretical paradigm.*

- *In terms of the studied themes, the new regionalism and old regionalism were both concerned about the driving forces that stimulated nations to join the regionalism and to divert national loyalty to regional loyalty.*

- *In terms of the main hypobook, the new regionalism and the old one were both based on the logic that regional cooperation was developing in order to solve certain needs of nations, and the ultimate tendency of this regional cooperation depended on whether the cooperative style adapted to these needs.*

Besides the origin of the new regionalism, literature also sought for the driving factors that prompted the new regionalism to evolve. Most Chinese and English-language literature agreed that the new regionalism derived from four factors: the end of the Cold War, the shifting balance of world economic power, the shift towards 'outward orientation' and the growing importance of non-tariff barriers to trade (Andrew, 1995, pp. 92-97). Only a few Chinese scholars sought for the origins of regionalism in the productivity and technological revolution of the late twentieth century, which were thought to make possible extensive economic activities far beyond national boundaries (Geng, 2001, p. 22).

Among Chinese scholars, Geng stood out for his contributions to the studies on the norms of the new regionalism. After making detailed analysis, he concluded that the core value of the new regionalism was regional supremacy. He explained this in three points: the supremacy of the regional interest, the priority of regional issues and the primacy of the regional community. In detail, they meant:

- *The regional interest was given the first consideration*

- *To resolve regional issues was given the first priority*

• *To realize regional integration and to build a regional community was set as the highest goal.*

So far, nobody has conducted any research on the norms of the new regionalism but Geng.

2.2.2   Several Key Concepts of the New Regionalism

Literature on the new regionalism not only explored such themes as its origin, driving forces and norms, but also tried to define the key concepts. Scholars made some comparison among those key concepts such as 'regionalism', 'regionalization' and 'integration', and pointed out their similarity and differences. In addition, they created the concept of 'regionness' to measure the degree of them.

2.2.2.1 Regionalism vis-à-vis Regionalization

Based on Chinese-language publications, some scholars argued that regionalism was the cross-boundary and mutually-dependent cooperation process of nation states' interaction; it could be a rigid international mechanism with a super-national nature, or could pause at the economic stage without institutional constraints (Wu & Li, 2003, p. 14). Other Chinese scholars interpreted regionalism as 'a kind of ideology or slogan in the strict sense', while they understood regionalization as 'a spontaneous regional formation, regional cooperation and regional integration, as well as other formations without regional consciousness' (Ren, 2005, p. 124). Many Chinese scholars agreed to use 'regionalism' to mean the theory/ideology/thought (Liu X. , 2004, p. 18) (Geng, 2003, pp. 36-37), whereas they used the term 'regionalization' to mean the process of regional integration (Xia, 2005, p. 22). This was a little different from what their western counterparts tried to do to in defining the concepts of 'regionalism' and 'regionalization'.

Based on English-language publications, most western scholars tried to distinguish regionalism from regionalization according to the role of nation-state actors and that of 'non-state' transnational actors, i.e. market, economic forces etc. in region building, although they defined the two concepts with multifarious emphasis on various aspects As early as 1995, Andrew Hurrell noticed the huge, albeit not that clear or exact, difference between regionalism and regionalization: regionalism was often analysed in terms of the degree of social cohesiveness (ethnicity, race, language, religion, culture, history, consciousness of a common heritage); economic cohesiveness (trade patterns, economic complementarity), political cohesiveness (regime type, ideology); and organizational cohesiveness (existence of formal regional institutions). In contrast, although seldom unaffected by state policies, the most important driving forces for economic regionalization came from markets, from private trade and investment flows, and from the policies and decisions of companies (Hurrell, 1995, pp. 38-39). In 1999, Edward D. Mansfield and Helen V. Milner warned that was necessary to differentiate policy-induced regionalism from that stemming primarily from economic forces (Mansfield & Milner, 1999, p. 600). In 2000, Björn Hettne and Fredrik Söderbaum also put forward two different concepts of 'formal' or *de jure* region and 'real' or *de facto* region, with the former underlining the state territorial borders and a state-centric logic while the latter highlighted the complex integration between many types of actors: market, private business and firms, transnational corporations (TNCs), transnational business networks, non-governmental organizations (NGOs), social movements and other types of social networks (Hettne & Söderbaum, 2000, pp. 462-463). In 2003, Raimo Väyrynen proposed two different concepts of physical region and functional region. Physical regions referred to territorial, military, and economic spaces controlled primarily by states, but functional regions were defined by non-territorial factors, such as culture and the market, which are often the purview of non-state actors (Väyrynen, 2003, p. 27). The most authoritative statement of regionalism and regionalization belonged to Shaun Breslin and Richard Higgot. According to them, 'regionalism connoted those state-led projects of cooperation that emerged as a result of inter-government dialogues and treaties. Regionalization referred to those processes of integration which, albeit '… seldom unaffected by state policies', derived their driving force 'from markets, from private trade and investment flows, and from the policies and decisions of companies' (Hurrell, 1995, p. 334), rather than the predetermined plans of national or local governments' (Breslin & Higgot, Studying Regions: Learning from the Old, Constructing the New, 2000, p. 344).

These definitions of 'regionalism' and 'regionalization' were conducive to understanding the relations between them. As mentioned above, regionalism and regionalization were two parallel ways leading to the ultimate outcome of regional integration, with various driving forces from different actors. However, Andrew Hurrell held a different view on this issue. He divided the notion of 'regionalism' into five different categories, of which regionalization was one, and the other four were regional awareness and identity, regional inter-state cooperation, state-promoted regional integration and regional cohesion (Hurrell, 1995, pp. 39-45). Here, regionalization became one category of regionalism. The view is distinct from the normal definitions of regionalism and regionalization.

2.2.2.2 *Regionalization vis-à-vis Regional Integration*

Although regionalization meant a cooperation process in a certain region, some scholars distinguished it from another concept of regional integration, which also connoted the cooperation process at times. As Ernest B. Haas pointed out, 'integration appears to be both a process and an outcome'. (Haas, 1970, p. 622) In comparison, regionalization meant nothing other than the process. 'It is the process, rather than just the outcomes, that are important here' (Breslin & Higgot, 2000, p. 345). English-language literature found the differences between them, while Chinese-language literature did not.

Some English-language literature claimed there was no need to 'exercise pedantic definitional thinking about the parameter of the region' in that regionalization/regionalism was a process instead of an outcome.

11

However, some other writers held a contrary argument and they tried to define the geographical scope within which regionalism/regionalization emerged and flourished in the east. For instance, Peter J. Katzenstein asserted the eastern regionalism had gone beyond the subregional integration in Southeast Asia and at present "superregional' constructs, such as Asia-Pacific, were gaining wider currency' (Katzenstein, Hamilton-Hart, Kato, & Yue, 2000, p. 1). In contrast, most Chinese-language literature insisted that the appropriate geographical scope for the eastern regionalism was East Asia (Zhang, 2005, p. 3) (Wang, 2003, p. 52) (Zhang, 2004, p. 3) (Fu, 2004, p. 68), in consideration of the substantive development of regional cooperation within the framework of ASEAN+3 in East Asia after the 1997-8 AFC. There was no agreement on this issue in the literature. 'Asian regionalism', 'East Asian regionalism' and 'Asia-Pacific regionalism' were extensively and interchangeably used in academia, which meant different regionalism processes were going on within different geographical scope. The author tries to find the most significant process and adopts it as the subject of her book

2.2.2.3 Regionness

In order to measure the different degrees of regionalism in Europe, America and Asia, Björn Hettne, a Swedish scholar, reconsidered the concept of 'regionness', which he originally put forward in 1999: regionness was a concept that implied the degrees of regionalization that had occurred in terms of, for example, spatiality, cooperation, and identity (Väyrynen, 2003, p. 40). In 2000, he further theorized the concept of regionness and divided it into five different levels: regional space, regional complex, regional society, regional community and region-state (Hettne & Söderbaum, 2000, pp. 463-468). In regional space, people were assumed to live in small isolated communities, with little contact. Early relations of interdependence constituted a regional complex and indicated the real starting point for the regionalization process. Regional society was the level where the crucial regionalization process developed and intensified, in the sense that a number of different actors apart from states appeared on different societal levels and moved towards transcendence of national space, making use of a more rule-based pattern of relations. The fourth level of regional community referred to the process whereby the region increasingly turned into an active subject with a distinct identity, institutionalized or informal actor capability, legitimacy and structure of decision-making in relations with a more or less responsive regional civil society, transcending the old state borders. The ultimate outcome could be a region-state, which in terms of scope and cultural heterogeneity could be compared to the classical empires. In a word, regionness was a useful variable, which could be utilized to conduct comparative studies among regionalism processes in Europe, American and Asia.

In summary, both Chinese-language and English-language publications showed that scholars discussed some important issues of new regionalism, such as the origin, driving factors and norms; besides, they tried to define several key concepts. Geng stood out because he conducted empirical studies on the norms of the new regionalism and pointed out that the core values of regionalism was regional supremacy; Breslin and Higgot stood out for their precise definition of regionalism and regionalization; and Hettne was distinguished because he introduced the concept of 'regionness' to measure the different degrees of development of economic integration. The author adopts these basic concepts and studies achievements in the specific case of regional integration in East Asia by probing into the relations and interactions among regional integration, regionalism and regionalization in East Asia.

2.3   Theoretical Framework for New Regionalism in East Asia

In contrast with a large number of Chinese-language and English-language publications that reported studies on the origin, driving forces and the norm of the new regionalism in a general sense, publications showed less interest in theoretical research on the new regionalism in East Asia in a specific sense. This could be attributed to two facts of the new regionalism in East Asia. One was that East Asian regionalism started much later than its counterparts in Western Europe and North America. There was not an evolving history long enough to come up with a systematic theoretical framework. The other was that there were so many workable mechanisms at various levels for East Asian regionalism, e.g. ASEAN plus One (ASEAN+1; ASEAN plus China/Japan/South Korea), ASEAN+3 (ASEAN plus China, Japan and South Korea), ASEAN plus Six (ASEAN+6; ASEAN plus China, Japan, South Korea and Australia, New Zealand and India) and APEC, etc.. Several regionalism processes at various levels were going on simultaneously in East Asia. It was not easy to identify which one played the dominant role at a certain level for a certain period; hence it was difficult for theorists to accumulate adequate facts from a certain mechanism. As a result, there was little choice for a systematic theory based on the mainstream facts to emerge. However, scholars did not give up their efforts to seek as appropriate a theoretical framework as possible for East Asian regionalism. Literature showed that both Chinese and Western scholars made efforts to look for a workable theory of East Asian regionalism. They tried to interpret East Asian regionalism from various theoretical perspectives, among which, neo-realism, neo-liberal institutionalism, constructivism and neo-functionalism were applied the most.

2.3.1   Neo-realism and New Regionalism in East Asia

Neo-realist theory highlighted the role of great powers in regionalism in East Asia. As a great power, China's role in East Asian regionalism attracted neo-realists' attention. They asserted that 'China, will inevitably challenge the United States' domination of the region and, in the process, became more expansionist and coercive as it sought to maximize its sphere of influence' (Khoo, R., & Shambaugh, 2005, p. 210). In the realist' view, the regional order is structurally asymmetrical and unstable. Realists of various stripes thus argue that China must be 'balanced', 'checked', 'offset', 'countered', or 'hedged against'.

However, this was not the case in East Asia. First of all, China did not maximize its sphere of influence in East Asia because this went against its strategic choice of peaceful rising. Beijing, on many occasions, publicly stated that China would never claim the hegemony in the region and in the world. Thus, there was no need for the United States to balance China together with other second rate great powers. Secondly, if China were the rising great power, other Asian countries did not either 'balance' or 'bandwagon' it; they 'engaged' it (Achaya, 2003, p. 152). This also ran against the key assumptions of neo-realist theory. According to David Shambaugh, 'realist theory seems particularly incapable of explaining such a complex and dynamic environment (in East Asia)'. (Shambaugh, 2004/2005, p. 99) It seemed that the realist theory did not conform to what happened to East Asia regionalism. However, realists clearly saw China's rising role as a great power in East Asia and in the world, this was very close to the fact that could not be ignored by studies on regionalism in East Asia.

2.3.2   Neo-liberal Institutionalism and New Regionalism in East Asia

Neo-liberal institutionalism featured two main assumptions. One was that it paid much attention to the role of institution in regional integration. 'For neo-liberal institutionalist, China's emergence is a natural phenomenon ...and China's emergence should be channelled and shaped through proactive engagement and integration in to existing and new institutions' (Khoo, R., & Shambaugh, 2005, p. 210). However, East Asian regionalism was characterized by a lack of hard institutions like those in Western Europe. 'The Asian reality was it lacked the economic and security institutions in the neo-liberal institutionalist sense' (Pang, 2001, p. 32); it was the soft cooperation institutions on which East Asian countries depended to march towards regional integration in East Asia. Therefore, this institutionalist assumption did not adhere much to the East Asian practices.

The other feature of neo-liberal institutionalism was that it took economically interdependent relations among participants into full consideration as the basis of regional integration. Neo-liberal institutionalist argued that 'due to the reinforcing economic interdependence and the intercorrelation of the transnational issues, the significance of military means in addressing bilateral and multilateral relations dropped' (Su, 2006, p. 10). Correspondingly, the importance of economic interdependence among participants of regional integrations grew, which laid a solid basis for the ultimate goal of integration. As to the trade and investment interdependence among East Asian countries in general and that between China and ASEAN in particular, the intra-regional trade values increased significantly before the 1997-8 AFC, which resulted in rising trade interdependence in East Asia. 'As China raises its investment profile in these countries (ASEAN members), increased trade flows will necessarily follow. Coupled with ASEAN's already substantial investments in China, a higher level of economic interdependence will be forged between the two regions' (Wu F. , 1994, p. 17). After the CAFTA agreement was endorsed, the trade and investment cooperation between China and ASEAN became closer and more intense; as a result, economic interdependence between China and ASEAN increased. A similar trend happened to ASEAN-Japan economic relations and ASEAN-South Korea economic relations.

Neo-liberal institutionalism drew a part of the whole picture of the economic integration in East Asia; although it was incapable of reflecting the other part, security integration. In light of her dense interest in *economic integration/regionalism* in East Asia, the author, in the second chapter of theory, reviews the some assumptions within neo-liberal institutionalist framework and rechecks whether they are applicable to studies on new regionalism in East Asia.

2.3.3   Constructivism and New Regionalism in East Asia

Besides realism and liberalism, constructivism was another alternative for theoretical frameworks on studies of new regionalism in Eat Asia. Firstly, constructivist publications positioned China in the region and in the world from a constructive perspective. They asserted that 'China became a confident country, who advocated cooperation and maintained the stability of the international order' (Xing & Zhan, 2006, p. 18). Moreover, they anticipated the future of East Asian regionalism. They argued that to establish the East Asian Community (EAC) was not only the ultimate goal of China, but also the 'consensus of the thirteen countries in East Asia. The Network of the East Asian Think Tanks (NEAT), as the Track Two organization, in some degree, reflected the East Asian mode of community construction through its negotiations and decision-making procedures: mutual respect, comfortableness and consensus (Qin & Wang, 2004, p. 8).

Thirdly and most importantly, constructivist literature placed much emphasis on the role of social factors in region building, although it interpreted the social factors using different expressions. Based on Chinese and English-language literature, constructivists denoted social factors for regional integration in East Asia by different expressions such as 'regional identity' (Liu X. , 2004, p. 18), 'the formulation and establishment of certain norms' (Achaya, 2003, p. 159), 'norm localization' (Achary, 2004, p. 239), 'the formation of the cultural circle' (Hu & Wang, 2002, p. 74), 'an ASEAN identity' (Jones, 2004, p. 140), 'common values' (Berkofsky, 2005, p. 20), 'citizens' values' (Blondel, 2006, p. 223) or 'collective identity' (Hemmer & Katzenstein, 2002, p. 575) (Niu, 2005, p. 1), 'the emergence and formation of the middle classes' (Shiraishi, 2006, p. 241) and sometimes even the fuzzy 'cultural familiar, geological and historical ties' (Ba, 2008/2009, p. 663), albeit with a similarity in the common social nature of various expressions. However, constructivists had no idea to what extent social factors played a role in regional integration in East Asia. This was a serious weakness of constructivist theory. Early on, constructivists overestimated the importance of regional identities and the discourse of regions and region-building (Hurrell, 1995, p. 66). As time passed, they admitted that it was not clear to what extent a sense of collective identity was necessary for the promotion of substantial regional cooperation (Terada, 2003, p. 253). In light of the low degree of regional identity in East Asia and the fact that the regional integration in East Asia was still at the initial stage, therefore, constructivism seemed not to be an optimal theoretical framework for studies on the new regionalism in East Asia.

2.3.4 Neo-functionalism and New Regionalism in East Asia

Neo-functionalism was adopted to investigate the effects of regional integration particularly in Southeast Asia, which was thought to be enlightening for regionalism in East Asia. Neo-functionalist literature looked into the 'positive implications of economic integration of ASEAN on economic and society development' and contended that this would enlighten the establishment of the CAFTA in three ways: 'firstly, the completion of the CAFTA would promote the in-depth cooperation between China and ASEAN; secondly, economic cooperation between China and ASEAN would have a far-reaching influence on regional integration in East Asia; and finally, political cooperation prompted by economic cooperation between China and ASEAN members was the best solution for land and sea disputes between them' (Cheng, 2006, p. 137). Through these three points, neo-functionalists saw the three effects of functional spill-over, geographical spill-over and political spill-over. However, there was no obvious analysis on whether East Asian integration was a geographical spill-over from Southeast Asian integration, and there lacked adequate discussions of how functional and political spill-over worked in East Asia. Thus, there was no obvious progress in solving the land and sea disputes between China and ASEAN members apart from the agreement on shelving the disputes and joint exploration; besides, there was no hard proof that showed the security problems was to be solved by benefiting a spill-over effect from economic cooperation between China and AESAN. Therefore, no clear spill-over effects could be seen from the economic field to the political or the security fields, which did not conform to the main assumptions of neo-functionalism.

To sum up, many theoretical frameworks such as neo-realism, neo-liberal institutionalism, constructivism and neo-functionalism were adopted to studies of new regionalism in East Asia. Each of them was useful in highlighting some aspects of regionalism in East Asia but at the same time they also showed their weaknesses. Neo-realism was good at explaining China's emergence by considering it as a rising great power; however, China was not balanced or bandwagoned by its neighbours, which went contrary to the realist assumptions. Neo-liberal institutionalism played a key role in analysing the economic interdependence relations among participants of regional integration in East Asia, although it lacked the capacity of analysing the rise of a great power. Hence, 'there are phenomena in Asia today that neither realist nor liberal international relations theory is able to capture, thus requiring deep grounding in area studies to be comprehended' (Shambaugh, 2004/2005, p. 99). Nevertheless, constructivism was not an ideal theoretical framework because it did not identify to what extent regional identity played a role in regional integration in East Asia, although it noted the significance of consensus. Neo-functionalist literature did not supply hard proof of the spill-over effect evolving from ASEAN to East Asia geographically, or from the economic fields to the security fields functionally, or from the national level to

16

the supranational level politically. In comparison, neo-realism and neo-liberal institutionalism seemed more consistent with the empirical facts of the new regionalism in East Asia and they were more capable of explaining it than constructivism and neo-functionalism. However, none of these existing theoretical frameworks could draw the whole picture of economic integration in East Asia, without help from others. The book, based on the empirical facts of the economic integration in East Asia during the 2000s, rechecks the main assumptions of neo-realism and neo-liberal institutionalism. And it applies the theoretical framework of complex interdependence theory because the theory was said to gathering the strength of both neo-realism and neo-liberalism (Men, 2003, p. 43).

2.4   China's Role in Regional Economic Integration in East Asia

China, as an ascending great power, played an increasingly important role in regional economic integration in East Asia. Both Chinese-language and English-language publications reported many studies on this issue. Their discussion concentrated on China's self-positioning in the region and in the world, China's strategic choice of peaceful rising; China's role in trade cooperation and investment cooperation with ASEAN after the proposal of the CAFTA was initiated in 2001. Special attention was given to Sino-ASEAN economic relations and the background, benefits and implications of the CAFTA. Then, China's role in regional economic integration in East Asia, which was embodied through economic cooperation between China and ASEAN, was ascertained.

2.4.1   China's Self-Positioning and Strategic Choice

Chinese-language publications paid much attention to China's self-positioning at the regional level because they thought it had a direct and decisive influence on China's regional policy in East Asia. However, Chinese-language literature did not reach an agreement on China's self-positioning. Although most of the Chinese-language literature agreed that 'China, was a great power in history at the regional level in East Asia and in wider Asia, and as a result of China's ascendancy in recent years, it became one of the great powers in Asia-Pacific ' (Men, 2003, p. 83), there were still a few authors who argued that 'China was a flourishing quasi-developed country with a strong comprehensive power in the world.' (Wei, 2007, p. 37) China's regional policy depended, to a great extent, on its self-positioning in East Asia and in the world. If China focused its positioning on the latter, as it did in the 1980s and 1990s, China put the priority on great powers in the West on its diplomacy; if China focused its positioning on the former, as it did in the 2000s, it gave the priority to the regional neighbours in East Asia.

Chinese policymakers' primary mission was to restore normal diplomatic relations and resume normal international exchanges with the world after China's 'open door' policy was implemented in 1978. Within the general context of the times in the 1980s it made sense for China to focus its attention of foreign policy on the great powers in the western world instead of on its neighbouring nations in East Asia. China put bilateral relations with the Western great powers in the first place in foreign relations, weakening the multilateral relations within East Asian region. (Zhang J. , 2006, p. 17) After the Cold War came to an end in the 1990s, China positioned itself as a 'within-institution', 'responsible' 'great power at a regional level' in East Asia region (Chen & Wang, 2001, p. 20). By the phrase 'within-institution', it meant China was willing to abide by the rules of the institutions co-founded together with other regional countries; by 'responsible' it meant China would like to take more into consideration than its own interests and was willing to provide public goods; by 'a great power at regional level' it emphasized China's current strategy focusing on surrounding members and meant China, as a great power at regional level, was going to take the responsibility of participation in and promotion of regional cooperation in East Asia.

Chinese leading groups of the second, third and fourth generations gradually transformed the great power strategy to a regional one after the Cold War ended in the early 1990s. At the core of Chinese second generation of group, Deng Xiaoping, the chief architect of China's reform and opening up, emphasized the importance of maintaining good relations with China's neighbours in East Asia in the 1990s. The third generation of leading group, with President Jiang Zemin at the core, centred China's foreign policy on its neighbouring countries and developed a specific foreign policy in East Asia at the very outset of the twenty first century. President Jiang proposed to set up friendship and partnership with China's neighbouring countries at the sixteenth National People's Congress (NPC) of the Communist Party of China (CPC) in Beijing in August, 2002. The fourth generation of leading group, with President Hu Jintao at the core, further visualized the specific regional policy. Premier Wen Jiabao pointed out that China was to 'become a good neighbour and a good partner, to strengthen good neighbourly ties, to intensify regional cooperation, and to push China's exchanges and cooperation with its neighbours to a new high' (Wen, 2003), when he attended the China-ASEAN Business and Investment Summit (CABIS) in October 2003.China's regional policy improved the bilateral relations between China and its neighbouring countries for a long time after the Cold War ended. However, the bilateral relations were frustrated when the 'China threat' theory spread all over Southeast Asia because of China's speedy ascendancy in the region. After Zhen Bijian, the former Chairman of China Reform Forum, used the phrase of 'China's Peaceful Rise' for the first time at the Bo'ao Forum for Asia Annual Conference in 2003, the phrase was cited repeatedly by Chinese leaders afterwards. Chinese decision-makers' acceptance and utilization of the phrase caused ASEAN's fear of China's rising.

In the meanwhile, China's strategic choice of 'peaceful rising' also stirred up a heated and extensive country-wide debate within country-wide academia in China. Many scholars strongly opposed the wording of 'China's peaceful rising', which they asserted would give rise to vigilance and fear in Southeast Asia.

They suggested it should be replaced with the phrase, 'China's peaceful development', in order to avoid adding fuel to the flames of the 'China threat theory'.[4] The great debate lasted for a while, and then the mainstream scholars came to an agreement that 'China's peaceful rising' was more appropriate to describe not only China's diplomatic strategy but also its diplomatic goals in consideration of the speed and size of China's development as well as the peaceful implications of China's Rise for region-wide and world-wide development'. (Yan, 2004, pp. 12-16) (Pang, 2004, pp. 1-8) (Cai, 2004, pp. 33-38) (Song & Yao, 2005, pp. 3-7) (Liu J. , 2006, pp. 36-40). After they came to an agreement on this issue, most scholars turned their interests to the potential implications of China's strategic choice of peaceful rising for China-ASEAN relations and China's role in regional integration in East Asia.

English-language literature also showed keen interest in the issue of 'China's peaceful rising'. After Zheng Bijian published his article titled 'China's 'Peaceful Rise' to Great-Power Status' in *Foreign Affairs* (sited in the United States) in 2005, western scholars' attention was attracted by the issue of China's strategy of peaceful rise. There were also some western scholars who predicted that Chinese leaders would replace the strategy of China's 'peaceful rise' with another phrase -- China's 'peaceful development' (Gaye, 2007, p. 501), which really was not the case. Nevertheless, eventually they accepted that the contents of both 'China's peaceful rise' and 'China's peaceful development' remained the same (Gaye, 2007, p. 501), and they agreed that it did not matter whether the terminology was changed or not. This coincided with what Chinese scholar argued.

As seen in both Chinese-language and English-language literature, there lacked a sufficient discussion and analysis about to what extent China's 'peaceful' strategy had influence on its in economic cooperation with ASEAN in East Asian region. The author, in this book, tries to investigate China's motives for changing its policy from its strategic choice of 'peaceful rise' and explores the implications of the 'peaceful rise' on China's role in East Asia and on Sino-ASEAN relations in particular.

2.4.2 China's Role in Regional Economic Integration in East Asia

As China's role in economic integration in East Asia was embodied through its economic cooperation with ASEAN, both Chinese-language publications and their English counterparts showed that scholars were

---

[4] The phrase '中国的和平崛起'sometimes is translated into English as 'China's Peaceful Rise' and sometimes as 'China's Peaceful Emergence'. The former is used more often than the latter and it is thought to be the reason why Western great powers and regional neighbours sought to jointly contain China. The phrase '中国的和平发展'is translated into English as 'China's Peaceful Development', which is thought to help alleviate the tendency of joint containing of China. Actually, the translation of 'China's Peaceful Emergence' also reflects such a consideration in this regard. In consideration of the speed and size of China's development, the most commonly used phrase in academia is still 'China's Peaceful Rise', assuming peaceful rise is also the ultimate goal of China's development.

keenly interested in studying Sino-ASEAN economic relations. Besides, particular attention was given to the proposal and establishment of the CAFTA when the economic relationship was analysed.

2.4.2.1 Sino-ASEAN Economic Relations

Both Chinese-language and English-language literature tended to analyse Sino-ASEAN economic relations from two aspects of trade and investment relations. According to Chinese-language literature, both China and ASEAN had their own characteristics of national resources and industrial structure which were highly complementary in nature, which led to an immense potential for economic and trade cooperation and promised a huge developing space (Liu Y. , 2007, p. 59). China had very close trade relations with the ten members of ASEAN, which was reflected in the degree of trade complementarity between China and ASEAN (Chen W. , 2003, p. 43). China's speedy trade growth (with ASEAN) was not a threat, but an opportunity for ASEAN countries (Zhang B. , 2004, p. 55). As to the investment relations between China and ASEAN, 'China and ASEAN members had few directly competitive relations' (Zhang B. , 2004, p. 56). 'As a matter of fact, China was an important investing area for ASEAN' FDI and meanwhile China also became a main source for some ASEAN members to attract FDI (Guo, 2006, p. 20).

As seen in Chinese-language publications, China and ASEAN had an overwhelmingly positive role in economic cooperation with ASEAN. However, English-language publications did not reach an agreement on those issues. Some English-language literature concluded 'that given the broad similarity in trade structures and the fundamentally competitive nature of China-ASEAN economic relations, there were more possibilities that China and ASEAN would compete, rather than complement one another' (Wong & Chan, 2003, p. 523). On the contrary, other literature asserted that 'the competition for FDI between China and ASEAN existed, but there was no obvious evidence that the rise of China had squeezed out the FDI inflow to ASEAN' (Wong, Zou, & Zeng, 2000, p. 9). Responding to arguments that the apparent competitiveness between China and ASEAN in the same sectors and industries acted as a constraint on cooperation, various authors like Tongzen, Chen, and Low, 'saw a significant degree of intra-industry trade taking place and thus more complementarity than initially meets the eye' (Ba, 2008/2009, p. 662).

As shown by both Chinese-language and English-language literature, there was not a general agreement on whether competitiveness or mutual complementarity dominated the trade and investment relations between China and ASEAN. As to the trade relations, they cannot be appropriately analysed without addressing the competiveness/mutual complementarity issue; while investment relations cannot be addressed reasonably without sorting out whether China crowded out ASEAN's FDI from developed countries. Therefore, in this book, the author reanalyses Sino-ASEAN economic relations from the two aspects of trade and investment by addressing the 'competitiveness/mutual complementarity' issue and the 'FDI crowd-out' issue.

2.4.2.2 The Benefits, Background and Implications of the CAFTA

When literature discussed Sino-ASEAN economic relations, particular attention was given to the decision to establish the CAFTA between China and ASEAN. Based on Chinese-language publications, the contents of CAFTA were very extensive, and included not only trade facilitation in goods, service and investment but also trade and investment liberalization (Wei M. , 2002, pp. 53-54). The CAFTA was thought to benefit China and ASEAN in political and economic dimensions. Economically, success in establishing and developing, the CAFTA would bring considerable economies of scale. At that time, there were 1.8 billion people in this area, with a gross domestic product (GDP) of 17 million US dollars and the total trade of 13 million US dollars. 'It was forecasted that after ten years, the population would increase to 2 billion with a promising GDP of more than 200 billion US dollars' (Zhang Z. , 2002, p. 23). Moreover, the CAFTA, as the first free trade area in East Asia, if it developed as planned, would encourage East Asian cooperation to take a big stride towards a more mature regionalism in East Asia. In addition, 'the CAFTA would play its role in promoting trade liberalization and economic cooperation in Asia pacific region' (Zhang Z. , 2002, p. 20). Finally, the establishment of the CAFTA 'would realize the long term objective of common prosperity both in China and in East Asia' (Wei M. , 2002, p. 51) and it 'would substantially reinforce China and ASEAN's significance in world economics' (Qiu, 2004, p. 19).

More importantly, the establishment of the CAFTA benefited China and ASEAN not only in economic terms but also politically. 'The establishment of the CAFTA was given the priority in China's geo-economic strategy and it played a role in bringing political spill-over to a considerable extent' (Qiu, 2005, p. 10). In terms of political benefits of the CAFTA, 'the decision to set up the CAFTA promoted the interactive development of political relations between China and ASEAN (Zhang Y. , 2006, p. 6), brought profound changes in Asia-Pacific international relations and further revealed the strategic intention and policy objectives of the United States, Japan and India in East Asia (Liu S. , 2008, pp. 65-69). Besides, the establishment of the CAFTA and economic cooperation between China and ASEAN in general 'would help lay a basis of trust for regional integration in East Asia and promote the integration process in East Asia' (Wei H. , 2005, p. 21).

Whilst anticipating a promising prospect for the CAFTA, some scholars also saw there were some unfavourable factors for the establishment of the CAFTA and the economic integration process in East Asia. For example, 'the complexity of Asian-Pacific cooperation, contradictory nature of ASEAN cooperation at intra-regional level, the competitive nature of similar economic structure in different countries and the arduousness to build mutual trust between different sides' (Zhao, 2002, pp. 28-30) would play a negative role in economic cooperation between China and ASEAN and in economic integration in East Asia. In addition, 'different conditions in various countries in East Asia, asymmetrical interdependence, outward-oriented economics, nationalism ideology, the so-called 'security dilemma' and so forth would hinder the regional integration process in East Asia' (Peng, 2006, p. 47).

English-language literature did not pay much attention to evaluating the benefits of the CAFTA. It was agreed that in the short run, the 'FTA (would) further promote the growth of trade between two sides' and 'reduce the dependence of China and ASEAN on other markets, especially on the US and EU markets' (Yin, 2004, p. 322), while 'the ASEAN-China Free Trade Area (would) benefit both sides in the long run' (Oxford Analytical, 2010). The establishment of the CAFTA would 'expedite the Asian economic integration'; helped 'economic integration to extend from East Asia (ASEAN plus three since 1997) to Asia'; made 'the leadership change from Japan to China' (Liou, 2007, pp. 197-199) and so on.

In contrast with Chinese-language literature, English-language literature had more interest in seeking for the motives underlying China's proposal of the CAFTA at the turn of the century. It was suggested that China took an initiative in putting forth the proposal of the CAFTA because of the four following motives. 'First, China wants to show its sincerity with other nations and pursue a win-win outcome in all its efforts. Second, China puts a high priority on the maintenance of security on its borders, and has wanted to maintain a stable relationship with ASEAN countries. Third, China may incur less frictional costs in political and economic terms with an ASEAN FTA as compared with a Northeast FTA or an East Asian one. Fourth, a more complementary relationship exists between China and ASEAN'. (Yin, 2004, pp. 320-321) Some literature sought for the internal dynamics and external dynamics of the CAFTA at the regional level in East Asia. It was argued that internal dynamics included the growing economic ties among East Asian economies, the impact of the Asian financial crisis in 1997, and the growing dissatisfaction of East Asian governments with the increasingly apparent limitations of the Asia-Pacific Economic Cooperation (APEC) forum and ASEAN in defending and promoting the interests of East Asia. External pressures included the expansion of European Union (EU) to include Eastern European countries and the enlargement of NAFTA (North American Free Trade Area) to form a Free Trade Area of the America and the fact that EU and NAFTA came to the bargaining table in multilateral trade negotiations as blocs (Cai K. G., 2003, pp. 388-399).

Of special note is that existing literature tended to explore China's motives at the regional level instead of at the national level; besides, scholars preferred to explore China's motives from an outward-looking perspective rather than from an inward-looking perspective to look into what happened *in* China that prompted China to change its attitude towards economic cooperation with ASEAN. In consideration of the fact that the proposal to set up the CAFTA was one of Beijing's critical domestic movements of economic diplomacy, it is quite imperative to look into China's motives from an inward-looking perspective at the national level. Therefore, in this book, the author pays particular attention to China's inward-oriented motives at the national level and explores the impact of domestic/national politics on regional politics and regional integration.

As we can see, there was not an adequate analysis of the background of the CAFTA in Chinese-language publications, English-language publications showed that scholars investigated the genesis and the background of the free trade agreement between China and ASEAN and found that its mindset was rooted deeply in the East Asian Economic Group (EAEG) proposal, was originally put forward by the former Malaysian Prime Minister, Mahathir Mohammad in 1990, which was based on his desire to set up an East Asian economic and political grouping in order to exclude the influence of the United States outside Asia (Cai K. G., 2003, p. 392). English-language literature also tried to investigate the implications of the CAFTA, which was considered positively significant and a driving force for East Asian regional integration. According to Kevin G. Cai, 'the CAFTA (would) impact significantly on the process of East Asian regional grouping, particularly exerting strong pressure on Japan and South Korea on the issue of creating an East Asian region-wide FTA. Thus, an East Asian FTA (would) invariably have substantial implications for the political economy of East Asia and beyond'. (Cai K. G., 2003, p. 402).

2.4.2.3 China's Role in Regional Economic Integration in East Asia

The CAFTA was the first FTA in East Asia, and the foundation stone for regional economic integration in East Asia. As Chinese premier, Wen Jiabao asserted, the East Asian Free Trade Area, based on the CAFTA, would be at the heart of the East Asian Community (EAC). The establishment of the CAFTA also attracted scholars' attention to China's role in regional economic integration in East Asia. Many Chinese-language and English-language publications agreed that China had increasingly become the 'engine of economic growth' (Zhang B. , 2004, p. 54) and 'facilitator for macro-economic stability' (Hu & Men, 2005, p. 26) in East Asian region and even 'a steady stellar of the globe' (Hira, 2007, p. 90). However, there were a few scholars who assumed the CAFTA was evidence of China's leading role in East Asian regionalism. 'If this is not a leading role in the EAC, then what is?' (Berkofsky, 2005, p. 22) Some scholars even predicted 'a perceptible US disengagement from Asia and subsequent displacement by China in the region' (Gaye, 2007, p. 502). Nevertheless, some other rational scholars asserted that 'China's role should not be exaggerated. *(Is China)* important? Yes. *(Is China)* Powerful? Perhaps not as much as many suggest. *(Does China play)* a leading role? Not yet and not for some time' (Breslin, 2006, p. 17).

There was no evidence in Chinese-language publications to show whether or not China acted as the leader in regional integration in East Asian. Yet we saw that Chinese scholars advocated China's predominant role in monetary cooperation in East Asia and the Chinese Ren Min Bi (RMB)'s leadership. In 2003, ten ASEAN members and three northeast countries- China, Japan and South Korea-all signed the Chiang Mai Initiative (CMI), which was considered the landmark of monetary cooperation in East Asia. 'Such a monetary cooperation mechanism had a practical significance on promoting the process of regionalization of RMB and helped better maintain the financial stability and protect the economic interests in Asian area.' (Zhang & Zhang, 2008, p. 43) 'As a great power at regional level, China should take active participation into the monetary cooperation and play a predominant role during the process.' (Ye, 2007, p. 65)

English-language publications showed that when the geographical scope of studies of economic relations extended from ASEAN and China to region-wide East Asia, ASEAN +3 was considered the most dynamic mechanism of economic cooperation as well as an useful vehicle to deal with any future financial crisis. 'The 'ASEAN+3' approach was perceived as an important means to strengthen ASEAN's status and relevance' (Cheng J. Y.-s., 2004, p. 257). 'The APT (ASEAN plus Three) process in many ways was simply the latest manifestation of evolutionary development of East Asian regional cooperation. For all the countries of East Asia, the best vehicle for developing a strategy for dealing with future crises appeared to be the embryonic APT.' (Stubbs, 2002, pp. 441, 449) In consideration of internal dispute in ASEAN +3 and external pressure from the United States, the book will rethink the feasibility, effectiveness and limitations of ASEAN +3 to locate its position on the way to East Asian integration by comparing it with another mechanism of the East Asia Summit (EAS).

To sum up, both Chinese-language and English-language literature reported extensive research on China's self-positioning, China's strategic choice of 'peaceful rising', the implications of the CAFTA and China's role in economic cooperation with ASEAN. However, as to China's self-positioning, there was no agreement about whether China positioned itself as a great power at the regional level or a great power at the international level. As to Sino-ASEAN economic relations, there was no agreement whether China and ASEAN were competitive or mutually complementraty in trade, and whether China crowded out ASEAN's FDI or not. As to China's role in economic cooperation with ASEAN in East Asia, there was no agreement whether or not China acted as a leader in the regional integration process. More importantly, there lacked sufficient analysis on China's motives for initiating the CAFTA proposal at the turn of the century from an inward-looking perspective at the national level instead of at the regional level. In light of these four gaps, the author rethinks China's position in East Asia, and reinvestigate China's role in economic integration in East Asia by looking for China's motives in proposing the CAFTA and analysing Sino-ASEAN economic relations.

In regard to China's role in regional economic integration in East Asia, the author, in this book, takes trade and FDI into account. The author repositions China's role in economic cooperation with ASEAN by assessing China's economic policy on trade and investment from the 1980s onward and analysing the Sino-ASEAN trade relationship. Special attention is given to the trade competitiveness and mutual complementarity between China and ASEAN in order to analyse the trade relationship between the two sides. Besides, special attention is also given to the investment relations between the two sides. Analysis of the investment relations between the two sides concentrates on whether China crowded out ASEAN's FDI flows from the developed countries. By describing China's economic policy, and analysing Sino-ASEAN relationship on trade cooperation and investment cooperation, the author repositions China's role in economic cooperation with ASEAN. With a view to seeking for China's domestic motives for setting up the CAFTA with ASEAN at the turn of the century, the author adopts an inward-looking perspective at the national level to evaluate the impact of the CAFTA on China's domestic development.

In regard to China's role in regional economic integration in East Asia, the author, as an East Asian scholar and Chinese scholar, conducts detailed research on this issue from an East Asian perspective and a Chinese perspective as well. The following questions are to be answered: Who are expecting/expected to be the leader in East Asia regional integration? Who really is the *de facto* leader? Who will successfully lead East Asian regional integration?

2.5 Conclusion

Both Chinese-language and English-language publications showed that scholars conducted extensive and deep studies on East Asian regionalism. Scholars discussed the origin, driving forces and norms of the new regionalism in East Asia; besides, they accurately defined the key concepts such as regionalism, regionalization, integration and clarified the similarities and the differences among them.

When seeking for a proper theoretical framework for studies on new regionalism in East Asia, scholars tested main assumptions of new-realism, neo-liberal institutionalism, constructivism and neo-functionalism with the evolving facts of the new regionalism in East Asia. They found that each of those theoretical frameworks had its own strengths and weaknesses in explaining what happened to regionalism in East Asia in the 1990s and 2000s. However, it was beyond the capability of any single theoretical framework to do this alone.

When analysing Sino-ASEAN economic relations, literature did not reflect an agreement on two problems. One was whether China and ASEAN were predominantly competitive or mutually complementary in trade relations; the other was whether China crowded out ASEAN's FDI from developed countries after its entry into the WTO. When identifying China's role in regional economic integration in East Asia, scholars were divided on whether China was the leader or not. More importantly, there lacked an adequate discussion/analysis of the motives for China's shifting attitude towards regional economic integration in East Asia at the turn of the century. At some times, the issue was, to some extent, ignored by scholars.

The author, in this book, reanalyses the disputes and fills in the gap on the basis of findings from collected sources. The main assumptions of existing theoretical frameworks are reassessed with a view to finding an appropriate theory or a combination of theories and to explain what happened to regionalism in East Asia. The author takes trade and investment relations between China and ASEAN during the 1990s and 2000s are taken into consideration and an attempt made to identity China's role in regional economic integration in East Asia. By comparing China's role in economic cooperation before and after 2001, the author attempts to identify the motives that prompted China to change its attitude towards bilateral economic cooperation with ASEAN and regional economic integration in East Asia at the turn of the century. Finally, the author detects the feature of East Asian regionalism embodied in bilateral economic cooperation between China and ASEAN during the 1990s and 2000s and assesses the outlook for the future.

3 Theoretical Framework: CIT and Methodology: GTM

The chapter consists of two parts: the theoretical framework and the research methodology. The theoretical part presents why and how the framework of complex interdependence theory (CIT) is applied in this book by examining its origin, key concepts and main assumptions. It explores the relevance to the bilateral economic relationship between China and ASEAN and China's role in economic integration in East Asia. The methodology section elaborates on why the grounded theory method (GTM) is applied to analyse data in this book by describing what is the GTM and its application. In addition, it dicusses methods to collect primary and secondary data and other methods which help to analyse data are also included in this part.

3.1 Theoretical Framework: CIT

In Chapter Two of Literature Review, the book investigated neo-realism, neo-liberal institutionalism, constructivism and neo-functionalism respectively and found that no one theory could explain all aspects of the new regionalism in East Asia. Such a review of mainstream theories proved very useful for empirical research of economic cooperation between China and ASEAN in East Asia. There was no similarly apt theoretical framework for studies of regional economic integration in East Asia as neo-functionalist theory to explain the regional integration in West Europe. None of the existing theoretical frameworks were originally created to explain the empirical interactions between/among actors in East Asia. East Asia was a newly emerging geo-political scope where new regionalism burgeoned after the Cold War ended. It did not take very long to get all East Asian states to participate in regional arrangements. Thus academia has not yet to come up with an appropriate theoretical framework to explain the proceedings in East Asia. Research was still rather limited (as illustrated in the Chapter Two). Hence the research project considered a range of different theoretical frameworks that might have been useful for analysis of regionalism in East Asia. Such a review of mainstream theories was conducive to selecting as appropriately useful as possible a theoretical framework, which could be adopted in the empirical case of the book.

In comparison, neo-realism and neo-liberal institutionalism seemed closer to the empirical facts of East Asia. 'Complex interdependence theory incorporates the strong points of both neo-realism and neo-liberalism' (Men, 2003, p. 43); therefore, it is more effective for analysing the new regionalism in East Asia. CIT highlights the interdependent relationship between/among countries in a region, while it does not ignore the role of national government in economic cooperation. It appreciates the power of hegemony while it emphasizes the interdependent characteristics of the world. It also anticipated an eroding hegemony. It presents simple models of economic process and overall power by which to analyse international regime changes and complements them with complex models of issue structure and international organization. Through a lens of CIT, roles of both national governments and international organizations (ASEAN in the case of this book) can be well understood. In addition, CIT is good at addressing economic issues rather than political/military issues, which is particularly applicable to the empirical studies of the bilateral economic relationship between China and ASEAN. Therefore, CIT is applied for the empirical study in this book.

The theoretical part of this chapter has four sections. The first section presents the origin, core concepts and key assumptions of CIT. The second checks its relevance to the Sino-ASEAN economic relationship. The third measures its relevance to China's role in economic integration in East Asia; and the final section identifies the weaknesses of applying CIT to the empirical studies of East Asian regionalism.

3.1.1 The Origin, Core concepts and Key Assumptions

CIT, elaborated by Robert O. Keohane, Stanley Hoffman and Joseph S. Nye in the late 1970s, shows great strength in analysing the conditions and evolution of regional politics in East Asia, the bilateral economic relationship between China and ASEAN and also China's role in economic integration in East Asia. Interdependence theory was derived from scholars' strong criticism of neo-functionalism, which prevailed in the 1970s. Keohane and Hoffman pointed out the weaknesses of neo-functionalism in their collaborative works. They observed that 'such an expansion (of spill-over) is by no means automatic; there are limits on spill-over'; they argued that 'successful spill-over requires prior programmatic among governments' (Keohane & Hoffmann, 1996, pp. 288-289). They disagreed with the neo-functionalist argument that the European Community was 'a political market characterized by arms-length transactions among independent entities, nor was it a hierarchy' (Hoffmann & Keohane, Conclusion: Community Politics and Institutional Change, 1996, p. 281). Instead, they referred to it as a 'network form of organization', where 'actors in a network have a preference for interaction with one another rather than with outsiders, in part because intense interactions create incentives for self-interested cooperation and for the maintenance of reputations for reliability' (Keohane & Hoffmann, 1996, p. 288). In addition, they asserted that the 'European Community is an experiment in pooling sovereignty, not in transferring it from states to supranational institutions' (Hoffmann & Keohane, Conclusion: Community Politics and Institutional Change, 1996, p. 277). Finally, they criticized neo-functionalists for failure to solve the problem 'of the degree to which the European Community can meet the aspirations of West Germany, its strongest member, while making those aspirations acceptable to its neighbours, both within the Community and to the east' (Keohane & Hoffmann, 1996, p. 288). As such, Keohane and Hoffman nearly negated the effectiveness of neo-functionalism in analysing European integration by criticizing its core concept and key assumptions.

Keohane not only criticized the weaknesses of neo-functionalism, but together with Nye, he developed a new theoretical framework, which was well known as the 'complex interdependence theory'. The core concepts and main assumptions of interdependence theory were mainly reflected in their work titled *Power and Interdependence (1977)*. By 'interdependence', they meant 'mutual dependence. Interdependence in world politics refers to situations characterized by reciprocal effects among countries or among actors in different countries' (Keohane & Nye, 1989, p. 8). Interdependence connoted not only the 'situation of mutual benefit', but also the 'cases of mutual dependence' (Keohane & Nye, 1989, p. 9). 'Interdependent relationship will always involve cost, since interdependence restricts autonomy; but it is impossible to specify *a priori* whether the benefits of a relationship will exceed the cost (Keohane & Nye, 1989, p. 9)'. With respect to the distribution of benefits among/between interdependent states, interdependence theorists believed emphasis should be placed on the 'relative gains' instead of 'the joint gains or joint losses' (Keohane & Nye, 1989, p. 10); furthermore, 'the politics of economic and ecological interdependence involve competition even when large net benefits can be expected from cooperation' (Keohane & Nye, 1989, p. 10). In regard to the structure of an interdependent relationship, the interdependence theorists thought most of the relations were characterized by 'asymmetrical interdependence', which could be 'a source of power' (Keohane & Nye, 1989, p. 11).

Following on the core concept, interdependence theorists put forth a number of main assumptions. Firstly, they summarized three main characteristics of complex interdependent conditions/relationships: multiple channels, absence of hierarchy among issues and the minor role of military force.

1. *'Multiple channels connect societies, including: informal ties between governmental elites as well as formal foreign office arrangements (interstate relations); informal ties among nongovernmental elites (trans-governmental relations); and transnational organization (transnational relations)'*

2. *'The agenda of interstate relationships consists of multiple issues that are not arranged in a clear or consistent hierarchy'*.

3. *Military force is not used by governments toward other governments within the region, or on the issues, when complex interdependence prevails. (Keohane & Nye, 1989, pp. 24-25)*

After examining the static characteristics of complex interdependence, theorists explored its dynamic process by offering four models of political process 'based on the changes in (1) economic processes, (2) the overall power structure in the world, (3) the power structure within issue areas and (4) power capabilities as affected by international organization' (Keohane & Nye, 1989, p. 38). The first two models were seen as simple models while the other two were complicated ones. CIT relied on the combination of simple and complicated models to constitute a complex analytical framework in order to understand the changes of international regime, on the ground that none of the four models could be relied upon to do this alone.

The economic process model of regime change had three premises: '1. Technological change and increases in economic interdependence will make existing international regimes obsolete; 2. Governments will be highly responsive to domestic political demands for a rising standard of living; and 3. The great aggregate economic benefits provided by international movements of capital, goods and in some cases labour will give governments strong incentive to modify or reconstruct international regimes to restore their effectiveness.' (Keohane & Nye, 1989, p. 40)

As far as the overall power structure model was concerned, theorists were struck by hegemony and leadership. They foresaw an eroding hegemony in this model and analysed the necessity of leadership under the conditions of complex interdependence. They argued that 'stable economic regimes require leadership. (Furthermore) an actor is most likely to provide such leadership when it sees itself as a major consumer of the long-term benefits produced by the regime', and it must have the 'willingness to forgo short-term gains in bargaining in order to preserve the regime (Keohane & Nye, 1989, p. 44).'

With respect to the issue structure model, its premise was that 'power resources in one issue area lose some or all of their effectiveness when applied to others (Keohane & Nye, 1989, p. 50).' Complex interdependence theorists shared similarity with the realists view that the powerful country made the rules; however, the differences between them was that the former did not believe that overall power country was necessarily likely to be the power on a certain issue, while the latter did.

Pertaining to the international organization model, theorists defined the term 'international organization' in a broad sense; it referred to informal and formal 'multilevel linkages, norms and institutions' (Keohane & Nye, 1989, p. 54). 'The international organization model assumes that a set of networks, norms, and institutions, once established, will be difficult either to eradicate or drastically to rearrange (Keohane & Nye, 1989, p. 55).' By applying these four process models, complex interdependence theorists generalized the changes of international regimes. Added by their accurate analysis of the three characteristics of the static world politics, complex interdependence theorists were able to reveal the structure of the world politics and its evolution of processes. This book applies the CIT to the study of the regional politics in East Asia, the bilateral economic relationship between China and ASEAN and China's role in economic integration in East Asia and economic cooperation with ASEAN before and after 2001.

3.1.2   CIT and the Bilateral Relationship between China and ASEAN

In general, the Sino-ASEAN relationship closely fits the three characteristics of CIT. After China's recognition of ASEAN as a viable regional entity in 1975, bilateral relations between China and ASEAN gradually developed. During the late 1970s, China began economic and trade exchanges with some ASEAN members such as Singapore, Malaysia and Thailand. However, the third Indochina War in 1979 more or less affected the normal proceedings of political and economic exchanges. Southeast Asian people showed strong aversion for China's usage of military force, to intervene in with Vietnam during the war. Within the general context of the Cold War, the Sino-ASEAN relationship did not see any breakthrough. It was not until the Cold War ended in the early 1990s, that Sino-ASEAN relations made significant progress. During the 1990s, China not only established/restored/upgraded its relationships with individual ASEAN members, but also developed a close relationship with ASEAN as a whole. A bilateral consultative relationship was established in 1991, and upgraded to a full dialogue partnership in 1996 and a strategic partnership in 2003. Therefore, the 1990s saw a stable, increasingly close bilateral relationship between China and ASEAN in a political/diplomatic sense. When the Asian financial crisis broke out in the late 1990s, the two sides began more interactions in financial areas in that it was the urgent needs during the crisis. After China entered the WTO, the two sides launched more economic cooperation with each other. At the time, ASEAN was worried that China would become a relatively strong competitor of ASEAN, so it agreed to China's proposal to set up the CAFTA in 2001. The two sides endorsed the Framework Agreement on Comprehensive Economic Cooperation, and subordinate Agreement on Trade in Goods (ATG), Agreement on Dispute Settlement Mechanism (ADSM), and Agreement on Trade in Service (ATS), Investment Agreement (IA) one by one in the 2000s in order to enhance bilateral trade and investment cooperation and completed the establishment of the CAFTA in 2010. In the economic sense, the 2000s saw an increasingly close relationship between China and ASEAN. Based on the historic evolution of bilateral relationship between China and ASEAN, it is safe to say that the two sides coexisted peacefully with each other by and large, except during the third Indochina War in the late 1970s. The 1990s saw stable and progressive bilateral political relations between China and ASEAN, while the 2000s saw a breakthrough in their economic relations due to the establishment and completion of the CAFTA. This clearly fits one of the three characteristics of world politics that CIT set forth: the minor role of military force.

Moreover, the enhancement and upgrading of bilateral economic and political relations between China and ASEAN necessitated more multiple channel connections between them. China and ASEAN managed to set up more formal/informal, governmental/nongovernmental institutions to meet this need. Firstly, China newly established/ restored formal diplomatic relationships with each ASEAN member during the 1990s, which laid a solid basis for regular interstate connections. ASEAN took the initiative in holding an annual ASEAN+1 (China) Summit after the 1997-8 AFC in order to seek help to survive the crisis as soon as possible; the annual Summit constructed a platform for leaders from the ten ASEAN members and China to communicate with each other. In addition to the interstate connections at the government leaders' level, those connections at the ambassador level also grew. The most striking event was that China sent an ambassador to the ASEAN Secretariat in 2008, which marked a new stage of interstate connections between China and ASEAN. In the meanwhile, the anticipated establishment of the CAFTA demanded more trans-governmental connections in the 2000s. A year after the Framework Agreement took effect, the China-ASEAN Expo (CAExpo) and the CABIS Secretariats were set up in 2004. They held trade fairs and investment summits for China and ASEAN members every year in order to further promote bilateral trade and investment connections and to help complete the CAFTA. In addition to the interstate and trans-governmental channels, transnational organizations contributed significantly to expand bilateral connections. As early as in 2001, the ASEAN-China Business Council (ACBC) was established to promote cooperation among industry/commerce chambers of the ten ASEAN members and China. After the Framework Agreement was endorsed in 2002, a great many of Chinese enterprises strengthened their transnational trade and investment cooperation with their counterparts in ASEAN by establishing foreign branches in ASEAN, merging with some ASEAN companies and investing in ASEAN. These interstate, trans-governmental and transnational connections between China and ASEAN led to a substantial increase in bilateral trade and investment exchanges. Take bilateral trade values and FDI flows as example, Table 3.1 displays some numeric evidence for the huge growth in trade values and FDI flows between China and ASEAN in the 1990s and 2000s. As seen in Table 3.1, China's total trade values with ASEAN in 1993 was only 4,528.7 million US dollars and accounted for 1.3% of total extra-ASEAN trade exchanges; it grew substantially to 32,315.9 million US dollars and with a 5.5% share in 2000. In 2008, the value grew by approximately six times that of 2000, to 192, 533.1 million US dollars, representing 15.37%. Both the trade value and the share saw large increases during the 1990s and 2000s. This reveals that ASEAN placed more dependence on China in terms of bilateral trade relationship. A similar growth tendency happened to bilateral FDI flows. In 2000, China imported 133.4 million US dollars from ASEAN, which accounted for 0.6% of total extra-ASEAN FDI flows. In 2008, China exported 1,497.3 million US dollars to ASEAN, which accounted for 2.5% of total extra-ASEAN flows in that year. This reveals that China turned from a net FDI recipient of ASEAN in the 1990s to be a net FDI exporter in the 2000s. These multiple channels of contact between China and ASEAN and their positive outcome fit the characteristics of complex interdependence.

Table 3.1 China-ASEAN Trade Value and FDI Flows

China-ASEAN Trade Value and FDI Flows and Share in Total Extra-ASEAN Exchanges in 1993, 2000 and 2008		
	Value and Flows: in million US$; Share: in percent	
Year	Trade Value (Share)	FDI Flows (Share)
1993	4,528.7 (1.3)	-
2000	32,315.9 (5.5)	-133.4 (-0.6)
2008	192,533.1 (15.37)	1,497.3 (2.5)

Source: ASEAN Statistics Yearbook 2003 and 2008 (Compiled and computed by the author)

Finally, the agenda of Sino-ASEAN relations shows a broad range of issues without a domination of military security concerns. For example, agricultural cooperation was never given any priority in bilateral cooperation between China and ASEAN during the 1990s; however, it was placed the first among five priority cooperation areas within the framework of the CAFTA in the 2000s. Bilateral trade in manufactured goods was paid much attention by China and ASEAN and it used to constitute the first major part of bilateral trade between them in the 1990s. However, no such domination occurred in the 2000s. This fits the last characteristics of complex interdependent relationship. In addition, according to complex interdependence theorists: 'many issues arise from what used to be considered domestic policy, and the distinction between domestic and foreign issues becomes blurred (Keohane & Nye, 1989, p. 25).' China's entry into the WTO was a case in point for this argument. In the complex interdependent relations between China and ASEAN, ASEAN, as the relatively weak party, was sometimes highly sensitive to the relatively strong party-China's domestic policy. On the eve and in the wake of China's entry into the WTO in 2001, ASEAN was very worried about its possible negative impacts. On the one hand, ASEAN worried that China would compete for trade with the advanced industrial countries in the West because China was an increasingly stable product supplier in the world after its accession to the WTO. On the other hand, ASEAN was concerned about whether China would crowd out ASEAN's FDI flows from the advanced industrial countries after the WTO accession. China's domestic policy of entry into the WTO, in some sense, played a decisive role in ASEAN's decision whether to agree to set up the CAFTA. ASEAN was highly sensitive to it because it thought this would change the relative gains/loss between the two sides within an interdependent context between them. ASEAN's decision to set up the CAFTA with China showed its general approval that the Sino-ASEAN relationship was likely being mutual benefit; and China probably was not an economic competitor of ASEAN. In this book, Chapter Four and Five analyse China's role in trade and investment cooperation with ASEAN respectively on an empirical basis in order to provide evidence for these theoretical assumptions.

3.1.3   CIT and China

Four political process models for international regime changes were set forth by CIT and they are applicable to analyse China's domestic policy, China's role and China's motive for changing its role in economic cooperation with ASEAN and in economic integration in East Asia. China's domestic policy focused dedicatedly on economic development for over three decades since the policy of reform and opening up was implemented in the late 1970s. At the thirteenth Communist Party of China (CPC) National Congress in 1987, Premier Zhao Ziyang made it clear in his speech that 'at the primary stage of socialism, the CPC's basic aim of building socialism with Chinese characteristics is to lead and unite people of all nationalities, consistently concentrate on economic development, stick to the Four Cardinal Principles, press ahead with reform and opening up and strive for building China into a prosperous, democratic and civilized modern socialist country (Zhao, 1987, p. 32).' This was well known as the basic line of the Communist Party of China (CPC): 'one central task and two basic points', which the CPC carried on with the aim of reinforcing China's economic strength and improving Chinese people's living level to a substantial extent. This basic line, focusing on promoting domestic people's welfare, was iterated many times by China's successive leaders. For example, at the latest 17th CPC National Congress (October 2007), President Hu Jintao articulated clearly that 'taking the path of socialism with Chinese characteristics means we will, under the leadership of the CPC and in light of China's basic conditions, take economic development as the central task, adhere to the Four Cardinal Principles and persevere in reform and opening up, release and develop the productive forces, consolidate and improve the socialist system, develop the socialist market economy, socialist democracy, an advanced socialist culture and a harmonious socialist society, and make China a prosperous, strong, democratic, culturally advanced and harmonious modern socialist country (Hu, 2007).' This reveals that Chinese government, led by the ruling CPC, took great responsibility for improving citizen's standard of living, which fits one of the assumptions of the economic process model that 'governments will be highly responsive to domestic political demands for a rising standard of living (Keohane & Nye, 1989, p. 40)'.

In addition, the increasing interdependence between China and ASEAN after the 1997-8 AFC caused the new cooperation institutions to come into existence. During the crisis, ASEAN pleaded for support from the United States, who, unexpectedly, responded lukewarmly. This stood in sharp contrast with the timely financial help China provided for Malaysia and Thailand, immediately after the crisis broke out. As a result, ASEAN was disappointed at the US's attitude and increased its economic interaction with China after the crisis. Before the crisis, China's trade with ASEAN hesitated at more or less 400 billion US dollars, accounting for approximately 1-5% of total extra-ASEAN trade with the world. After the crisis, trade between them increased to a significant extent, to reach about 1,200 billion US dollars in 2008, accounting for over 15% of total extra-ASEAN trade. The increasing economic interaction made old cooperation institutions obsolete. During the process of economic cooperation, China and AESAN set up new cooperation institutions during and after the crisis. Of special note is the establishment of the ASEAN+1 (China) cooperation mechanism in 1997 and the practical cooperation of interstate, trans-governmental and transnational cooperation institutions within the framework of the CAFTA. They laid a solid basis not only for individual domestic economic growth in China and AESAN, but also for an increase in economic interdependence between them. This fits the other two assumptions of the economic process model of CIT that 'technological change and increases in economic interdependence will make existing international regime obsolete' and that more economic interactions 'will give governments strong incentive to modify or reconstruct international regimes to restore their effectiveness (Keohane & Nye, 1989, p. 40)'. Based on the aforementioned analysis, China's domestic policy and its subsequent increasing interdependence with ASEAN fit all the three assumptions of the economic process model of CIT. Therefore, it will be taken into consideration as a theoretical framework for the empirical studies in this book.

When negotiating to set up the CAFTA, China expressed its good will towards ASEAN by making economic concessions to its members. Firstly, China promised to give the MFN treatment to those ASEAN countries that were not WTO members. Moreover, ASEAN-4 members were given another five years to finally complete their free trade area with China in 2015. In addition, ASEAN-4 were allowed to set out their exclusion list of products which would be exempted by China in the Early Harvest Plan (EHP), and ASEAN-6 were permitted to list specific products which would not be excluded from the EHP by China. China's economic concession made to ASEAN members were rooted in its assumption that neighbourly stability and development was a *sine qua non* of China's domestic stability and development, which was articulated in its regional diplomacy strategy. In the long term, China was striving for domestic and neighbourly stability and development by maintaining the existing regional regime; in the short term, China was willing to make necessary economic concessions in order to realize its long-term aims. This fits the definition of 'leader' proposed by the CIT, that 'leading states forgo short-run gains in bargaining in order to secure the long-run gains associated with stable international regimes (Keohane & Nye, 1989, p. 231).'

By making economic concessions to ASEAN, China induced ASEAN to help stabilize the existing regional regime. After the crisis, ASEAN's economic policy had obvious characteristics of outward-oriented development. It negotiated to set up a free trade area with Australia and New Zealand around the Pacific while it took the CAFTA in East Asia into consideration. When it was puzzled about which side to rely on between Asia-Pacific and East Asia, China's great concessions undoubtedly helped it to choose, and *vice versa*. After initiating to establish the CAFTA, China really needed ASEAN to cooperate. Happily, ASEAN agreed to the proposal of the CAFTA a year after China's initiative in 2001 and the two sides endorsed the CAFTA agreement in 2002. This reveals that, at that time, ASAN believed that it would benefit from the establishment of the CAFTA by reducing the negative impacts of China's entry into the WTO. In other words, ASEAN took for granted that the newly built CAFTA cooperation institution between China and ASEAN would benefit ASEAN and ASEAN approved the legitimacy of the newly built regime between them. It makes mush sense that China was a hegemonic player in security building between China and ASEAN in realist lens (Dosch, 2007, p. 213). Meanwhile, assumptions of CIT made China's role in economic cooperation with ASEAN also close to the definition regarding the non-hegemonic leader[5]. According to CIT, a non-hegemonic leader 'is based on action to induce other states to help stabilize an international regime. Large states are most likely to make short-run sacrifices, because they are likely to be major beneficiaries of the regime...other states must cooperate somewhat...Cooperation by middle-level states, will depend in turn on the legitimacy of the regime (Keohane & Nye, 1989, p. 231).' Therefore, on the one hand, the overall power model is taken into consideration as another theoretical alternative to identify China's role in economic integration in East Asia; furthermore, on the other hand, the characteristics of the non-hegemonic leader offered by CIT is conducive to identify to what extent China or Japan fits the model of a non-hegemonic leader in economic integration in East Asia. If a non-hegemonic leader means it is contested by other players, then both China and Japan's roles are to be considered. And it is for sure that Japan's role must be paid more attention if the book was related to economic integration in East Asia in the 1970s, 1980s and 1990s. However, since the book focuses on economic integration in East Asia in the 2000s, then China's role must be stressed. China and Japan's role in East Asian economic cooperation will go in detail in Chapter Seven.

Within the analytical framework of the issue structure, China impressed its East Asian neighbours with its capability of issue-setting and agenda-making when negotiating to establish the CAFTA. China initially put forth the proposal to set up a free trade area relationship at the fourth ASEAN+1(China) Leaders Summit in 2000; and it made it a formal proposal at the fifth ASEAN+1(China) Leaders Summit in 2001. The CAFTA proposal was the first free trade area arrangement in East Asia. During the next ten years, China and ASEAN made great efforts to negotiate and come to agreements first on trade in goods, then on trade in service and finally on investment. Unlike the free trade area in Western Europe and in North America, these agreements on trade and investment were not done simultaneously; one was negotiated while the others were agreed or implemented. This step-by-step, issue-by-issue, incremental approach was applied to the whole process of the CAFTA establishment. For example, when the overall agreement on trade in goods was being negotiated, the EHP programme of agricultural product trade had been implemented. When the investment agreement was being negotiated, the agreements of trade in goods and in service had taken effect and come into practice. All these showed strong evidence for China's success of issue-setting and agenda-making. This fits the assumption on issue structure that 'the strong states (in an

---

[5] Here, non-hegemonic means the leadership is contested.

issue area) will make the rules (Keohane & Nye, 1989, p. 50)'.

However, during the cooperation process between China and AESAN, China, as the relatively powerful party, did not try to link any issue to the establishment of the CAFTA, as the CIT presumed. On the contrary, it was ASEAN, the relatively weak party that tried to link the building of the ASEAN Economic Community (AEC) to the establishment of the CAFTA. When negotiating for the CAFTA agreement, ASEAN demanded China's full support to the Community and prioritized it over the establishment of the East Asian free trade area in the future. ASEAN also linked the Community issue to the establishment of the free trade area between ASEAN and Japan and that between ASEAN and South Korea. Within such a context, the assumption that 'the strong makes the rules' was not fulfilled. The issue structure shows that 'this link from the below (poor, weak states) is an anomaly which neither structural model adequately explains (Keohane & Nye, 1989, p. 53)'.

Regarding the international organization model, international organization refers to multilevel linkages, norms, and institution, including formal networks at the government level and informal sectoral association/enterprise networks at the trans-government level. In the case of East Asia, the economic integration saw more clearly the role of formal organizations such as governmental cooperation institutions than that of informal network such as the cooperation intuitions at the sectoral association/enterprise level. East Asian economic integration started from the 1997-8 AFC, when the role of governments in managing regional financial crisis and promoting the regional economic cooperation was highlighted. As a result, economic integration in East Asia during the next years was more embodied in inter-governmental regionalism instead of sectoral/transnational regionalization. This is a feature of the process of East Asian economic integration, which will be discussed in further detail in Chapter Seven.

To sum up, the four models of CIT have their own strengths in analysing economic cooperation between China and ASEAN and China's role in economic integration in East Asia. The economic process model focuses the analysis on China's motives for proposing to establish the CAFTA on China's domestic policy and concentrates on the evaluation of Sino-ASEAN economic relationship on an interdependent basis. The overall power structure model highlights China's power in East Asia; furthermore, its definition of the non-hegemonic leader is conducive to identity to what extent China fits the model of leadership in East Asia. Although the issue structure model could not explain the issue linkage from below, it was good for analysing the incremental approach China applied to economic integration in East Asia. Therefore, the CIT is an effective theoretical framework for empirical studies of the economic relationship between China and ASEAN, China's role in economic integration in East Asia and the approach and outlook of East Asian economic integration. However, applying the CIT to studies on regional politics in East Asia has inevitable weaknesses like other theoretical frameworks that were adopted in empirical studies. The author has to manage to make up for the deficiencies. This matter is considered in detail in the next section.

3.1.4   Weakness and Remedy

Applying CIT to the empirical studies of regional politics in East Asia, China's role and China's motives for changing its role in East Asia poses great challenges to the theory *per se*. Firstly, '(complex interdependence theory) seems less relevant to communist states and many less developed states than it does to advanced industrial countries (Keohane & Nye, 1989, p. 226).' If this is the case, then China, as a communist state and a developing country, may be unsuitable for applying a theoretical framework of complex interdependence. In addition, as the complex interdependence theorists asserted, 'they do not focus directly on national policy, but on the development and decline of international regimes...Our level of analysis is the world system, rather than national policy (Keohane & Nye, 1989, p. 223)' or regional regimes. However, applying the theory to studies of China's role in economic cooperation with ASEAN and that in economic integration in East Asia would focus the analysis on national policy of China in East Asian region, which obviously goes against the original intention of the interdependence theorists.

China, like advanced industrial countries the interdependence theorists investigated, took great responsibility for domestic economic welfare. Although it maintains a communist political system, the central government's focus is still on economic development, as analysed in the previous section. China is a perfect example of the assumption of CIT that 'governments in nearly all types of countries have increasingly been held responsible for economic development more than military. Governments will continue to be held responsible for economic welfare (Keohane & Nye, 1989, p. 226)'. Given this and the fact that interdependence theorists did not clearly explain the reasons why their theory were less fitful for communist states and more for developed countries, it is safe to apply the interdependence theory to studies of China.

Interdependence theorists thought that if the interdependence theory was applied to studies of the policy of a nation under interdependent conditions, the severity of the external constraints and the comparative analysis of the domestic structures and political process of the particular nations must be investigated (Keohane & Nye, 1989, p. 223). In the case of East Asian economic integration, the United States, who was keen to get involved in it, yet preferred regional liberalization (rather than economic integration) in the wider geographical Asia-Pacific (instead of East Asia), was evidently an independently external variable for East Asia. The United States used to predominantly lead economic liberalization in Asia-Pacific within the framework of APEC organization during the Clinton administration (1992-2001). However, when the US's initiative of Early Voluntary Sectoral Liberalization (EVSL) met with a lukewarm response from ASEAN and Japan in the late 1990s, the US and the APEC did not make any breakthrough, either in economic liberalization or economic integration in Asia-Pacific. 'During the George W. Bush administration (2001-2008), Washington was busy in anti-terrorist war in Iraq and Afghanistan and failed to take an active part in regional integration in Asia-Pacific. After Barack Obama cam into power in 2008,

Washington invested more in Asia-Pacific region in order to increase exports and go out of the crisis as soon as possible. The most representative event was that the US joined the Trans-Pacific Partnership (TPP) Agreement with a view to reintegrate the overall Asia-Pacific region according to the American roadmap'[6]. In consideration of the US's proactive role in economic integration in Asia-Pacific region, it was likely to be an external variable for China-led economic integration in East Asia. However, in terms of its disappointing support for East Asian countries during the 1997-8 AFC, it made sense for ASEAN to place more hope and reliance on China. Therefore, China, as an internal factor, is likely to play a more significant role than the US as an external variable. When conducting empirical studies, the author takes into consideration the US's role in East Asian economic integration and explores how severe the external constraint of the US is in Chapter Seven.

Furthermore, as interdependence theorists asserted if the theory was applied to studies of a nation's policy, the domestic politics must be investigated (Keohane & Nye, 1989, p. 223). Therefore, the author conducts comparative studies of China's domestic economic policy on trade and investment before and after 2001 so as to overcome the weakness of applying the interdependence theory to studies of a nation's policy. In 2001, China officially put forth the proposal to set up the CAFTA between China and ASEAN within ten years, which displayed a dramatic change in China's attitude towards economic cooperation with ASEAN and economic integration in East Asia. Beijing used to emphasize the promotion of political and security relations with ASEAN, given their newly built/restored diplomatic relationship after the Cold War ended and the historic territorial disputes with some ASEAN members during the 1990s. In contrast, Beijing diversified its focuses of relationship with ASEAN after 2001 by taking into consideration more economic cooperation with ASEAN and showed great eagerness to get involved in economic integration in East Asia by initiating the establishment of the first free trade area there. The comparative studies of China's economic policy before and after 2001 are anticipated to identify clearly and exactly the different roles of China in East Asia. This in turn lays a basis for exploring the domestic motives that induced China to change its attitude towards economic cooperation/integration with ASEAN in East Asia. By applying CIT in study of East Asian regionalism and fixing its weaknesses, the author is able to analyse China's role in economic integration in East Asia and explore China's motives for shifting its attitude towards it from a Chinese perspective.

In summary, the CIT proves to be very suitable theoretical framework to explain economic cooperation between China and ASEAN, although both of them were non-Western actors. First and foremost, the economic relationship between China and ASEAN was part of the world-wide economic relations, which, argued by complex interdependence theorist were mutually interdependent. In further words, the Sino-

---

[6] Interview with an official from the Institute of the American Studies, China Institute of Contemporary International Relations (CICIR), Beijing, 15 July, 2010

ASEAN economic relations fit the three main characteristics of mutual interdependence: multiple channels, absence of hierarchy among issues and the minor role of military force; and three of the four political modes were able to explain the regime changes between China and ASEAN at the regional level. Moreover, the CIT was suitable to investigate the relative gains/losses in the economic cooperation between China and ASEAN. Whether China was competitive for ASEAN in the third export markets and whether China crowded out ASEAN's FDI from developed economies were good examples for the relative gains/losses subject. In addition, China, as a communist country and an economy in transition, could be a research object of CIT after its domestic politics were explored to remedy the weaknesses of CIT. Finally, the United States and Japan could be treated as external factors within complex interdependence framework by looking into their implications for economic cooperation between China and ASEAN and for China-led economic integration in East Asia. Therefore, the CIT proves to be a very suitable theoretical framework, within which Sino-ASEAN economic relations, China's motives to shift its attitude towards economic cooperation with ASEAN and China's role in it can be studied effectively and efficiently.

> *'However, when we adopt international relations theory which originally came up in a Western academic environment, we need to be especially careful about it application in an Eastern/China subject. The complex interdependence theory assumed global people were living ina complex interdependent world, which hinted the possibility that it could be adopted in the East/China. Nonetheless, this does not exclude the possible mistake that it could be applied mechanically in China, which were always called on to avoid by Chinese scholars. When we conduct research of China-related issue within the complex interdependence theory, those cases which do not conform to the assumptions of the theory must be taken into special consideration. Only by this, can the mistakes of adopting the theory mechanically to an Eastern/China subject be avoided and the weakness of applying a Western theory to the Eastern/China-related subject can be remedied'.*[7]

Therefore, in the case of this book, the author took special consideration of China's domestic politics

---

[7] Interview with a professor of international relations theory in School of International Studies, Nanjing University, Nanjing, 12 August, 2011

before and after 2001 and saw the United States and Japan as the external factors for China-led economic integration with ASEAN in East Asia, which hopefully could remedy the weaknesses of the CIT in an Eastern academic environment.

3.2   Methodology: the GTM

In social science research, theory and method inevitably interplay (Maanen, SØrensen, & Mitchell, 2007, p. 1145). Political science research is no exception. This is why the methodological part was placed immediately following the theoretical part in this chapter. As mentioned in the Literature Review, there is no theory in studies of East Asian integration/regionalism as applicable as in the case of neo-functionalism for European integration studies. Although CIT was applied in this book, this hardly changes that fact. Furthermore, CIT has some weaknesses when applied to research of economic integration in East Asia. Firstly, CIT focuses on international regime changes at the world level, instead of at the regional level. Secondly, during the process of economic integration in East Asia, people valued significantly the role of national governments; however, the domestic politics of national governments are comparatively ignored by CIT. Finally, CIT is said to be less relevant to communist/less developed countries (as China in the case of this book) than to advanced industrial countries. In some sense, application of CIT to studies of East Asian economic integration, whose substance was Sino-ASEAN economic cooperation, is likely to overlook some essential features of it. The weaknesses of applying CIT to studies of East Asian economic integration played a potentially significant part in the method chosen for this book. The grounded theory method, which aims to grasp a large quantity of data and generalize the data in order to induce a new theory, seems appropriate, given the lack of a proper theory applicable to East Asia. According to Keith F. Punch, 'if a satisfactory theory already exists on a particular topic, there is little point in mounting a study to generate a new theory about that topic. The rationale for doing a grounded theory study is that we have no satisfactory theory on the topic and that we do not understand it enough to begin theorizing (Punch, 1998, pp. 167-168)'. Therefore, this book adopted the GTM to investigate the basic facts as much as possible and summarize related theoretical issues and analyse them. Of special note is that the objective of adopting the grounded theory method was not to generate a new theory; instead, the main principles of the GTM were adopted in this book so that the author was able to collect as much as possible data and summarize related theoretical issues and verify them within the theoretical framework of complex interdependence.

As far as the data sources are concerned, data from both primary and secondary sources informed the analysis. The primary data sources included individual anthologies of Chinese leaders; government publications, agreements, declarations and resolutions made by China and ASEAN, etc. as well as elite interviews, and the secondary sources included monographs, newspapers, periodicals, statistical yearbooks and so on.

Two methods of data collection were used: extensive search of documentary sources and in-depth interviews of pertinent elites. China-related data relied more on in-depth elite interviews, while ASEAN-related data depended more on documentary sources (partly because of lack of access to ASEAN elites). Data was mainly processed by two methods: documentary/textual analysis and grounded theory analysis. Other methods such as narrative analysis, policy evaluation analysis and content analysis also contributed to the research project.

This methodological part proceeds with four sections. The first one discusses what the GTM is and how it was applied in this book. The second presents the methods of data collection. Next follows a discussion of data analysis methods. Finally, a brief summary concludes this part.

3.2.1   What Is the GTM and How Is It Applied?

At first glance, the GTM is sometimes misunderstood as a theory. As a matter of fact, it is not a theory, but a method. 'Grounded theory is best defined as a research strategy whose purpose is to generate theory from data. 'Grounded' means that the theory will be generated on the basis of data; the theory will therefore be grounded in data. 'Theory' means that the objective of collecting and analysing the research data is to generate theory…Theory will be developed inductively from data (Punch, 1998, p. 163).' An important point to make is that in this book, the aim of applying GTM is definitely not to create a theory. Instead, it aims to refine data, summarize relative theoretical issues and then analyse the issues within a theoretical framework of complex interdependence, which is thought the closest and most relevant theory to economic integration in East Asia.

Data collection and data analysis proceed simultaneously when the GTM was applied. Guided by the initial research questions, the first set of data collection began. After the initial data collection, even if it was of a small amount, the data was immediately analysed before more data was collected. The process was iterated to constitute a cycle of data collection followed by data analysis. Thus, after the first round of data analysis, the second cycle of data collection started, guided by the issue directions emerging during the first cycle of data analysis. It continued until new data revealed no new theoretical elements. Following this procedure, the author, in this book, applied GTM by doing data collection and data analysis cycle by cycle until theoretical saturation was reached where no new theoretical issues came up from the data.

Of special note is that 'grounded theory is essentially an inductive technique, but it uses deduction as well. It stresses induction as the main tool for theory development, but, in developing the theory, deduction will also often be necessary (Punch, 1998, p. 167)'. In light of the special aim of applying GTM in this book, deduction was used more than induction, particularly when the summarized theoretical issues were analysed within the theoretical framework of complex interdependence.

3.2.2   Data Collection

This section discusses what kinds of data were collected in this book, and by what means.

Generally speaking, data were collected from a range of primary and secondary sources. The primary sources included:

1.   In-depth elite interview

2.   Individual anthologies of Chinese leaders and their speeches/reports at the CPC National Congress

3.   Official government publications of China

4.   Declarations, resolutions and other relevant documents of ASEAN at various conferences

5.   Official websites of ministries of China

6.   Official websites of ASEAN and nonofficial websites for Track Two Diplomacy of ASEAN

7.   Official agreements endorsed by China and ASEAN

8.   Other relevant primary sources

The secondary sources included:

1.   Monographs, newspapers, periodicals, magazines and so on in both Chinese-language and English-language

2.   Relevant statistical data from governmental and non-governmental institutions

3.   Other relevant secondary sources

Two methods of data collection were applied: documentary search and personal interview. Documentary and archival sources offer great opportunities for political scientists to develop novel accounts and interpretations of significant events; therefore, documentary research was the primary choice for data collection. Documentary data was searched for thirty years from the 1980s onward. In terms of the general context in the world and the regional context in particular, searching for data from the 1980s onward made sense. This was because a significant turning point occurred in to both China and ASEAN's domestic policies and foreign policies from the 1980s onward. As explained earlier, Chinese policy of reform and opening up was implemented in 1978 at home and regional cooperation was launched after the 1997-8 AFC. ASEAN set about sub/intra-regional cooperation in the 1980s and its outward-looking policy went beyond Southeast Asia also after 1997-8 AFC. Data during the 1980s and 1990s were conducive to describing what role China and ASEAN played before bilateral regional economic cooperation proliferated and the data after the 2000 provided evidence for why and how their roles changed. For the earlier period, secondary sources could be usefully applied, while for the post-crisis period, primary sources were more helpful. For China-related data, more reliance could be placed on primary sources, given the advantage of the author's Chinese-language and the high feasibility of elite interviews in China. In contrast, for ASEAN-related data, more dependence was placed on secondary sources, due to the financial constraints related to travelling for interviews. This book focuses on a Chinese perspective of Sino-ASEAN economic relations and investigates China's motives for changing its attitude and role in economic integration in East Asia from an inward-oriented perspective. ASEAN perspective research was supplementary rather than the focus of the book. Given this, it was safe to place more reliance for China-related data on primary sources and more reliance for ASEAN-related data on secondary sources.

Another useful way to collect primary data was via interviews. Data collected via interviews is specific and unique, which will significantly contribute to the depth of the book. In order to obtain the first hand data, which were rare in the empirical literature, the author applied the elite interview in this book. From summer 2009 onward, the author began to contact the potential interviewees. Many difficulties, however, were foreseen in carrying out interviews in China. Those difficulties were taken into careful consideration and solutions were found.

The first challenge was who would be interviewed, in terms of the book subject. Interviewees were constrained to the elites, primarily with a Chinese focus, who came out as decision-proposers, decision-makers and decision-executers as well as pertinent academic scholars, who were also in close contact with the former. In China, sometimes, decision-proposers were also academic scholars, e.g. members of the ASEAN-China Expert Group on Economic Cooperation (EGEC) and the ASEAN-China Eminent Persons Group (EPG). In this case, the senior expert members of EGEC were potential interviewees. Moreover, the former minister of Ministry of Foreign Affairs, Qian Qichen, was among the most important members of the Eminent Persons Group. In consideration of the difficulty in gaining access to him, perhaps, his assistant would be another potential interviewee. When she was invited to attend the 5th China National Association of International Studies (CNAIS) doctoral forum in Nanjing in April 2010, the author met Mr. Qin Yaqin, the special assistant of Qian Qichen, who also attended the forum as a reviewer. Fortunately, the author was given the chance to interview him. Decision-makers in China tended to be at the central governmental level. For example, Zhu Rongji, the former Premier of China, who witnessed the initiation, establishment and final completion of the free trade area, was a perfect potential interviewee, although it was difficult to bypass the gatekeepers to gain access to him. Meanwhile, some senior officials of Ministry of Commerce, China also participated in the decision-making process, therefore, they were possible interviewees too. In contrast, decision-executers were from both central governmental and local/provincial level in China. At the central level, the Ministry of Commerce (MOC) and its predecessor Ministry of Foreign Trade and Economic Cooperation (MOFTEC) were good sources of potential interviewees. Specifically, the former minister, Shi Guangsheng, who participated to promote the establishment of free trade area at the early stage, would be a good potential interviewee. However, not any official of the MOC responded to the interview query after the author tried two or three times to contact them via written letters and emails. Luckily, a former official of the MOC, who was at that time a senior leader of of Guangxi Provincial Department of Commerce, sited in Nanning, agreed for the interview, and the author successfully interviewed him when she stayed at Nanning during summer 2010. At the local level, City of Nanning, the capital of Guangxi Province, where many executing institutions of CAFTA at provincial level are located, would be a good source of potential interviewees. For example, the CAExpo Secretariat and the CABIS Secretariat were good sources of potential interviewees. The author tried to meet Mr. Gong Qijun, the vice director of the Bureau of the CAExpo and Mr. Deng Shijun, the director of the International Conference of the CABIS Secretariat in August, 2010. Three strategies of interview- unstructured, semi-structured and structured interviews-were used. Semi-structured interviews were the main method, supplemented by the other two. The length of every interview, depending on structure of the interview, was originally estimated to be forty five minutes. The preferred location for the interview was the office of the interviewees.

The second big challenge was how to form a rapport between the interviewer and the interviewees in light of the big gaps in different dimensions between them. Difference in age and experience, social status, and sometimes, even gender, posed great challenge to forming rapport between the interviewer and the interviewees. For example, 'a big age differential, where the researcher is considerably younger than the respondent, can make it difficult for the interviewer to be taken seriously (Odendahl & Shaw, 2002, p. 312)'. In this case, the interviewer's overseas study experience might be able to help overcome the problem. Educated and trained systematically and strictly overseas in the UK, the interviewer had access to a large number of sources about her subject; many of which might not be available to the interviewees. This could balance knowledge and reduce the risk of age and (in) experience; and ultimately help establish rapport between the interviewer and the interviewees.

A gap in social status between the interviewer and the interviewees would add another difficulty in the expected rapport. This seldom posed a big problem if an interviewee also came from academia. In this case, 'both interviewee and interviewer were social scientists sharing a prevailing academic attitude. There were shared expectations of research processes manifest in expectation of research competency and intellectual curiosity (Stephens, 2007, p. 207).' This was expected to reduce the social status gap. Moreover, many of the elites from academia were also supervising Ph.D. students; the interviewer could benefit from mimicking a supervisor-Ph.D. student relationship for the interview setting. As far as those elites from political realm, i.e. the policy-makers and policy-executers, were concerned, less similarity existed between them and the interviewer. Nevertheless, what the researcher was studying in academia was highly relevant to the policies they were implementing. It was hoped this would stimulate their interest in the interview.

Another interesting challenge related to gender. Each of the interviewees was male, who would be less comfortable if the female interviewer controlled the pace of the interview. According to Neil Stephens, 'where a women researcher is interviewing other women, this is a situation with special characteristics conducive to the easy flow of information (Finch, 1999, p. 70)'. It is argued that where the interviewer is female (as in this case) and the interviewee is male, there 'is a threat in as much as an interviewer controls the interaction, asks questions that put these elements of manly self-portrayal into doubt, and does not simply affirm a man's masculinity displays (Schwalbe & Wolkomir, 2002, p. 312)'. For example, the author encountered such difficulty when she interviewed Mr. Sun Jianqiu, the deputy director of Guangxi Provincial Department of Commerce. The author failed to follow the pre-designed interview questions at a planned pace to do the interview with him. The interviewee made a plan for this after he asked the author to send him the questionnaire, where all the planned questions were listed. As soon as he met the author, he began his presentation on his own. The author was not given a chance to ask any more questions. After his presentation for forty-five minutes, the author was informed that there was a conference urgently waiting for the interviewee, and he had to leave. Then this interview ended up with unstructured questions. In spite, in most of the interview cases, the author tried to take care to be more polite and more respectful to these elites (but without undermining their status as interviewees). In the process of interviews, tape recording is a good way to save the conversation and keep the data. Further review of the tape recordings and more detailed conversation analysis after the event would help to reduce the gender-induced risks.

Despite the difficulties mentioned above, the elite interview was a good alternative for collecting the primary data. In summer 2010, the author went to Nanjing, Beijing and Nanning, China to do elite interviews. Twenty of the forty originally contacted interviewees responded the author. Although some difficulties emerged, the author overcame the difficulties and interviewed twenty elites. They included those policy-proposers/senior experts from EGEC, EPG, China Association of Southeast Asian Studies (CASAS), policy-makers from MOC, Ministry of Foreign Affairs (MFA) sited and policy-executers from CAExpo, CABIS and ACBC. Moreover, the author managed to interview some elite practitioners of Nanning (China-ASEAN) Commodity Exchange (NCCE) sited in Nanning. In addition, the author succeeded in interviewing a number of elites from the biggest official think tank: China Institute of Contemporary International Relations (CICIR) although some elites interviewed asked for anonymity in light of the high sensitivity of their workplace in China. In all, although the number of the interviewed elites was limited due to the availability of experts on the subject in this book and financial constraints sometimes, in all cases, interviews were conducted in depth with highly knowledgeable individuals. Within one and a half hours interviews at average, those interviews supplied a great deal of primary data for the study in this book. They, together with documentary research, enable the author to have adequate primary and secondary data for her book.

3.2.3   Data Analysis

When analysing collected data, the author applied many methods to do qualitative analysis, such as the grounded theory analysis, analytical induction, documentary analysis, narrative analysis and policy evaluation analysis and so forth.

The grounded theory helped to abstract theoretical issues from the practices of East Asian integration. The analysis proceeds in three steps. 'The first is to find conceptual categories (substantive codes) in the data, at a first level of abstraction. The second is to find relationships (theoretical codes) between these categories. The third is to conceptualize and account for these relationships (core codes) at a higher level of abstraction (Punch, 1998, p. 210).' In the case of East Asian integration, the 'substantive codes' constituted several significant events on the way to East Asian integration, i.e. China and ASEAN began a dialogue in the early 1990s, 1997-8 AFC broke out, China entered the WTO in 2001, China and ASEAN endorsed bilateral agreement cooperation in 2002, and the two sides completed the CAFTA in 2010, just to list a few. The 'theorizing codes' are evidence of the relationship between these events. For example, the first dialogue in the early 1990s provided opportunities for both sides to begin economic cooperation; the 1997-8 AFC acted as catalyst in stimulating both sides to take bilateral economic cooperation into consideration; China's accession to the WTO in 2001 posed a direct pressure for ASEAN to cooperate with it, and the bilateral agreement on economic cooperation in 2002 was the most crucial step for East Asian integration. Finally, the 'core codes' were evidences of the role of national states (China) in regional integration, motives that stimulated China to set out economic cooperation with ASEAN, conditions on which China was willing to make economic concessions, the role of multi-governmental institutions between China and ASEAN and so forth. In the case of CIT, these issues can be abstracted as 1. Whether China played the role of (a non-hegemonic) leader in East Asian economic integration; 2. What changes happened to the power structure in East Asia when China and ASEAN decided to set up the CAFTA; 3. Whether China was willing to forgo short-run gains in order to obtain the long-term gains; and 4. What kind of role trans-governmental institutions played in economic integration in East Asia. These questions related to the core assumptions of CIT and they were also the 'core codes' of the grounded theory method.

On the basis of these three steps, the research was able to summarize some theoretical issues such as those mentioned above. However, the grounded theory analysis is weak in responding to these theoretical issues within an existing theory because it is an entirely inductive process; it does not verify findings and it somehow 'molds' the data to the theory (rather than the reverse) (Berg, 1989, p. 111). Thus, this raised the issue of how questions/hypotheses could be addressed and whether these hypotheses were suitable to other cases beyond the significant events from which they were inferred. In such cases, the method of analytical induction helped to verify these hypotheses. Analytical induction directs 'researchers to study evidence that challenges or disconfirms concepts or ideas they are developing, paying particular attention to the negative cases, or exceptions (Punch, 1998, p. 202)'. This allowed the researcher to further verify whether the hypotheses were correct, or to revise them if they were not. For example, based on the summarization of core codes, China was a non-hegemonic leader in consideration of China's issue-setting and agenda-making capability, and the economic concessions China made to ASEAN. However, as a matter of fact, China's leaders strongly promoted ASEAN's leading role in East Asia. At this point, China seemed not to have the willingness to act as a leader. While the GTM focused attention on the evidence for China's leading role in East Asian economic integration, the analytical induction method showed evidence that was not consistent with the argument. This is quite necessary in research.

During the process of the grounded theory analysis and analytical induction analysis, the documentary and narrative analysis reminded us of the need to pay more attention to the basic and hard evidence, which showed us something closer to the real facts. Because documentary and textual communicative practices are a vital way in which organizations constitute 'reality' and the forms of knowledge appropriate to it (Atkinson & Amanda, 1997, p. 47), documentary and textual analysis is of particular importance in data analysis. In addition, because official publications constituted a large part of the primary sources, primary sources had to be approached from an 'interpretive' stance instead of a 'critical' and 'evaluative' stance (Atkinson & Amanda, 1997, p. 49). A comprehensive agreement and four subordinate agreements signed by ASEAN and China in the 2000s constituted the most important primary sources on the subject of the book; therefore, content analysis was an imperative means by which these agreements and their context were analysed.

In addition to the grounded theory analysis, inductive analysis and content analysis, narrative analysis also contributes to the data analysis in this book. China's roles in economic integration in East Asia before and after were embodied through contexts when bilateral agreements between China and ASEAN were negotiated and endorsed. To narrate the changes of the context is one of advantages of narrative analysis. Therefore, it was adopted in this book. Narrative analysis identifies the basic story which is told, focusing on the way an account or narrative is constructed, the intention of the teller and the nature of the audiences as well as the meaning of the story or 'plot' (Spencer, Ritchie, & O'Connor, 2003, p. 200). It was useful for describing ASEAN and China's general context and economic policy after the 1980s. Other than documentary analysis, content analysis and narrative analysis, many other analysis methods were also applied to analyse collected primary and secondary data. For example, conversation analysis was applied when interview transcripts were analysed. Since the book is essentially an analysis of China's economic policy, the method of policy and evaluation analysis were also applied to interpret the changes in China's policy of economic cooperation towards ASEAN.

Thus, many methods, mainly the grounded theory analysis, analytical induction, supplemented by documentary and textual analysis, narrative analysis, conversation analysis and policy and evaluation analysis jointly helped to summarize theoretical assumptions from East Asian integration and verify them within the framework of CIT.

3.2.4 A Brief Summary

The methodological part presented the grounded theory method, which was applied in this book due to the absence of a satisfactory theory totally applicable in the case of East Asian economic integration.

Although CIT was applied as an effective theoretical framework in this book, its effectiveness was reduced when analysing China's domestic economic policy at the national level. With resort to the GTM and analytical induction, the author was able to summarize some theoretical issues/hypotheses from practices of East Asian economic integration and verify them within the theoretical framework of complex interdependence.

Regarding data collection, primary and secondary data were collected by documentary research and in-depth interview. Although many difficulties were foreseen in the elite interview, the author found means to overcome them.

With respect to data analysis, grounded theory analysis and analytical induction were applied, supplemented by documentary analysis, content analysis, narrative analysis and policy evaluation analysis. The GTM contributed to abstract significant events of East Asian economic integration, find the relations among them and conceptualize them in a theoretical dimension. This was a deductive process. Analytical induction was carried out in an inductive process and helped to verify the issues summarized in the previous process within the CIT. During the two processes of deduction and induction, content analysis, narrative analysis and policy analysis were applied in narrating the context changes, analysing the agreements between China and ASEAN and evaluating China's policy towards ASEAN. They all contributed to the data analysis in the book.

4 Background for Economic Cooperation between China and ASEAN from the 1980s onward

This chapter describes what happened to the general context and ASEAN's economic policy with respect to trade and investment during the past three decades from the 1980s onward and how the former influenced the latter, in order to investigate the background for trade and investment promotion between ASEAN and China. By exploring the changes in general context at the international and regional levels, the chapter discusses economic policy changes of ASEAN (supplemented by those of China) as well as the new mechanisms for economic cooperation between them.

During the Cold War, ASEAN tried to gain international acceptance as a viable regional organization, made efforts to enlarge its membership and promoted intra-regional economic cooperation, while China implemented an 'open door' policy to develop its domestic economy. After the dark clouds of the Cold War dissipated, ASEAN devoted itself to intra-regional integration by setting up the ASEAN Free Trade Area (AFTA) and to expanding to include all ten members in Southeast Asia. The end of the Cold War provided ASEAN and China with more opportunities to develop their external relationship normally and independently. The two sides officially built the consultative relations in 1994, and upgraded it to be a full dialogue partnership in 1996 and a strategic relationship in 2003.

The evolution of this external relationship facilitated bilateral economic cooperation on aspects of trade and investment. Bilateral trade and investment values saw a gradual increase after the Cold War ended. However, they suffered a heavy setback from the 1997-8 AFC, which exposed the fragility of high GDP growth in East Asia. During the crisis, East Asian countries built up ASEAN+1 (China/Japan/Korea) and ASEAN+3 (China, Japan and Korea) institutions to integrate East Asian countries' strengths to survive the crisis. China promised not to devalue the Chinese currency and supplied financial support for three crisis-plagued ASEAN members, which impressed ASEAN with an image of a great power, a good neighbour and a benign partner.

Shortly after the crisis, in 2000, China took the initiative in proposing to set up a free trade area to enhance bilateral economic cooperation, based on two general considerations. One was that China was standing at the door of the WTO, which would probably intensify the competition between China and ASEAN; and obviously the competition was not in favour of ASEAN. The other was that China forecast the negative impact the WTO accession would have on China's domestic economic development, and China believed enhanced economic cooperation between China and ASEAN would help to address this. At that time, ASEAN got aware of the imperativeness of external economic cooperation with partners and followed a parallel approach of promoting intra-regional and extra-regional economic cooperation, which gave China the chance to turn its proposal into reality. The two sides agreed to set up the CAFTA by 2010.

A further glance at ASEAN suggested that ASEAN was an inter-governmental but not a supranational-governmental organization since the inception of its foundation in the 1960s. Therefore, the ASEAN Secretariat did not play an impressive role in negotiating and endorsing the CAFTA agreement with China. Instead, individual ASEAN member governments played their impressive roles in economic cooperation with China. Particularly, the negotiations and endorsement of the CAFTA agreement were based on bilateral economic cooperation between each ASEAN member and China at the governmental level rather than the regional level between ASEAN as a whole and China.

Before ASEAN and China decided to set up the CAFTA, the ASEAN-China Joint Committee on Economic and Trade Cooperation (JCETC) and the EGEC provided supportive justifications for the establishment of the CAFTA from an academic perspective. This laid an academic basis for the final decision of the CAFTA. After the CAFTA agreement was signed, the ACBC, CAExpo and the CABIS made great contributions to the virtual completion of the CAFTA by introducing, encouraging and facilitating enterprises to participate in the establishment of the CAFTA. These concrete institutions within the framework of ASEAN+1 (China) played a critical role in completing the CAFTA.

The structure of this chapter is as follows: the first section presents the changes in the general context, in which the end of the Cold War in the very early 1990s, the regional economic crisis in Asia in the late 1990s and China's entry into WTO in 2001 are given particular consideration. The changes in the general context had a significant influence on the economic policy of ASEAN; so the second section examines the resulting changes of economic policy in ASEAN and China respectively. ASEAN's economic policy on trade and investment is analysed in details, supplemented by the brief description of China's economic policy. Evidence suggests that ASEAN implemented a parallel approach of promoting both intra-regional and extra-regional economic cooperation during and after the 1997-8 AFC. It looked beyond Southeast Asia and towards East Asia/Asia-Pacific after it became aware of the imperativeness of external economic cooperation with neighbours in Northeast Asia/Asia-Pacific during the crisis. The third section takes a further glance at the institutional nature of ASEAN as a regional organization, the role of ASEAN Secretariat in negotiating and endorsing the CAFTA agreement and the individual member states in ASEAN's relations with China (particularly the Sino-Singapore and Sino-Indonesia relations with regards to the negotiations of CAFTA.) The fourth section includes the new cooperative institutions between ASEAN and China within the framework of ASEAN+1 and ASEAN+3, including detailed account of the JCETC and EGEC, the ACBC, and the CAExpo and CABIS. The fifth section provides a summary.

4.1 General Context

China and ASEAN enhanced bilateral economic cooperation in the 2000s after they endorsed the

Framework Agreement of Comprehensive Economic Cooperation (Framework Agreement) in 2002. Before that, three events in the general context in the region and in the world had great influence on their economic relations. They were the Cold War and its conclusion, the 1997-8 AFC and China's accession to the WTO in 2001. ASEAN devoted itself to enlarging its membership, obtaining international acceptance as a viable regional organization, and developing its domestic economy after it was founded in 1967 until the Cold War ended in 1991. In the meanwhile, China focused on developing its domestic economics as well, after it implemented reform and opening up in 1978. As to political relations between China and ASEAN, China exported revolution to ASEAN and was seen as a threat to ASEAN during the Cold War. China and ASEAN had great opportunity for economic cooperation after the Cold War ended. China restored/newly built normal diplomatic relations with each of ASEAN members individually and with ASEAN as a whole after the conclusion of the Cold War. This partly resulted in promotion of economic cooperation between the two sides; however, the 1997-8 AFC destroyed the promising situation. Some ASEAN members were heavily attacked by the AFC and it took them several years before they could recover from it. In contrast, China was less affected by the AFC; instead it provided as much support as possible to help its neighbours survive the crisis. Thus, China's image as a responsible great power, a good neighbour, and a good partner in East Asia impressed all Southeast Asian countries. In contrast, the United States was eclipsed by China because of its failure to help crisis-hit countries out of the crisis. Nonetheless, China's good image did not last long before its accession to the WTO. ASEAN was very concerned about China's accession because they thought China would compete with them for exports to the west and crowd out ASEAN's FDI flows from advance economies. China officially proposed to set up the CAFTA in 2000 in order to diminish ASEAN's worries. Bilateral economic cooperation was enhanced after the two sides signed the Framework Agreement in 2002.

4.1.1   ASEAN and China during the Cold War

During the Cold War, the two camps were in confrontation and Southeast Asia became the objective they competed for. Regardless of the confrontation in the world, ASEAN was devoted to domestic political affairs (Xu, 2007, p. 56). It was preoccupied with its enlargement to include all ten countries in Southeast Asia and with gaining international acceptance as a viable and energetic regional organization after it was founded in 1967. At the very outset of foundation, ASEAN's founding fathers had the ambitious dream to enlarge ASEAN to include all ten countries in Southeast Asia. There was not much progress on this during the 1980s, when only Brunei applied and was accepted as a new member of ASEAN in 1984. Comparatively, ASEAN succeeded in seeking international acceptance by taking a common stand in international political and economic matters. After Vietnamese occupation of Cambodia at the end of the 1970s, ASEAN kept looking for a just political solution. ASEAN'S initiative resolution, which included withdrawal of foreign forces from Cambodia and the exercise of the right of the self-determination by the

Cambodian people, was unanimously accepted at the 39th session of the United Nations General Assembly in 1984. By its determined efforts to find a just political solution to the Vietnamese occupation of Cambodia, ASEAN succeeded in gaining international acceptance as 'a successful example of a viable and dynamic regional organization' (ASEAN Secretariat, 1983-1984) in the early 1980s.

Economically, the members of ASEAN also began to hold a common position on international economic matters and speak in one voice (Wang, 2006, p. 6). When ASEAN took part in the General Agreement on Tariffs and Trade (GATT) Ministerial Meeting in November 1982, they 'took a common position on nine priority topics' (ASEAN Secretariat, 1982-1983). Besides, ASEAN expressed common views 'on trade liberalization, the proposed new round of Multilateral Trade Negotiations (MTNs), problems relating to commodity, debt problems and high interest rate' at the London Summit in June 1984, which demonstrated ASEAN's joint stand and common approach to dealing with the international economic matters. In addition, ASEAN members asked for their special interest *as a whole* to be considered in the new MTNs at the international level. They jointly conveyed their common concerns on the need to reduce protectionism in developed countries, the seriousness of the debt problem, the continuing instability of commodity prices and the importance of reviving the North-South dialogue' (ASEAN Secretariat, 1984-1985) at the Bonn Summit of G7 in May 1985, where problems facing developing countries were highlighted.

The year 1987 was significant for ASEAN because it was in this year that ASEAN obviously changed its economic policy to one of intra-regional economic cooperation. In 1987, ASEAN members discussed 'various issues of concern, such as political, economic and functional cooperation, ASEAN's relationship with dialogue partners, the machinery for ASEAN cooperation and finalized common positions' (ASEAN Secretariat, 1987-1988) at the Manila Summit. They released the Manila Declaration, which 'outlined the objectives and plans of ASEAN for the immediate present and charts the future course of ASEAN cooperation' (ASEAN Secretariat, 1987-1988) after the Summit. Since then, ASEAN focused on continuing enlarge its members and intra-regional cooperation and integration.

At that time, China implemented reforming and opening-up, after the third Plenum of the 11th Central Committee of the CPC in 1978. Later, in 1982 and 1984, Deng Xiaoping, the general secretary of CPC, made two speeches respectively titled '*To Concentrate on Economic Development*' (Deng, 1993, pp. 9-11) and '*To Maintain World Peace and to Promote Domestic Construction*' (Deng, 1993, pp. 56-57), which demonstrated that China's focus had shifted to domestic economic development on the basis of political peace. As a result of these policies, China achieved high gross domestic product (GDP) growth during the whole 1980s, except in 1989. In 1989, China was criticized by western countries because the People's Liberation Army (PLA) cracked down on the protestors on Tiananmen Square on 4th June. The Tiananmen Square Incident and the subsequent isolation of the western countries resulted in a substantial reduction of bilateral and multilateral economic activities between/among China and the advanced industrial economies.

This gave rise to the lowest annual GDP growth of 3.9% in China in 1989 since 1978.

4.1.2   ASEAN and China after the Cold War Ended

After the Cold War ended, ASEAN continued to enlarge its membership. During the first half of the 1990s, all the existing six ASEAN members achieved high GDP growth through economic cooperation after the Manila Summit in 1987. The remaining four Southeast Asia countries were deeply attracted by ASEAN's economic vitality and high GDP growth. They applied to become members of ASEAN shortly after the Cold War ended. Eventually, they all were accepted to join ASEAN one by one in the 1990s (Viet Nam in 1995, Burma and Laos in 1997 and Cambodia in 1999), which finally realized the great founding fathers' dream of enlarging ASEAN to include all ten Southeast Asian countries.

The Cold War's conclusion speeded up ASEAN's pace towards establishing the AFTA. The AFTA was originally planned to be completed within 15 years, beginning from 1992. Then in 1994, the ASEAN Economic Minister Meeting decided to accelerate the AFTA, with 'the original members (Brunei Darussalam, Indonesia, Malaysia, Philippines, Singapore and Thailand) to advance implementation to 2002' (ASEAN Secretariat, 1998-1999).

The Cold War's conclusion in 1991 relaxed political tensions all around the world. It left a power vacuum in East Asia, which provided China and ASEAN with more chances to recover/newly build normal diplomatic relationship with each other (Guo, 2007, p. 6). During the 1990s, China promoted its relations with those Southeast Asian states, with whom it had already set up normal diplomatic relationship in the 1950s and 1960s, e.g. Cambodia (19th July, 1958), Indonesia (13th April, 1950), Laos (25th April, 1961), Myanmar (8th June, 1950) and Viet Nam (18th January, 1950). Moreover, China repaired its relationship with those with whom it had set up a normal relationship in the 1970s but which had been destroyed during the Cold War. Among them were Malaysia, the Philippines and Thailand, with whom China set up relationship respectively on 31st May, 1974, 9th June, 1975 and 1st July, 1975. What is more important was that China set up new diplomatic relationship with the two remaining states of ASEAN: Singapore (3rd October, 1990) and Brunei (30th September, 1991). Thus, by the early 1990s, China had normal diplomatic relations with all ten ASEAN members.

China not only promoted its bilateral relationship with each of the ten ASEAN members, but also enhanced its relationship with ASEAN as a whole after the Cold War ended. China began a formal dialogue with ASEAN when Qian Qichen, the former Foreign Minister of China, was invited by Malaysia to attend the 24th ASEAN Ministerial Meeting (AMM) in 1991. At this meeting, Qian Qichen proposed to establish programmes for cooperation in science and technology, trade and economic relations with ASEAN, which opened the door of economic cooperation between China and ASEAN. Later, ASEAN sent a delegation to Beijing to explore China's proposals and potential areas of cooperation. In 1994, the ASEAN-China 'consultative' relationship was formalized when the Secretary-General of ASEAN and the Chinese Foreign Minister exchanged views by letter. China was upgraded to the status of a full dialogue partner with ASEAN in July 1996, with the continuous development of bilateral political exchanges. China, for the first time, attended the meeting between ASEAN and its dialogue partners in 1996. When Jiang Zemin, the former President of China, attended the first ASEAN-China Summit in December 1997, he and the ten ASEAN leaders signed the Joint Declaration to establish a good-neighbour partnership in the 21st century. Greater and closer economic cooperation between ASEAN and China strengthened both sides to deal with the increasing challenges of regionalism development in other areas such as Asia-Pacific, West Europe and North America (Writing Group of Guangxi Academy of Social Science, 2006, p. 1). The slow progress of Uruguay Round MTNs in the late 1980s and the early 1990s stimulated Asia-Pacific, West Europe and North America to increase regional economic cooperation. In the Asia-Pacific region, the first session of the APEC Ministerial Meeting strongly advocated by the United States, was held in Australia in 1989. The foundation of the APEC, more or less, dwarfed and weakened ASEAN's role in economic cooperation in East Asia/Asia-Pacific. The United States placed so much hope in the APEC and it was so deeply dedicated to economic cooperation and liberalization within the framework of the APEC that it, to a great extent, ignored ASEAN as a potentially workable organization for regional cooperation. It even postponed the regular annual dialogue meeting with ASEAN in 1989 to the following year because it was too preoccupied in the APEC affairs. In West Europe, the members of the European Community signed the 'Maastricht Treaty' in 1 February, 1992, which marked the final establishment of the single market in West Europe. This added to the regional pressure for economic cooperation in Asia-Pacific. In North America, the United States and Canada began to negotiate to set up a free trade area in 1989. Later, Mexico joined them. After fourteen months of negotiation, in 1992, the United States, Canada and Mexico signed the 'North America Free Trade Agreement' (NAFTA), which came into effect on 1 January 1994. This marked the establishment of a FTA in North America, which again placed added pressure on ASEAN for economic development and cooperation. These pressures at the international and regional levels threatened ASEAN's status in the world and in the region in the early 1990s; besides, the ravaging 1997-8 AFC again exacerbated the situation ASEAN was struggling to survive. At that time, China played an important role in helping ASEAN survive these pressures.

4.1.3 ASEAN and China after the 1997-8 AFC

The regional economic crisis exposed the fragility of high GDP growth in Southeast Asia and heavily attacked many East Asian countries. However, the crisis did not eliminate the Asian countries' enthusiasm for economic cooperation and integration. On the contrary, ASEAN was determined to further speed up the pace towards AFTA. On 1 January 2003, ASEAN declared the completion of the AFTA. When realizing economic integration, ASEAN also paid attention to political and social integration. ASAEN members 'agreed to consider the proposed ASEAN Economic Community (AEC) as an end goal for the Roadmap for the integration of ASEAN and Vision 2020' (ASEAN Secretariat, 2002-2003) at the 9th ASEAN Summit held in Phnom Pen, Cambodia in November 2002.

During the AFC, ASEAN gained much support from China. Firstly, China promised not to devalue the Chinese currency-Ren Min Bi (RMB), which stopped the crisis from spreading further; moreover, China provided financial support for Indonesia, Malaysia and Thailand to help them survive the crisis. Finally, China and ASEAN decided to further promote their political relations at the critical moment of the crisis. They issued a statement shortly after the crisis broke out, and forecast ASEAN-China strategic dialogue relations into the 21st century at the 2nd Informal Summit held in Malaysia in December 1998. This demonstrated ASEAN and Chinese people's determination to overcome the difficulties hand in hand. As a result, China was not seen as a threat to ASEAN; instead, China's image as a responsible great power, a good neighbour and a good partner was established. Nonetheless, this did not last long before China's accession to the WTO in a near future brought about economic worries for ASEAN.

4.1.4   ASEAN and China after China's Accession to the WTO

ASEAN was very worried about the challenges posed by China's accession to the WTO. On the one hand, ASEAN and its members were worried that China would compete with ASEAN for exports to the western countries given China's rising status as a stable international supplier for exports. On the other hand, they were much concerned that China would divert ASEAN's FDI from advanced economies, given China's increasing status as an attractive investment destination. In light of ASEAN's worries, China officially proposed to set up the CAFTA in 2001 in order to diminish the potential implications of China's WTO-accession for ASEAN and to promote bilateral economic cooperation. After two years' negotiation, both sides agreed to establish the CAFTA within ten years and endorsed the Framework Agreement in 2002. Shortly, a series of concrete agreements were negotiated, signed and implemented. In January 2004, the Early Harvest Programme (EHP) came into effect. The Agreement on Trade in Goods (ATG) and the Agreement on Dispute Settlement Mechanism (ADSM) were signed in November 2004, and became effective on 1 January 2005. The Agreement on Trade in Service (ATS) was signed in January 2007 and went into operation on 1st July 2007. The CAFTA Investment Agreement (IA) was signed on 15 August 2009 by Commercial Ministers from the ten ASEAN members and China, which finalized all the main negotiations to establish the CAFTA between ASEAN and China. On 1 January 2010, ASEAN and China declared the virtual completion of the CAFTA, and the biggest FTA in the world came into being.

At the same time, bilateral political relations between China and ASEAN developed smoothly. They upgraded bilateral political relations to a strategic partnership by signing the 'Joint Declaration on Strategic Partnership for Peace and Prosperity at the Bali Summit in 2003'. This marked another critical leap in the bilateral relationship, following the 'full dialogue partnership' in July 1996.

Greater cohesion in economic and political relations between China and ASEAN helped them be more confident when responding to international and regional challenges; such confidence had been weakened to a great extent after the AFC. At the turn of the century, the United States and Europe were suffering from a serious slowdown of economic growth and Japan was experiencing the most painful period of its ten-year-long economic recession after the 1997-8 regional economic crisis in East Asia,. In comparison, both ASEAN and China achieved a historic GDP growth through persistent efforts on domestic economic development and bilateral economic cooperation. That China and ASEAN decided to enhance bilateral economic cooperation supplied East Asia with an enhanced chance to rise, to see a tri-polarity of East Asia, West Europe and North America in the world.

In summary, ASEAN and China concerned themselves with domestic affairs during the Cold War. Regardless of the international confrontations, both ASEAN and China concentrated on domestic development. ASEAN focused on enlarging its membership to include all ten Southeast Asian countries, and on gaining international acceptance as a viable regional organization and intra-regional economic integration, while China focused on implementation of the reform and opening-up policy to develop the domestic economy. After the Cold War ended, ASEAN and China had more chance of developing normal political relations. China not only restored/newly built political relations with each of the ASEAN members after the Cold War ended, but also developed bilateral relations with ASEAN as a whole. China was upgraded from a consultative partner for ASEAN in 1994 to a full dialogue partner in 1996. The 1997-8 AFC witnessed ASEAN's increasing need for China's help. During 1997-8 AFC, China impressed ASEAN with an image of a responsible great power, a good neighbour and a good partner because of its support to ASEAN to help survive the crisis. China's accession to the WTO in the early 2000s gave rise to ASEAN worries about China. In order to diminish such worries, China took the initiative in proposing the establishment of the CAFTA and enhancement of bilateral economic cooperation. This was a turning point for China-ASEAN economic relations. Thereafter, China and ASEAN launched a comprehensive economic cooperation, which constituted the substance of regional economic integration in East Asia and supplied East Asia with great opportunity to rise, with a view to forming a tri-polarity world with Western Europe and North America.

4.2 ASEAN's Economic Policy

The end of the Cold War had further impact on ASEAN-China political relations. Both sides restored/newly built normal political relations between individual ASEAN members and China and also between ASEAN as a whole and China after the Cold War ended. This provided more chances for ASEAN and China to promote their bilateral economic cooperation. In contrast, the 1997-8 AFC had more influence on ASEAN's economic policy. Before the AFC, ASEAN's economic policy was characterized by an inward-oriented preference because ASEAN concentrated on intra-regional economic integration during the decade after the Manila Summit in 1987. Nevertheless, after the AFC, while it paid attention to intra-regional economic integration, it also began to look for extra-regional economic partners in the Asia-Pacific and East Asian areas. The parallel approach of promoting inra-regional and extra-regional economic cooperation was embodied through ASEAN's trade and investment policy. With respect to ASEAN's trade policy, it underlined the intra-regional trade liberalization after the Manila Summit in 1987, paid attention to intra-regional trade integration by deciding to establish the AFTA in 1992 and then highlighted extra-regional trade cooperation as much as intra-regional integration together with intra-regional trade cooperation after the 1997-8 AFC. In simple words, ASEAN's trade policy featured two parallel preferences of intra-regional trade integration and extra-regional trade integration in East Asia/Asia-Pacific. With respect to ASEAN's investment policy, it focused on expanding intra-regional investment flows within ASEAN and strengthening ASEAN's competitiveness as an attractive investment destination when the AFTA was being established; meanwhile it highlighted the needs to attract extra-regional investment inflows particularly from China after the decision to set up the CAFTA in the early 2000s. In summary, ASEAN's trade and investment policies both reflected the parallel approach of intra-regional and extra-regional economic cooperation after the 1997-8 AFC.

4.2.1   Trade Policy

ASEAN's trade policy since the 1980 was divided into three phases. The first phase lasted throughout the 1980s until the Cold War ended in the early 1990s. During this period, ASEAN's trade policy was characterized by trade liberalization, aiming at enhancing intra-ASEAN trade. In the second phase, which lasted from the Cold War ended until the outbreak of the AFC in 1997, intra-regional trade integration within ASEAN held a dominant role. The regional economic crisis changed ASEAN's trade policy considerably. While ASEAN was still on the way to intra-regional trade integration, it also took extra-regional trade integration into consideration. In other words, ASEAN's focus on intra-regional trade integration geographically expanded from the inside to outside ASEAN and reached Asia-Pacific and East Asia. While ASEAN was establishing the AFTA within the framework of ASEAN, it also launched negotiations of trade cooperation with two neighbours in Asia-Pacific-Australia and New Zealand and another three neighbours in Northeast Asia-China, Japan and Korea after surviving the 1997-8 AFC.

During the 1980s, ASEAN devoted itself to trade liberalization and tried a number of measures to enhance intra-ASEAN trade. On the one side, ASEAN removed many items from the Exclusive List (EL) of items on which tariffs did not need to be reduced and added them to the Inclusive List (IL) of tariff reduction; on the other side, they reduced the tariff on traded goods on the IL to a substantial extent. In 1988, 1,679 items were removed from the EL, which brought the total IL items to 14.462. In addition, 3,261 items on the existing Preferential Trade Arrangement (PTA) list were accorded deeper margins of preference (MOP). In 1989, 'a total of 500 new items have been introduced with a minimum Margin of Preferences (MOPs) of

25%. This has brought the total number of items which are accorded preferential tariff to 15,295' (ASEAN Secretariat, 1989-1990). At the same time as ASEAN was taking efforts to remove tariff barriers, it also paid attention to the non-tariff barriers (NTBs). 'Although the TPNG (Trade Preferential Negotiating Group) has yet to render (any) concrete result, individual member countries have been undertaking unilateral actions to further liberalize their trade regimes. This has resulted in the removal of a number of Non-Tariff Barriers (NTBs) (ASEAN Secretariat, 1989-1990)'. In some sense, ASEAN succeeded in implementing the economic policy of trade liberalization by increasing items of phased-out goods and enlarging tariff preferences, although it did not make great progress in removing NTBs.

When the Cold War ended, ASEAN diverted its focus on intra-regional trade liberalization to intra-ASEAN trade integration so as to strengthen ASEAN's trade status in response to pressure from other regions such as Western Europe, North America and Asia-Pacific. '1991-92 has been a watershed for ASEAN' (ASEAN Secretariat, 1989-1990). In the early 1990s, the Cold War's conclusion precipitated a radically changed global economic configuration. Regional integration newly emerged in Asia-Pacific, Western Europe and North America. Pressurized by external challenges in other regions, ASEAN made a critical and visionary decision in 1992 to set up an AFTA within 15 years beginning from 1993. During the 1990s, 'in the area of ASEAN economic cooperation, the most significant event that took place was the launching of the Common Effective Preferential Tariff (CEPT) Scheme for AFTA in January 1993 (ASEAN Secretariat, 1992-1993)'. ASEAN members discussed the implementing details of the CEPT for the AFTA Agreement, including the rules of the origin, principles and lists of products for accelerated tariff reduction, operational procedures, and products for inclusion at their 24th AEM Meeting in October 1992. Thereafter ASEAN members made great efforts to accelerate the establishment of the AFTA. The originally planned 15 years were in fact finally shortened to 10 years; namely the six original members would implement the AFTA by 2003 (other four new members would fully implement it by 2010). Among the external motives for ASEAN's acceleration of the AFTA, the 1997-8 AFC could not be ignored.

While ASEAN immersed itself in establishing the AFTA, the 1997-8 AFC severely hit many ASEAN members' economies. Nevertheless the crisis did not stop ASEAN's pace of regional economic integration. On the contrary, ASEAN decided to accelerate the establishment of the AFTA. It was during the 1997-8 AFC that ASEAN was determined to shorten the period of time to establish the AFTA and accelerate the pace of regional trade integration. ASEAN made great efforts to strengthen the rules and disciplines of the CEPT Agreement, facilitate customs as well as eliminate technical barriers during the AFC. Particularly, in 1997, ASEAN was 'drafting a Framework Agreement on Mutual Recognition Arrangement which would provide the basis for accelerating the development of both bilateral and regional mutual-recognition agreements on standards and conformance among ASEAN member countries (ASEAN Secretariat, 1997-1998)' and would ultimately enhance intra-ASEAN trade cooperation. In December 1998, ASEAN leaders agreed to accelerate the establishment the AFTA with the decision that 'the original members would advance the implementation of AFTA by one year from 2003 to 2002 (ASEAN Secretariat, 1998-1999)'. In 1999, 'ASEAN agreed in principle to advance the elimination of all imports duties by 2010, ahead of the original schedule of 2015, for the six original signatories to the CEPT scheme of the AFTA (ASEAN Secretariat, 1999-2000)'. In 2002, the AFTA was finally completed in six original ASEAN members. 'The six original signatories reduced tariffs on all products listed in their 2002 Inclusion List (IL) to 0-5 percent. The newer members of ASEAN still had to reach the 0-5 percent tariff for intra-ASEAN trade-Viet Nam in 2006, Lao PDR and Myanmar in 2008, and Cambodia in 2010 (ASEAN Secretariat, 2002-2003)'.

The 1997-8 AFC also reminded ASEAN of the increasing significance of economic cooperation with extra-regional partners. Therefore, ASEAN paid attention to the external economic cooperation with partners in East Asia/Asia-Pacific, while it still kept an eye on its intra-regionale economic integration (Narine, 2002, p. 11). After surviving the AFC, ASEAN began to look for potential external partners, which it was believed, could help ASEAN when another crisis came in the future. Australia and New Zealand were the first two partners with whom ASEAN negotiated to set up free trade areas. ASEAN sent a Task Force to explore the feasibility of a free trade arrangement with Australia and New Zealand in 1999. However, protracted negotiations had taken place among ASEAN, Australia and New Zealand yet without break-through progress, when China took an initiative in putting forth the proposal to set up the CAFTA in November 2001. China took into special consideration ASEAN members' various economic levels and promised to make great concessions to ASEAN in certain sectors at some points. Therefore, ASEAN accepted China's proposal and both sides signed the Framework Agreement of Comprehensive Economic Cooperation after two years' negotiations. Following China, Japan and Korea also signed free trade area agreements with ASEAN later. Thus, three bilateral free trade areas were established or being established during the 2000s. The CAFTA was completed in 2010, the Korea-ASEAN FTA is anticipated to be completed in 2012 and Japan-ASEAN FTA is set for completion in 2013. By establishing three bilateral FTAs, ASEAN diverted its trade policy beyond Southeast Asian region and towards a wider East Asian region.

Table 4.1 provides statistical data showing evidence of ASEAN's trade policy. In general, intra-ASEAN trade value was basically on an ascending trend due to ASEAN's trade policy of intra-regional liberalization and integration during the 1980s and 1990s; while extra-ASEAN trade value was generally on a descending trend. The former increased to a historic high of 206,731.6 million dollars, accounting 25.1% of ASEAN's total trade in 2003 when the AFTA was declared of complete for the six original ASEAN members; while the latter decreased to a historic low correspondingly. Due to the parallel approach of promoting both intra-regional and extra-regional economic cooperation in the 2000s, the extra-ASEAN trade saw a gradual, yet unstable increase until 2008, when the global economic crisis broke out and it dropped to another new historic low.

Table 4.2 supplies some data of ASEAN's trade with three Northeast Asian countries-China, Japan and South Korea. After ASEAN's trade policy implemented the parallel approach of promoting both intra-regional and extra-regional trade cooperation particularly after the 1997-8 AFC, its trade with these three Northeast Asian countries saw a stable increase. During the AFC, ASEAN's trade with Northeast Asia dropped to a historic low (455,189.8 million dollars) from 1995 onwards, and it then increased substantially after the AFC. It stood at 1,252,307.8 million dollars in 2008 after ten years stable increase. Also, the share of ASEAN's trade with Northeast Asia in ASEAN's total trade saw a gradual, though fluctuating rise; it grew from 31.43% in 1995 to 38.35% in 2008. The numeric evidence illustrates, on the one hand, that ASEAN succeeded in enhancing intra-ASEAN trade cooperation by implementing intra-regional trade liberalization and integration; and on the other hand, that ASEAN managed to make great progress in promoting extra-ASEAN trade cooperation with these three Northeast Asian countries because of its parallel approach of promoting both intra-regional and extra-regional trade cooperation in the 2000s. It also illustrates that the trade interdependence between ten Southeast Asian counties and three Northeast Asian countries was increasing during the 2000s, in words of complex interdependence theorists.

Table 4.3 presents evidence for ASEAN's efforts in promoting bilateral trade value between China and ASEAN during the 2000s. As clearly shown in Table 4.3, China-ASEAN trade value was increasing from 1993 to 2008. During the 1990s, it increased from 4,528.7 million dollars in 1993 to 32,315.9 million dollars in 2000 and its share of total ASEAN trade value grew from 1.3% in 1993 to 5.5% in 2000. During the 2000s, China-ASEAN trade rose from 31,915.2 million dollars in 2001 to 192,533.1 million dollars in 2008. Even when the global economic crisis broke out in 2008, China-ASEAN trade was increasing. This fully supported the success of China and ASEAN's promotion of bilateral trade cooperation with the establishment of the CAFTA.

To sum up, ASEAN economic policy on trade experienced three phases: during the first stage from the 1980s to the early 1990s, ASEAN focused on trade liberalization within ASEAN to promote intra-ASEAN trade cooperation. During the second phase, from the end of the Cold War till the 1997-8 AFC, ASEAN underlined trade integration within ASEAN with the same objective of enhancing intra-ASEAN trade cooperation. During the third phase, after the 1997-8 AFC, ASEAN attached as much importance to trade integration outside AESAN as to that within ASEAN. To some extent, the former was taken into special consideration, since the latter had achieved a landmark success with the preliminary realization of the AFTA. In a word, ASEAN re-orientated its trade policy, based on the changes of the general context.

Table 4.1   Intra-ASEAN and Extra-ASEAN Trade Value and Share, 1991-2008

Intra-ASEAN and Extra-ASEAN Trade Value and Share, 1991-2008				
			Value: in US$ million; Share: in percentage	
Year	Intra-ASEAN Trade		Extra-ASEAN Trade	
	Value	Share	Value	Share
1991	n/a	n/a	n/a	n/a
1992	n/a	n/a	n/a	n/a
1993	82444.1	19.2	347503.6	80.8
1994	105483.5	20.5	408523	79.5
1995	123780.9	20.1	491470.5	79.9
1996	145184.7	21.5	528782.6	78.5
1997	149972.8	21.5	548668.8	78.5
1998	120917.9	21	455189.9	79
1999	132674.5	21.3	490483.3	78.7
2000	168902.5	22.3	587617.9	77.7
2001	152127.9	22.1	535646.1	77.9
2002	159908.8	22.4	553908.2	77.6
2003	206731.6	25.1	617807.1	74.9
2004	260697.5	24.3	811150.3	75.7
2005	304893.2	24.9	919996.2	75.1
2006	352771.3	25.1	1052034.3	74.9
2007	401920.3	25	1208867.1	75
2008	458113.9	26.8	1252307.8	73.2

Source: Data from 1993 to 2001 were available from ASEAN Statistical Yearbook 2003; data from 2002 to 2007 were available from ASEAN Statistical Yearbook 2008; and data of 2008 were available at: http://www.aseansec.org/Stat/Table18.pdf. (Compiled and computed by the author)

Table 4.2 ASEAN's Trade with Three Northeast Asian countries, 1995-2008

ASEAN's Trade with Three Northeast Asian countries, 1995-2008

Tade: in million dollars; Share: in percentage

| Year | ASEAN's Trade with China, Japan and Korea | | | | Total Extra-ASEAN Trade | Share |
	China	Japan	Korea	Sum		
1995	13,330.6	121,215.9	19,920.0	154,466.5	491,470.5	31.43
1996	16,691.7	116,460.4	22,741.1	155,893.2	528,782.6	29.48
1997	22,650.8	113,272.8	25,525.2	161,448.8	548,668.8	29.43
1998	20,414.1	81,410.5	17,080.4	118,905.0	455,189.9	26.12
1999	21,922.5	89,153.1	23,168.7	134,244.3	490,483.3	27.37
2000	31,150.6	120,371.1	29,635.3	181,157.0	587,617.9	30.83
2001	45,511.3	101,637.8	28,191.8	175,340.9	535,646.1	32.73
2002	42,759.7	97,587.1	30,533.2	170,880.0	553,908.2	30.85
2003	59,636.9	113,400.6	33,548.1	206,585.6	617,807.1	33.44
2004	89,066.0	143,263.0	40,543.8	272,872.8	811,150.3	33.64
2005	113,393.6	153,834.4	47,971.8	315,199.8	919,996.2	34.26
2006	139,961.2	161,780.5	55,942.3	357,684.0	1,052,034.3	34.00
2007	171,117.7	173,062.0	61,184.0	405,363.7	1,208,867.1	33.53
2008	192,533.1	211,988.2	75,721.4	480,242.7	1,252,307.8	38.35

Source: Data from 1993 to 2001 were available from ASEAN Statistical Yearbook 2003;
data from 2002 to 2008 were available from ASEAN Statistical Yearbook 2008
(Compiled and computed by the author)

Table 4.3 ASEAN-China Trade Value, 1991-2008

ASEAN-China Trade Value, 1991-2008			
		Value: in million US$; Share: in percent	
Year	ASEAN-China Trade	Total Extra-ASEAN Trade Value	Share
1991	n/a	n/a	n/a
1992	n/a	n/a	n/a
1993	4,528.70	347,503.60	1.3
1994	5,303.80	408,523.00	1.3
1995	13,330.60	491,470.50	2.71
1996	16,691.80	528,782.60	3.16
1997	22,650.80	548,668.80	4.13
1998	20,414.10	455,189.90	4.48
1999	21,922.50	490,483.30	4.47
2000	32,315.90	587,617.90	5.5
2001	31,915.20	535,646.10	5.96
2002	42,759.80	553,908.20	7.72
2003	59,637.00	617,807.10	9.65
2004	89,066.00	811,150.30	10.98
2005	113,393.60	919,996.20	12.33
2006	139,961.20	1,052,034.30	13.3
2007	171,117.70	1,208,867.10	14.16
2008	192,533.10	1,252,307.80	15.37

Source: ASEAN Statistics Yearbook 2003 and 2008
(Compiled and computed by the author)

4.2.2 Investment Policy

Taking the 1997-8 AFC as a benchmark, ASEAN's investment policy had two phases. Before the AFC, ASEAN placed emphasis on intra-regional investment cooperation with a view to establishing the AFTA. However, no concrete and feasible measures were implemented because ASEAN paid main attention to intra-regional trade cooperation instead of investment cooperation. Therefore the whole 1990s did not see a substantial increase in intra-regional investment values. After the 1997-8 AFC broke out, ASEAN members signed the ASEAN Investment Area (AIA) agreements in order to fight jointly against the crisis and strengthen ASEAN's status as an attractive investment destination as a whole. In the meanwhile, ASEAN also looked for external opportunities to attract as much investment flows as possible from its dialogue partners.

Since the 1980s, ASEAN had kept underlining the significance of expanding ASEAN's investment flows and of promoting ASEAN as an attractive investment destination. In order to do that, ASEAN economic ministers signed the Agreement for the Promotion and Protection of Investments (PPI) at the Manila Summit in 1987. This was the first investment-related document that ASEAN endorsed to promote intra-regional investment cooperation and strengthen ASEAN's investment status. Regrettably, however, this document did not result in any further concrete measures or actions to enhance investment cooperation among ASEAN members. Not until in 1992 when ASEAN decided to establish the AFTA, did ASEAN discuss the feasibility of investment cooperation among ASEAN members. ASEAN economic ministers agreed that 'the officials responsible for investment promotion should conduct regular consultations with a view to increasing the inflows of foreign direct investment in ASEAN (ASEAN Secretariat, 1992-1993)' at the 25th AMM in July 1992. Later, a Consultative Forum for the Promotion of Foreign Direct Investment was held by the Investment Coordinating Board of Indonesia, and a Memorandum of Understanding (MOU) was endorsed to guide the ASEAN member countries on incorporating mechanisms, objectives, and plans of action for investment. The year 1995 witnessed another leap in ASEAN's investment measures. In 1995, ASEAN members decided at the 5th Summit to 'work towards establishing an ASEAN investment region, which will help enhance the area's attractiveness and competitiveness for promoting direct investment (ASEAN Secretariat, 1995-1996)' among ASEAN members or from external economic partners. Besides, they endorsed the ASEAN Plan of Action on Cooperation and Promotion of Foreign Direct Investment and Intra-ASEAN Investment at the Summit. In addition, the Heads of ASEAN Investment Agencies also met twice to enhance their investment cooperation. As a result of the measures taken to promote investment cooperation in 1995, ASEAN's total FDI flows saw a steady rise from 1995-1997. As shown in Table 4.4, ASEAN's total FDI flows increased from 23,389.4 million dollars in 1995 to 29,612.3 million dollars in 1997.Due to the severe impact of the 1997-8 AFC, ASEAN's total FDI saw a substantial decrease and it did not recover to the pre-crisis level until 2000.

Table 4.4 Intra-ASEAN and Extra-ASEAN FDI Flows and Share, 1995-2008

Intra-ASEAN and Extra-ASEAN FDI Flows and Share, 1995-2008

					Value: in US million dollars; Share/Growth Rate: in percent	
Year	Intra-ASEAN FDI		Extra-ASEAN FDI		Total Value	Annual Growth
	Value	Share	Value	Share		
1995	3,516.90	15.0	19,872.50	85	23,389.40	-
1996	3,121.70	12.2	22,432.80	87.8	25,554.50	9.26
1997	3,962.90	13.4	25,649.40	86.6	29,612.30	15.88
1998	2,073.10	9.5	19,705.50	90.5	21,778.60	-26.45
1999	934.60	4.2	21,235.20	95.8	22,169.80	1.80
2000	761.90	3.2	22,964.90	96.8	23,726.80	7.02
2001	2,526.50	12.2	18,103.90	87.8	20,630.40	-13.05
2002	3,812.90	21.4	13,974.70	78.6	17,787.60	-13.78
2003	2,702.00	11.2	21,364.70	88.8	24,066.70	35.30
2004	2,958.60	8.4	32,242.50	91.6	35,201.10	46.26
2005	4,217.70	10.8	34,738.30	89.2	38,956.00	10.67
2006	7,602.30	14.2	45,767.90	85.8	53,370.20	37.00
2007	9,408.60	13.7	59,106.00	86.3	68,514.60	28.38
2008	11,070.80	18.3	49,355.20	81.7	60,426.00	-11.81

Note: FDI flows of Cambodia were not calculated due to the data lack.

Source: ASEAN FDI Database of July 2009 (Compiled and computed by the author)

In response to the 1997-8 AFC, ASEAN signed the Framework Agreement on ASEAN Investment Area (AIA) at the 30th AMM in July 1998, which was seen as a milestone in the progress of ASEAN investment cooperation. 'The Framework Agreement on AIA was expected to complement the 1987 ASEAN Agreement for the Promotion and Protection of Investments and its 1986 Protocol (ASEAN Secretariat, 1998-1999)'. This was one of the boldest steps ASEAN had taken with respect to investment cooperation since the 1980s. In the late 1990s, ASEAN launched more concrete investment promotion activities with a view to promoting ASEAN's investment flows and strengthening ASEAN's status as an attractive investment destination. ASEAN released the first ASEAN Investment Report in November 1999 and issued another report on investment guidance titled *Investing in ASEAN: A Guide for Foreign Investors.* Besides, the Investment map and an investment promotion brochure were also published. In support of investment promotion, ASEAN also began work to harmonize the FDI statistics of ASEAN Member Countries. The FDI Statistical Task Force disseminated the first publication on investment statistics, 'Statistics of Foreign Direct Investment in ASEAN', which was believed to provide 'a comprehensive set of comparable statistics on FDI in ASEAN' (ASEAN Secretariat, 1999-2000). From then on, publications on investment guidance and statistics were released every year, which provided a platform for information exchange between the investors and the investing destinations. As a result of ASEAN's measures, reports and guidance, ASEAN saw a stable rise in investment values in general and FDI flows in particular after the AFC.

ASEAN achieved the highest FDI growth in the world in 2003, despite facing the spreading SARS, avian influenza and a global FDI downturn. This encouraged ASEAN to take more measures to expand FDI flows. More sectors were opened to FDI investment, strengthened institutional facilitation was arranged, and ownership equity given to foreigners was further relaxed in 2004. All expectations accumulated were realized in 2006, when the annual growth rate of FDI 'notably surpassed the growth rate of ASEAN FDI flows in pre-crisis 1997' (ASEAN Secretariat, 2006-2007). 'Ten years after the signing of the AIA Agreement, the AIA Council agreed in August 2007 to revise and integrate the Framework Agreement on the ASEAN Investment Area with the ASEAN Agreement on the Promotion and Protection of Investments into a single ASEAN Comprehensive Investment Agreement (ACIA) (ASEAN Secretariat, 2007-2008)'. This became another legal document after the PPI and the Framework Agreement on AIA, which laid the legal basis for FDI promotion and cooperation in ASEAN. As displayed in Table 4.4, with the exception of those years when financial/economic crisis (1998 and 2008) and global economic recession spread (2001 and 2002), ASEAN's FDI kept increasing. It stood at 24,066.7 million dollars in 2003, increasing by the highest growth rate of FDI in the world of 35% over 2002. In 2004, ASEAN achieved another new high with its FDI flows arriving at 35,201.1 million dollars, an increase of 46% over 2003. The good momentum went on until 2008, when the global economic crisis caused a decline in ASEAN's total FDI flows, which dropped to 60,426 million dollars.

If it is the case that ASEAN focused key attention on intra-ASEAN investment in the 1990s, it included among its concerns investment cooperation with its external partners (Qin & Chen, 2006, p. 122) after the AFC. ASEAN sent investment missions to Japan, the United States and Europe in 1999. 'The missions held investment seminars to inform current and potential foreign investors of business opportunities in ASEAN. The seminars provided opportunities for ASEAN to reassure investors of ASEAN's continued commitment to regional economic integration and open regionalism (ASEAN Secretariat, 1999-2000)'. In March 2003, ASEAN convened the first ASEAN-China Investment Consultations in Singapore, where 'both sides agreed on the need to cooperate and work together in exchanging statistics and in holding further consultations on investment regime and regulatory framework (ASEAN Secretariat, 2002-2003)'. As a result of ASEAN's efforts to enhance extra-ASEAN investment, extra-regional FDI flows increased and it helped ASEAN survive the 1997-8 AFC and the global economic recession in 2001. As Table 4.4 shows, ASEAN's total FDI in 1999 had a great increase after a substantial drop in 1998. This helped ASEAN survive the crisis. In total, ASEAN attracted 22,169.8 million dollars of FDI in 1999, of which intra-ASEAN FDI accounted for only 4.2%, even lower than that in 1998 (9.5%) and extra-ASEAN FDI accounted for 95.8%, much higher than that in 1998 (90.5%). A similar case happened in 2003, when ASEAN recovered from the impact of the global economic recession. If it was true that the FDI flows contributed to helping ASEAN get out of the economic crisis/recessions, then extra-ASEAN FDI contributed more significantly than intra-ASEAN FDI did.

Table 4.5 supplies statistical evidence for ASEAN's investment cooperation with three Northeast Asian countries. After the 1997-8 AFC, ASEAN recognized the importance of attracting FDI inflows from extra-ASEAN partners. The global economic recessions from 2001 strongly highlighted the importance of its neighbours in Northeast Asia-China, Japan and Korea. As displayed in Table 4.5, ASEAN's FDI inflows from these three partners in East Asia saw a substantial albeit fluctuating rise from 2000 to 2008 and so did its share in total extra-ASEAN FDI inflows. In 2000, ASEAN was a net FDI source for China, Japan and Korea; it invested 151.1 million dollars in them totally. Then ASEAN turned to be a net FDI recipient for these three countries in 2001, when it attracted 808.5 million dollars from them, accounting for 4.47% of total extra-ASEAN FDI inflows. When it came to 2008, ASEAN attracted 49,355.2 million dollars from China, Japan and Korea, which accounted for 21.13% of total extra-ASEAN FDI inflows. This evidence suggests that ASEAN succeeded in enhancing its investment cooperation with three Northeast Asian neighbours and meanwhile the investment interdependence between the ten Southeast Asian countries and three Northeast Asian countries was increasing during the 2000s.

Moving on to ASEAN's FDI from China, Table 4.6 provides data for it from 2000 to 2008. According to the data, two arguments could be made. Firstly, China turned from a net FDI recipient country of ASEAN to a FDI source country for ASEAN. China became from an importing to an exporting country after 2002, which thoroughly changed the direction of FDI flows between China and ASEAN. As clearly shown in Table 4.6, China attracted 133.4 million dollars of inward FDI flows from ASEAN in 2000 and it invested 1,497.3 million dollars of outward FDI to ASEAN in 2008. Secondly, China tended to invest more FDI in ASEAN after the Framework Agreement took effect in 2004. China invested 735 million dollars of FDI in ASEAN in 2004. When it came to year 2008, China invested 1,497.3 million dollars of FDI in ASEAN. Although the global economic crisis took place in 2008, ASEAN's FDI from China still saw an increase by more than 20% compared to 2007. Meanwhile, ASEAN's FDI from China accounted for more proportions in ASEAN's total FDI flows. It increased over threefold, from 0.8% in 2003 to 2.5% in 2008. Of special note is that the share of ASEAN's FDI from China increased to a smaller extent than that of ASEAN's trade with China, as seen by comparing Table 4.3 and Table 4.6. Part of the reason may be that the IA was still under negotiations until 2009, when it was endorsed by the ASEAN members and China. As for bilateral trade between China and ASEAN shown in Table 4.3, it was reasonable for ASEAN's FDI from China to see a steady increase after the Framework Agreement took effect in 2004. In the investment case, it is safe to predict there will be a FDI increase not only in the value but also in the share in the future.

Table 4.5 ASEAN's FDI Inflows from Three Northeast Asian countries, 2000-2008

ASEAN's FDI Inflows from Three Northeast Asian countries, 2000-2008						
				Tade: in million dollars; Share: in percentage		
Year	ASEAN's FDI Inflows from China, Japan and				Total	Share
	China	Japan	Korea	Sum	Extra-	
2000	26.4	-135.0	-42.5	-151.1	22,964.9	-0.66
2001	148.3	900.5	-240.3	808.5	18,103.9	4.47
2002	-71.9	3,026.4	176.5	3,131.0	13,974.7	22.40
2003	186.6	3,908.4	550.0	4,645.0	21,364.7	21.74
2004	735.0	5,667.4	828.2	7,230.6	32,242.5	22.43
2005	537.7	6,655.0	507.0	7,699.7	34,738.3	22.16
2006	1,016.2	10,222.8	1,253.8	12,492.8	45,767.9	27.30
2007	1,226.9	8,382.0	3,124.7	12,733.6	59,106.0	21.54
2008	1,497.3	7,653.6	1,279.1	10,430.0	49,355.2	21.13

Source: Data from 1993 to 2001 were available from ASEAN Statistical Yearbook 2003; data from 2002 to 2008 were available from ASEAN Statistical Yearbook 2008 (Compiled and computed by the author)

Table 4.6 FDI Inflows into ASEAN from China, 2000-2008

FDI Inflows into ASEAN from China, 2000-2008			
		Value: in million US$; Share/Growth Rate: in percent	
Year	FDI Value	Annual Growth Rate	Share of ASEAN's FDI from China in Total Extra-ASEAN
2000	-133.4	-	-0.6
2001	144	-	0.7
2002	-71.9	-	-0.4
2003	186.6	-	0.8
2004	735	293.89	2.1
2005	537.7	-26.84	1.4
2006	1,016.20	88.99	1.8
2007	1,226.90	20.73	1.8
2008	1,497.30	22.04	2.5

Note: The above figures do not include FDI from Taiwan or Hong Kong.

Source: ASEAN Statistics Yearbook 2008 (Compiled and computed by the author)

To summarize, ASEAN concentrated on promoting intra-regional investment before the 1997-8 AFC and many measures were adopted in an effort to ultimately strengthen ASEAN's status as an attractive investment destination. After the AFC, ASEAN, on the one hand, continued to pay attention to intra-regional investment flows; and on the other hand, took extra-regional investment flows from its economic partners into consideration. As a result, extra-regional FDI flows played a more important role than intra-regional FDI flows did in helping ASEAN survive the economic crisis in the late 1990s and late 2000s and the global economic recession in the early 2000s.

An overview of ASEAN's economic policy reveals two characteristics. One is that ASEAN implemented regional economic integration in an incremental approach. It classified traded goods on the Inclusive List (IL), Temporarily Exclusive List (TEL), Sensitive List (SL) and General Exceptions List. Items on different lists were subject to different phase-out timetables. With respect to investment, ASEAN also had Temporary Exclusion Lists and Sensitive Lists according to different sectors and gave them different priority of investment. Moreover, ASEAN also classified the ten members into two groupings according to their economic level and the time they joined ASEAN: the six original members and four new members. Taking relatively underdeveloped economic levels into consideration, ASEAN permitted each new member to have its own time plan of tariff reduction and the AFTA completion. 'Individually, each country (of *the six original members*) will commit to achieve a minimum of 85% of the Inclusion List with tariff of 0-5% by the year 2000. Thereafter, this will be increased to a minimum of 90% of the Inclusion List in the 0-5% tariff range by the year 2001. By 2002, all of items in the Inclusion List will have tariffs of 0-5% with some flexibility... The *newer members* of ASEAN shall expand the number of tariff lines in the 0% category by 2006 for Viet Nam and 2008 for maximize their tariff lines, between 0-5% by 2003 for View Nam and 2005 for Laos and Myanmar (ASEAN Secretariat, 1998-1999).' Finally, ASEAN implemented trade integration and investment integration step by step. After ASEAN implemented the CEPT in 1993 to promote trade integration, it signed the Framework Agreement on AIA in 1998 to promote investment integration. In all, ASEAN implemented intra-regional economic integration in an incremental way, which was copied by its neighbours in East Asia, such as China, Japan and Korea. Thus, gradually, regional economic integration spread in a wider geographical scope in East Asia.

The second feature is that ASEAN attached greater importance to economic integration geographically beyond the Southeast Asia, to reach Asia-Pacific and East Asia although ASEAN was hesitating and wavering between the two geographical scopes of Asia-Pacific and East Asia. On the one hand, ASEAN took an active role in the Asia-Pacific region within the framework of APEC. 'ASEAN member countries continued to participate and coordinate their positions in the APEC process with the fundamental objective of sustaining the growth and dynamism of the *Asia-Pacific region*' (ASEAN Secretariat, 1991-1992). Meanwhile, ASEAN began to explore the possibility and feasibility of establishing free trade areas with Australia and New Zealand in the wake of the 1997-8 AFC because ASEAN believed this would help

ASEAN should it face regional economic crisis again in the future.

On the other hand, ASEAN took the initiative in proposing economic integration in East Asian region. Shortly after the Cold War ended, Mahathir Mohammad, the former Malaysian premier, proposed to found the East Asia Economic Group (EAEG) to enhance economic cooperation among countries in *East Asian* region. Although the idea was aborted because of the strong opposition from the United States, ASEAN members 'agreed to the convening of the EAEC (East Asia Economic Caucus) to discuss issues common concern to *East Asian* economies and to meet as and when the need arises.' Just before the 1997-8 AFC took place, ASEAN leaders held the 2nd informal ASEAN Summit in Malaysia, where they discussed the issue of regional economic cooperation respectively with China, Japan and Korea. As a result, ASEAN and China issued a statement that forecast the evolution of ASEAN-China dialogue relations into the 21st century, setting the stage for greater bilateral cooperation in economic relations. Among the three countries in Northeast Asia, it was China who took the initiative in proposing to set up a free trade area with ASEAN and to establish the final East Asian free trade area in the future. Following China, Japan and Korea also launched negotiations with ASEAN in order to establish bilateral free trade areas with ASEAN. During the 2000s when the East Asian countries were establishing free trade areas, economic cooperation in the Asia-Pacific region seemed, to some degree, to be marginalized particularly after the US-initiated EVSL programme encountered great frustration in 1998. China provided the impetus for ASEAN to choose East Asia with its proposal to establish a free trade area between China and ASEAN. ASEAN, stimulated by three bilateral free trade areas, between China and ASEAN, Japan and ASEAN, and Korea and ASEAN, promised to 'take a proactive role in strengthening *East Asian* cooperation' (ASEAN Secretariat, 2004-2005) during the 2000s. It modified the original goal of 'promoting peace, prosperity and progress in *Southeast Asia*' , set at its foundation in 1967 to 'sustaining peace, prosperity and progress in Southeast Asia and *East Asia*' at the first East Asia Summit (EAS) in 2005.

In summary, 'as ASEAN (came) upon the full realization of the AFTA, it (ran) against the limits of regional (Southeast Asian) integration. The next step (involved) reaching beyond the confines of South China Sea and moving towards an East Asian destiny' (The EGEC, 2001, p. 6). Therefore, ASEAN promoted intra-regional and extra-regional economic cooperation in parallel in the 1990s and 2000s. Its passion in enhancing extra-regional economic cooperation in Easi Asia/Asia-Pacific supplied not only more chances for bilateral economic cooperation between China and AESAN, but also a driving force for economic integration in East Asia. ASEAN accumulated abundant experience in regional economic integration and it was copied by East Asian countries when they made efforts to promote East Asian economic integration. ASEAN *per se,* as an engine, provided unexpected impetus for East Asian economic integration by looking beyond Southeast Asia and towards East Asia. Although ASEAN played an important role in promoting economic integration in East Asia, it was not the dominant power (Cao, 2007, p. 15), asserted by some scholars. When ASEAN was hesitating and wavering between Asia-Pacific and

East Asia after the 1997-8 AFC, it was China that stimulated it to choose East Asia by proposing to establish the CAFTA. However, this is not to deny that 'ASEAN's status as a key regional institution was further strengthened; ASEAN would play a greater part in regional affairs' (Hu, 2001, p. 51) in East Asia and 'would play a catalytic role in economic cooperation in Asia-Pacific (Li & Wang, 2005, p. 112)'.

4.3   A Further Glance at ASEAN

In order to identify ASEAN's role in economic cooperation with China and that in economic integration in East Asia, it is necessary to take a further glance at the institutional nature of ASEAN, the role of ASEAN Secretariat and individual member states in ASEAN's relations with China (particularly with regards to the negotiation of the CAFTA). Therefore, in this section, ASEAN was further investigated in regards to its nature and the role of the Secretariat when negotiating the Framework Agreement with China. Particularly attention was given to the bilateral relations between individual ASEAN member and China. Among ASEAN members, Singapore and Indonesia were chosen as examples because the former played an obviously proactive role in negotiations with China while the latter did nothing but took passive participation into the negations. They individually indicated proactive and passive relationships with China.

Since its inception in the 1960s, ASEAN was an inter-governmental rather than a supra-national organization, unlike the European Union. According to Denis Hew, 'ASEAN still maintains a very loose institutional structure although there has been a strengthening of its institutions in the recent years. ASEAN does not presently operate on the overriding principle of using a formal, detailed, and binding institutional structure to prepare, enact, coordinate, and execute policies for economic integration' (Hew, May 2006). Despite of decades of institutional evolution as a regional organization, ASEAN did not promote to be a closely connected supra-national organization in terms of 'the lack of political will in most (Southeast Asian) region because of widespread uncertainty among policy makers and business executive about the end goal of economic integration and its benefits for individual countries. The lack of political will is also reflected in ASEAN's past reluctance to create regional institutions to expedite decision making and raise investor confidence in the integrity of the groups' commitments. ASEAN remains primarily a government-led trade group.' (Schwarz & Villinger, 2004, p. 43).

According to Michael G. Plummer, there was little possibility for ASEAN to come up with as such a supranational institution as that in Europe due to reasons as follows: '(1) nation-state formation was much later than in the European context, and in some countries must still be given strong priority; (2) divergence in socio-political institutions are far greater than they were in Europe, especially as some European countries had to recreate these institutions after World War Two; (3) it is not clear that European institution building has been particularly successful in all areas, though it would receive high marks in economic-related matters (though this hypobook might also be tested); and (4) European institutions are quite expensive with ASEAN government budgets much smaller (fortunately, ASEAN would not have to employ an army of translators, as the EU does. (Plummer, 2006, p. 8)'

ASEAN's status as a loose inter-governmental regional organization gave rise to the two outcomes concerning its role in economic integration in Southeast Asian and East Asian region. One was that ASEAN Secretariat played a nominal role in promoting economic integration in Southeast Asia and East Asia due to its weak institutional structure. In Southeast Asia, 'the ASEAN Secretariat had neither the power nor the resources to formulate and propose policies, coordinate their implementation, monitor compliance, and settle disputes (Schwarz & Villinger, 2004, p. 43)'. The Secretariat was hindered from an effective part in erstwhile initiatives to reduce tariffs and eliminate non-tariff barriers (Plummer, 2006, p. 54). In East Asia, the ASEAN Secretariat was eclipsed by individual member governments when negotiating and endorsing the CAFTA agreement with China. The other outcome was that those individual ASEAN members' governments took the place of the Secretariat and played an imperative and significant role in the establishment of the free trade areas with China, Japan and South Korea. 'The current spate of agreements, however, has not been extended throughout ASEAN+3, but rather derives more from ASEAN to individual countries (Plummer, 2006, p. 8).' Take FTA negotiations between ASEAN and China as example. China negotiated with each ASEAN member government to come to conclusion of the Framework Agreement, the ATG, and the ATS, which symbolized the burgeoning of bilateralism in East Asia. When negotiating the IA, Chinese government sent negotiating represent group to negotiate with those from ten ASEAN members and finally they went to the agreement concerning the IA, which symbolized the emergence of multilateralism in East Asia. However, no matter where bilateralism or multilateralism dominated the negotiations and agreements, it was the eleven national governments at the governmental level, instead of the ASEAN Secretariat at the sub-regional/regional level that dominated and finalized the integrating process. The FTA negotiations between ASEAN and Japan was another good case in point for the governments' role in promoting economic integration in East Asia. ASEAN demanded of taken as a whole in at the outset of negotiations of the FTA agreement with Japan. Otherwise, they argued, it would 'undermine ASEAN's solidarity and collective strength' (Yue, 2003, p. 89). Disappointingly, the ASEAN Secretariat did not have the capability of incorporating all ten ASEAN members' interest and base its negotiations as a whole with Japan on it. In the end, Japanese government negotiated with ten ASEAN member governments and signed the agreement one by one. The FTA agreement between ASEAN and South Korea was also an outcome of governmental negotiations between ten ASEAN member governments and South Korea. In all, the ASEAN Secretariat did not play an impressive role in negotiating and endorsing the FTA agreement with China, Japan and South Korea, and promoting economic integration in both Southeast Asian and East Asian region although it had the demand that ASEAN should be taken in to consideration as a whole.

Among ASEAN, Singapore was among those members who took proactive participation into the CAFTA negotiations with China (together with Thailand and Malaysia) at the very outset while Indonesia belonged to those who passively joined the negotiations very late. Here, Singapore and Indonesia were chosen in order to check the individual relations between ASEAN members and China, particularly with regards to the negotiations of CAFTA. Singapore was the most active player and promoter of the CAFTA negotiations with China in terms of its wish to bandwagon China's fast economic growth, its strategic plan to have the balance influence of great powers such as the United States and China in Southeast Asia and its expected great benefits from the CAFTA establishment (Pan, 2005, p. 18). Singapore kept a high profile in leading ASEAN to participate the CAFTA negotiations with China. However, it did not maintain good negotiating relations with China. It requested more concessions from China than any other ASEAN did so that a Chinese trade negotiator privately described Singapore as a clown (Tiaoliangxiaochou) in the CAFTA negotiations (Jiang, 2010, p. 244). Actually, Singapore government hoped to get every single benefit from the CAFTA establishment by increasing its trade with China, help ASEAN grow in economic sense and maintain stability in political sense in Southeast Asia. Therefore, Singapore was not satisfied with the gradual negotiations of the CAFTA establishment. Instead, it decided to set up Singapore-China Free Trade Area and launched the separate negotiations with China during the CAFTA negotiations. Finally, on 31 October, 2008 Singapore and China endorsed an overall FTA agreement, which included the articles of ATG, ATS, IA and ADSM. Moreover, China promised to make sure that Singapore would enjoy more preferential tariff than the Framework Agreement between ASEAN and China would provide. In simple words, Singapore did believe that the CAFTA and Singapore-China FTA would benefit it both economically and politically; and in order to realize the benefits, it carried out tough negotiations with China, which induced China's resentment. Fortunately, this did not stop them from further economic cooperation through establishing their separate bilateral FTA.

Indonesia was a passive player in the CAFTA negotiations with China. 'Indeed, although the early phase of an FTA with China was already in place in 2004, it was only then that the Indonesian government finally decided to consolidate its free trade strategy' (Candra, 2005, p. 542). At that time, all ASEAN members joined the CAFTA negotiations with China, but Indonesia. Indonesia feared to be left out of the CAFTA establishment, its policy-makers decided to join the negotiations, though very late (Candra & Lontoh, 2011, p. 7). Domestically, Indonesia did not prepare itself well in participating FTA negotiations due to the lack of FTA strategy before; in terms of the timing, it launched the negotiations too late. As a result, the CAFTA agreement was at place in such a hurry for Indonesian people that Indonesian government encountered objections from the people, the sector associations, small and medium-sized enterprises. All of them complained that they would suffer heavily from the preferential tariff of the CAFTA agreement to such a great extent that would go beyond what they could afford (Candra A. C., 2009, p. 11). The direct result of the resentments was that the Indonesia government demanded of postponing the complete fulfilment of the

CAFTA agreement in Indonesia on 1 January, 2010, when the CAFTA was declared of complete in the six original members of ASEAN and China. The demand resulted in China's promise to set up an expert group with Indonesia to investigate the potentially negative effects of the CAFTA on Indonesian economy. However, both Indonesia and China missed the deadline for convening the expert group. The Indonesian performance in the CAFTA negotiations and establishment stood at a sharp contrast with Singapore. The former asked for a delay of the fulfilment of the CAFTA agreement while the latter took an initiative in setting up an individual FTA with China during the CAFTA negotiations. This also indicated the loose structure of ASEAN. Its members had various domestic economy and they felt difficult to coordinate their own interest within the framework of ASEAN.

In all, ASEAN's nature as a loose inter-governmental institution hindered, to a great extent, the ASEAN Secretariat from playing a significant role in economic cooperation with China and promoting economic integration in East Asia. Instead, the individual ASEAN members' governments played an impressive role in negotiating and establishing the CAFTA with China. Different performance of those ASEAN members' governments in negotiating the CAFTA with China illustrated the different domestic interests in them on the one hand and on the other hand, indicated the loose institutional structure of ASEAN. The governments' significance in negotiating the CAFTA between China and ASEAN was also embodied through the cooperation institutions between them. Most of the cooperative institutions were comprised at governmental level. This goes in detail in the next section.

4.4 Cooperation Institutions on Economic Issues between ASEAN and China

Bilateral cooperative activities between China and ASEAN started in 1991, when the consultative relationship was formalized. Most of the original cooperation was focused on, if not limited to, the political and security fields, although a few cooperative committees were set up to enhance bilateral economic cooperation. Generally speaking, ASEAN and China worked together on economic issues through bilateral and multilateral institutions. Bilateral institutions referred to those within the framework of ASEAN+1 (China) while multilateral institutions connoted those within the framework of ASEAN+3. In comparison, the former were more relied on by the two sides to promote their bilateral economic cooperation. ASEAN and China promoted their economic cooperation through five important institutions within the framework of ASEAN+1, which were the ASEAN-China Joint Committee on Economic and Trade Cooperation (JCETC, founded in 1994) and ASEAN-China EGEC (founded subordinate to the ACJCETC in 2001), ASEAN-China Joint Cooperation Committee (JCC, founded in 1997), ACBC (founded in 2001), CAExpo (started in 2004) and the CABIS (started in 2004). These six institutions made considerable contributions to promoting the economic cooperation between ASEAN and China by discussing the possibility and feasibility of CAFTA before 2001 and facilitating the establishment of CAFTA after the Framework Agreement was endorsed in 2002. Among them, CAJCC was not only in charge of economic cooperation between China and ASEAN; it was a comprehensive institution, which also took charge of political and security cooperation between China and ASEAN. JCETC and EGEC were started before the endorsement of the Framework Agreement and in fact they played a critical role in proposing to set up the CAFTA. Members of the EGEC drafted the report, suggesting establishing the CAFTA, which confirmed Chinese leaders' thinking about the CAFTA from an academic perspective. ACBC was also founded before the Framework Agreement as a cooperative institution at the enterprises and commercial chamber level. CAExpo and CABIS were set up after the endorsement of the Framework Agreement with a view to promoting bilateral economic cooperation on trade and investment and facilitating the establishment of CAFTA as concrete actions. Here, JCETC and EGEC are given special attention because of their contribution to directly causing Chinese proposal to establish the CAFTA at the governmental level. The ACBC, CAExpo and CABIS are also taken into special consideration, due to their efforts to help introduce enterprises and commercial chambers in China and ASEAN to participate into the establishment in the CAFTA.

4.4.1   The JCETC and EGEC

When Beijing was invited as a 'guest' by the ASEAN Standing Committee (ASC) to attended the 25th AMM meeting in Manila in 1992, Qian Qichen, the Chinese vice Premier and foreign minister at the time, proposed to design programmes for cooperation in science and technology, economic and trade relations with ASEAN. Later, the first ASEAN-China consultations on economic and trade, science and technology cooperation was convened on 13th-14th September 1993, where both sides made the decision to set up two joint committees with a view to promoting bilateral cooperation and exchanges on economic and trade matters as well as science and technology. Then, with permission from Qian Qichen and Tan Sri Dato' Ajit Singh, the general secretary of ASEAN (January 1993-December 1997) from Malaysia, the ASEAN-China JCETC was founded, and an agreement was signed on 23rd July 1994. The establishment of JCETC, together with the other Joint Committee on Science and Technology (JCST), marked the formalization of the ASEAN-China consultative relationship in 1994. Based on the JCETC agreement, regular meetings were organized alternatively in ASEAN member countries and China to conduct studies and discuss approaches to further enhancing bilateral cooperation in economic and trade relations and also in science and technology.

The function of the JCETC is to: a) revaluate the implementation of economic and trade cooperation between ASEAN and China; b) conduct more research on approaches to enhance bilateral economic and trade cooperation and make proposals on how to promote it; and c) discuss other regional and international issues, on which both ASEAN and China have common concerns. (S.a., 2001)

The first meeting of JCETC was held in Jakarta, Indonesia, on 7 August 1995, where ASEAN proposed to jointly set up an economics and trade information centre and ACBC. The second meeting was convened in Beijing in 1997, but no specific items emerged. The third meeting was organized in Kuala Lumpur, Malaysia on 28th March 2001, shortly before the 5th ASEAN and China Leaders Summit in Brunei on 6th November 2001. On this occasion, both sides approved the establishment of the ASEAN-China EGEC within the framework of JCETC and they came to common views on its task scope, function and research subjects. It was planned that the EGEC would look into further impact of China's entry into WTO on ASEAN and put forth potential approaches to further enhance ASEAN-China economic cooperation and integration, including the possibility of establishing a free-trade area between ASEAN and China.

Ten months after EGEC was established, it submitted its first report to the 5th ASEAN and China Leaders Summit in November 2001, in which the CAFTA was proposed so as to further promote bilateral economic cooperation between the two sides. The report the EGEC submitted conducted detailed research on the implications of China's WTO-accession for the ASEAN economy and the feasibility of establishment of the CAFTA and made an exact evaluation of its potential benefits and challenges for both China and ASEAN. In a sense, the report laid an academic basis for the establishment of the CAFTA. According to the report, ASEAN would have to build on market opportunities that would arise from China's liberalization efforts as well as the dynamism of the Chinese economy to ensure that economic cooperation could continue to grow and prosper (The EGEC, 2001, pp. 1-7), given the growing interdependence between ASEAN and China, the increasing bilateral trade and the great trade potential between China and Cambodia, Laos and Viet Nam, which borders China, the competition between China and ASEAN for FDI in the manufacturing sector and the more intensified competition foreseen after China's WTO-accession. In simple words, the EGEC believed more intensified competition between China and ASEAN, particularly after China's WTO accession, would force ASEAN to take advantage of the opportunities of China's liberalization after the accession. Therefore, they strongly recommended establishing the CAFTA and promoting bilateral economic cooperation. Finally China and ASEAN endorsed the Framework Agreement to set up the CAFTA within ten years in 2002, shortly after the report was submitted to the JCETC. This report confirmed the far-sight wisdom of Zhu Rongji, when he originally proposed to set up the free trade relationship between China and AFTA in 2000, from a governmental perspective. The JCETC and the EGEC played a promoting role in the establishment of the CAFTA.

4.4.2 ACBC

The ACBC is one of the five great dialogue institutions[8] between China and ASEAN, which was founded

---

[8] The other four dialogue institutions are ASEAN-China Senior Officials Consultation Meetings, ASEAN-China Joint Cooperation Committee (ACJCC), ASEAN-China Joint Committee on Economic and Trade Cooperation (ACJCETC) and ASEAN-China Joint Committee on Science and Technology (ACJCST).

in November 2001 after ASEAN proposed it at the first JCECET meeting in 1995. It is a cooperative institution standing for commerce industry in ASEAN and China, constituted of the China Council for Promotion of International Trade (CCPIT), ASEAN Chamber of Commerce (ACC) and leaders from individual ASEAN members' commercial chambers, well-known entrepreneurs and experts. Generally, CCPIT and ACC respectively represent part of China and ASEAN; they work closely with each other within the framework of the ACBC. ACC is a multilateral institution, made up of the most representative associations in the ten individual ASEAN member countries, such as the Brunei National Chamber of Commerce & Industry (BNCCI), Cambodia Chamber of Commerce (CCC), The Indonesia Chamber of Commerce and Industry (ICCI), the Laos National Chamber of Commerce & Industry (LNCCI), National Chamber of Commerce and Industry, Malaysia (NCCIM), The Union of Myanmar Federation of Chambers of Commerce and Industry (UMFCCI), the Philippine Chamber of Commerce and Industry (PCCI), Singapore Business Federation (SBF), the Federation of Thai Industries (FTI), the Vietnam Chamber of Commerce and Industry (VCCI).

The objectives of the ACBC are to: a) boost the dialogue and cooperation among enterprises in ASEAN and China; b) enhance trade and investment cooperation between ASEAN and China; and c) promote individual domestic economic development and the establishment of the CAFTA.[9]

In order to realize its objectives, the ACBC functions by a) providing information on trade and investment for ACBC members and member countries, and commercial consultations for government divisions, sector associations and enterprises; b) organizing/undertaking meetings to promote commercial cooperation between China and ASEAN, including forums, seminars and economic fairs, etc.; c) coordinating the CAExpo and offering necessary assistance; d) enhancing bilateral personnel exchanges in form of mutual visiting of entrepreneur delegations of both sides, personnel training and others; and providing a training service to human resources; e) boosting Chinese members' reputation in Southeast Asia to benefit them by effectively developing commercial connections with Southeast Asian enterprises; f) supplying legal-related service for both Chinese and ASEAN enterprises, including mediation, and arbitration to enable enterprises to solve trade disputes in a friendly atmosphere.

The inaugural meeting was convened in Jakarta, Indonesia on 8 November, 2001, and was attended by Zhu Rongji, the Chinese former Premier and Indonesian President Megawati Sukarnoputri, who declared the foundation of ACBC. So far ACBC had held six meetings, in 2001, 2003, 2004, 2005, 2006 and 2008. Among them, the most important was the fourth one held at Nanning, China in 2004, where the CCPIT and ACC discussed the future directions of ACBC, made a plan for new projects for 2006, 'further discussed on how the council could play an important role in improving ASEAN-China relations (S. a., 2005-2006)'

---

[9] Interview with the executive deputy general secretary of the Chinese Secretariat of the CABC, Beijing, 13 July, 2010

and finally signed the Nanning Joint Declaration. As a cooperative institution at the enterprise and sector association level, the ACBC contributed significantly to enhance economic cooperation among enterprises and sectoral associations in ASEAN and China. To establish the CAFTA was basically a decision made by the governments of ASEAN and China at the governmental level; nevertheless, relying on governmental cooperation alone, the CAFTA could not have been established. The ACBC introduced, encouraged and helped enterprises and sector associations to take active part in the establishment of the CAFTA, which was a great contribution that could not be ignored. Therefore, the ACBC was well placed as a promoter at the enterprise and sectoral association level to help establish the CAFTA.

4.4.3   The CAExpo and CABIS

The CAExpo and CABIS were two governmental/official cooperation institutions on trade and investment issues between ASEAN and China. Both of them were founded in 2004 after the Framework Agreement between China and ASEAN took effect. A year after the Framework Agreement was signed in 2002, Chinese Premier Wen Jiabao proposed to that the CAExpo and CABIS fairs to be held annually in Nanning, Guangxi, China, as a practical action toward setting up the CAFTA at the seventh China-ASEAN Summit on 8 October, 2003. The proposal was approved unanimously by the ten ASEAN members and included in the Chairman Statement in 2003. Then the CAExpo and CABIS held their first fair and summit in 2004.

The CAExpo aims at promoting the building of the CAFTA, striving for mutual benefits and common prosperity, focusing on regional economic and trade cooperation and providing tremendous opportunities for the business communities from all over the world (CAExpo, 2006). The goal of the CABIS is to promote the all-round economic cooperation between China and the ASEAN countries and accelerate the development of the CAFTA. It aims to offer government officials, entrepreneurs and scholars in China and the ASEAN countries an opportunity to publicize their trading policies, promote projects and share views. By conveying the ideas of business circles to government leaders, the Summit will facilitate the formulation of new policies, and offer more opportunities for global purchasers, producers and investors to make a fortune, thus giving an impetus to the development of China-ASEAN economic cooperation (CABIS, 2009).

The two institutions worked very closely to co-promote trade and investment exchanges between China and ASEAN. They were held simultaneously every year. So far, each has held seven events from 2004 onward. They have attracted more and more enterprises to participate, who signed higher and higher contract values during the events. For example, the CAExpo supplied 2,506 booths for 1,505 exhibiting enterprises who signed contracts to the value of 1,080 million dollars at the first fair and it supplied 4,600 booths for 2,200 enterprises who signed contracts worth 1,712 million dollars in 2008. The CABIS also made great efforts to increase the bilateral investment value by over ten times from 2004 to 2010. The CAExpo and CABIS, as the practical action to promote the establishment of the CAFTA played a direct role in it. Although to establish the CAFTA was a governmental decision, the CAExpo and CABIS also contributed substantial to constructing platform for enterprises in China and ASEAN to participate, like the ACBC.

An overview of the cooperative institutions between ASEAN and China shows that most of them seemed at first glance to be bilateral. However, closer investigation revealed that all cooperative institutions were multilaterally constituted by China and individual ASEAN ten members. For example, the report of the EGEC to suggest establishing the CAFTA in 2001 was drafted together by eleven parties; the ACBC also was a multilateral cooperative institution because eleven parties of chambers of commerce in China and ten ASEAN members took part in it and worked closely; the CAExpo and CABIS were hosted by China and undertaken with help from ten parties of ASEAN members. This makes sense, given the fact that ASEAN was a soft and loose association of ten member countries in Southeast Asia. Since the ACC was not able to stand for all the individual interests of ten members, it made sense for such multilateral cooperative institutions to emerge between ASEAN and China. These institutions played their part in suggesting the establishment of the CAFTA and directly boosted it in an effort to provide more chances for enterprises and sectoral associations in ASEAN and China to participate in it.

4.5 Conclusion

After the 1980s, the whole world, including the countries in Southeast and East Asia, went through radical changes of the general context. The Cold War ended in the early 1990s and the Asian economic crisis broke out in the late 1990s, both of which substantially affected the economic policy of ASEAN and China. Before the ending of the Cold War, ASEAN fought for international acceptance as a viable and energetic regional organization, which came into reality in the mid-1980s. Meanwhile, ASEAN also chased another goal, to expand to include all ten Southeast Asian countries, which was finally achieved when Cambodia, as the last member, joined in 1999. More importantly, ASEAN focused on intra-regional economic integration by deciding to set up the AFTA within fifteen years beginning from 1993 after the conclusion of the Cold War.

Sino-ASEAN relations also benefited from the conclusion of the Cold War. They were formalized as a consultative relationship in 1994, upgraded to a full dialogue relationship in 1996 and finally ended with a strategic relationship in 2003. Normal political relations laid a solid basis for promotion of economic exchanges between the two sides. Bilateral trade and investment value between Chin and ASEAN saw a gradual, albeit slow increase after the Cold War ended. However, it was attacked by the 1997-8 AFC.

In response to the regional economic crisis in Asia in late 1997, ASEAN, on the one side speeded up its pace to establish the AFTA; and on the other side, looked beyond Southeast Asia and began to attach importance to economic integration in a geographically wider scope of East Asia and Asia-Pacific, which it was thought could help ASEAN survive a potential economic crisis in the future by economic cooperation with its dialogue partners there. Both ASEAN's trade and investment policies featured a parallel approach of promoting the economic cooperation in Southeast Asia and East Asia. China took the opportunity of the diversion and originally put forth the proposal to establish the CAFTA with ASEAN in 2000. Forecasting the implications of China's WTO-accession and the subsequent intensified competition from China, ASEAN agreed to enhance bilateral economic cooperation with China and set up the CAFTA by 2010.

That ASEAN carried out a parallel approach of promoting the economic cooperation not only in Southeast Asia but alsl in East Asia supplied more chances for economic cooperation between ASEAN and China and provided a driving force for economic integration in East Asia. ASEAN's gradual approach of economic integration was copied by its three Northeast Asian neighbours when they promoted economic integration in East Asia. China took an initiative in putting forth a proposal for the establishment of the first free trade area in East Asia. It helped and stimulated ASEAN to focus on economic cooperation in East Asia instead of the Asia-Pacific region when ASEAN was outward-looking, yet wavering between East Asia and Asia-Pacific. Both ASEAN, as the engine, and China, as an influential great power, provided a driving force foe economic integration in East Asia.

However, ASEAN was not a powerful engine in terms of its loose institutional structure as an intergovernmental organization. The ASEAN Secretariat did not play an impressive role in negotiating to set up the CAFTA with China. Instead, government negotiations between individual ASEAN members and China dominated the process. Moreover, most of the cooperation institutions between China and ASEAN on economic issue were also comprised at the governmental level. Before China's proposal of the CAFTA was accepted by ASEAN, JCETC and EGEC, which drafted the supportive report, provided a critical basis for it from the academic perspective; after the Framework Agreement was endorsed, ACBC, CAExpo and CABIS respectively contributed to introducing, encouraging and helping enterprises and sectoral associations to take part in enhancing trade and investment cooperation between ASEAN and China. As a governmental decision, the establishment of the CAFTA benefited significantly from the participation of enterprises and sectoral associations in China and ASEAN members. These seemingly bilateral, yet essentially multilateral cooperative institutions played a direct role in the initiation, establishment and completion of the CAFTA.

5 China's Role in Trade Cooperation with ASEAN before and after 2001

5.1 Introduction

This chapter examines China's role in trade cooperation with ASEAN during the last decade of the 20th century and the first decade of the 21st century. By describing Beijing's economic policy from the 1990s and discussing the status quo of China-ASEAN trade cooperation, this chapter analyses the Sino-ASEAN trade relationship and observes whether competitiveness or complementarity dominated the bilateral trade relationship between China and AESAN. Beijing was overwhelmingly preoccupied with the multilateral negotiations to enter the WTO during the last decade of the 20th century, after it formally applied to resume its position as an original contracting party of the GATT in July 1986. Therefore, China's efforts towards regional economic cooperation with ASEAN were relatively less due to lack of a clear and targeted policy on economic cooperation at the regional level. China had fairly low, though slowly increasing trade exchanges with ASEAN partners in 1990s, given the high tariffs between two sides and the recent recovery of their initial political and diplomatic relations. In 2001, Beijing officially proposed to set up the CAFTA, which marked a tremendous change in China's attitude towards economic cooperation with ASEAN. Thereafter, a clear policy on economic cooperation at the regional level in East Asia quickly unfolded. As a result, bilateral trade cooperation between China and ASEAN was gradually enhanced and trade value in particular began to increase. The total trade value between China and five main ASEAN members[10] in 1995 was 18,408 million dollars, which increased by 96%, arriving at 36,096 million dollars in 2000. It reached as high as 120,002 million dollars in 2005, over three times the 2000 level. The chapter describes a totally different engagement of China in trade cooperation with ASEAN before and after 2001, by comparing the trade value before and after 2001 in different dimensions. With the trade value increasing, both the competitiveness and the complementarity of trade between China and ASEAN were also intensified. Taking three classifications of traded goods, S1-7 Machinery and Transport Equipment, S1-6 Manufactured Goods and S1-0 Food and Live Animal, as examples, the chapter looks into the competitiveness and complementarity of trade in goods between China and ASEAN. The description of China's economic policy on trade cooperation with ASEAN and the relationship analysis between China and ASEAN lead to the conclusion that China has been playing an increasingly complementary partner of ASEAN in the 2000s. Also, China, following Japan in the 1960s, 1970s and the early 1980s as well as

---

[10] Hereafter, ASEAN-5, which includes Singapore, Malaysia, Thailand, Philippines and Indonesia.

U.S.A in the 1980s and 1990s, acted as the third core promoter in East Asia regionalism since the 1960s.

The chapter has three sections. The first section focuses on Beijing's economic policy on trade cooperation with ASEAN, which was also part of China's economic policy on economic integration at the regional level in East Asia. Beijing was characterized by lack of a clear regional policy on economic cooperation before 2001. However, Beijing put forth a clear policy of setting up the CAFTA in 2001 and implemented it quickly during the next decade. Beijing endorsed the Framework Agreement and other five sub agreements with ASEAN from 2002 to 2009. The objective was to take measures to promote bilateral trade and investment between China and ASEAN. The second section compares trade value between China and ASEAN before and after 2001 from various aspects in order to set up a well-founded basis for analysis of trade relationship between China and ASEAN. The third section evaluates the competitiveness and complementarity of trade relationship between China and ASEAN on the basis laid in the second section and identifies China's role in trade cooperation with ASEAN and in economic integration in East Asia before and after 2001.

All the data, whether quoted originally or computed by the author, are collected from:

1.   Official databases, e.g. ASEAN Statistics Database, UN COMTRADE Database, the WTO International Trade Centre (ITC) Database, Asian Development Bank (ADB) Database, and etc.

2.   Annual statistics yearbooks, e.g. China Statistical Yearbook (1991-2009), China Customs Statistics Yearbook (1991-2009) and so on.

3.   Official websites of international organizations or national governments, e.g. International Monetary Foundation (IMF), World Bank, Ministry of Commerce of China, etc.

4.   Some other reliable data sources such as the Department of Statistics of Singapore, National Institute of Statistics of Cambodia etc.

When the Sino-ASEAN relationship on trade is analysed, five countries, Indonesia, Malaysia, the Philippines, Singapore and Thailand (ASEAN-5) are chosen as the main representatives of ASEAN, for three reasons. First, ASEAN *per se* kept enlarging with new members joining in. Taking new members into consideration adds to the difficulties of data collection, computation and comparison. Second, some trade data of four new members of ASEAN are not available, especially the data before 1995. Finally, the trade value between these five countries and China accounted for more than 90% of the total trade value between China and ASEAN in most years since 1990. In 2000, for example, the export value of ASEAN-5 accounted for 95.4% of the total ASEAN export to China, and import value accounted for 94.1% of China's total imports with all ASEAN members. Therefore, changes of exports and imports of ASEAN-5 with China largely reflected the tendency of all ten ASEAN members.

When the Sino-ASEAN trade relationship is discussed, focus was placed on trade in goods between two sides because, first, bilateral trade in service was still at a low level in the 2000s; and second, the ATS did not took effect until 2009, which resulted in an minor impact. Three classifications of traded goods on basis of Standard International Trade Code (SITC) are chosen as examples. Although the Harmonized Commodity Description and Coding System (HS) was applied in the Agreement on Trade in Goods between China and ASEAN, SITC is applied in this chapter due to the fact that most data are from the UN COMTRADE Database, where SITC facilitates data statistics. China's export and import of S1-6 the Manufactured Goods with ASEAN had the highest trade value in 1990s, which is why S1-6 is chosen as an example to explore the Sino-ASEAN trade relationship. Also S1-7 Machinery and Transport Equipment, is chosen as another example because it had the highest trade value between China and ASEAN in the 2000s. Based on the fact that China and ASEAN gave agricultural cooperation the first priorityand the classification of S1-0 Food and Live Animal includes most agricultural products[11], S1-0 is chosen as the third example. Thus, China's export and import trade with ASEAN are focused on these three SITC products: S1-6, S1-7 and S1-0.

When the competitive and mutually complementary characteristics of trade structure between China and ASEAN are measured, Revealed Comparative Advantage (RCA)[12] index is adopted, in order to explore respective advantage in S1-6, S1-7 and S1-0 of China and ASEAN. The American market was the biggest single export destination outside the East Asian region for both China and ASEAN in the 1990s and 2000s. China exported 21.5% of its total exports to the United States, 15.5% to Europe and 16.6% to Japan in

---

[11] According to the definition of 'agricultural products' from the Food and Agricultural Organization of the United States (FAO) in FAO Statistical Yearbook 2004, agricultural products refers to products in food and live animals (Chapter 00-09 of SITC), beverage and tobacco (Chapter 11 and12), non-food materials (21, 22, 23EX, 26EX and Chapter 29, except fuels), mineral fuels and lubricants and related material (Chapter 41-43) (EX means parts are excluded). Therefore, the three classifications S1-0 food and Live Animals, S1-1 Beverage and Tobacco and S1-4 Mineral Fuels and Lubricants and Related Material make up of the most part of the agricultural products. Among the three classifications, since S1-0 constitutes most of the trade of the agricultural products between China and ASEAN, it is chosen as the third example.

[12] Bela Balassa, Trade Liberalization and 'Revealed' Comparative Advantage, *The Manchester School*, Vol. 33, 1965, pp. 99-123 and Bela Balassa, 'Revealed' Comparative Advantage Revisited: An Analysis of Relative Export Shares of The Industrial Countries, 1953-1971, *The Manchester School*, No. 4, Vol. 45, December 1977, pp. 327-344. In these two papers, Bela Balassa conducted in-depth research on the RCA of Manufacturing Goods and that of the research-intensive product in several economies: the United States, Canada, the European Common Market, the United Kingdom, the Continental member countries of EFTA, and Japan. Bela Balassa suggested not applying RCA to primary products due to 'the subsidies, quotas and special arrangements' for them. However, in terms of the joint endeavour of China and ASEAN in eliminating the above-mentioned subsidies, quota and tariff barriers between them after the *Framework Agreement* in 2002 and of their great achievements by reducing the custom rates of more than 90% of classifications of their bargained goods to zero by 2010, it is safe here also to apply the RCA to the goods classification of S1-0 Food and Live Animals and S1-7 Machinery and Transport Equipment. In addition, the final computed data show evidences that there is little shift in tendency of China's and ASEAN's RCA of S1-7 and S1-0 between the 1990s and 2000s, which further diminishes the hesitation to apply the RCA index to S1-7 and S1-0.

1999; while ASEAN exported 20.5% of its total exports to the United States, 16.3% to Europe and 11% to Japan in 1999. Therefore, the American market is chosen as the third market to calculate ASEAN and China's relative advantage in the three product classifications. All these are applied in order to investigate the competition and mutual complementarity of trade between China and ASEAN.

5.2   Beijing's Trade Policy with ASEAN before and after 2001

As asserted by complex interdependence theorist, if the interdependence theory was applied to studies of the policy of a nation under interdependent conditions, the comparative analysis of the domestic policy of the particular nations must be investigated (Keohane & Nye, 1989, p. 223). Therefore, before analysing the specific Sino-ASEAN relations on trade, it is necessary to sketch in the general orientation of China's economic policy before and after 2001.

5.2.1   Beijing's Trade Policy before 2001

China has been implementing an 'open door' policy for more than three decades since 'reforming and opening-up' was designated as the national policy at the third Plenary Session of the 11th Central Committee of the CPC in 1978. Beijing focused mainly on multilateral trade cooperation at the global level, as demonstrated by its efforts to become a member of the WTO after 1978. Meanwhile, its trade cooperation with ASEAN at the regional level was marginalized because both sides were trying to resume their diplomatic relations after the end of the Cold War. China was among the very few countries who had not become a member of any regional free trade areas by the early 2000s.

Beijing officially applied in July 1986 to resume its position as an original contracting party of the GATT, since when it began the more-than-fifteen-year negotiations with concerned parties of the GATT. This 'Century Negotiation' exhausted their time and efforts; they were unable to take any other trade plan into consideration. More importantly, 'China's accession to the WTO was one of the prerequisites for China being a member of any regional trade areas. Therefore, there is not a big chance for China to set up any free trade area with any partner before its WTO accession'[13]. The negotiations proceeded from 1986 to 2001 and were suspended only for two years after the Tiananmen Square Incident in 1989. Finally, China was accepted as one of the members of the WTO on 11 November, 2001.

During the negotiations, the international context encountered radical changes, among which, the most important was the end of the Cold War. As aforementioned in Chapter Three, China not only newly built/restored normal diplomatic relationship with each of ASEAN members, but also developed a

---

[13] Interview with the director of the EGEC, Beijing, 9 July, 2010

consultative partnership with ASEAN as a whole after the Cold War ended. China was upgraded to be a full dialogue partner with ASEAN in July 1996, with the continuous development of bilateral political exchanges. China, for the first time, was invited to attend the meeting between ASEAN and its dialogue partners in 1996. When Jiang Zemin, the former President of China, attended the first ASEAN-China Summit in December 1997, he and ten ASEAN leaders signed the 'Joint Declaration' to establish a good-neighbour partnership in the 21st century. Since then, China-ASEAN relationship entered a new stage. However, the promotion of diplomatic relations between China and ASEAN did not result in a corresponding increase of economic exchange. The trade value between two sides did not see a huge increase. On the contrary, the trade value between China and the Western world increased substantially because the WTO negotiations came to near completion by the end of the 1990s.

5.2.2   Beijing's Trade Policy after 2001

At the turn of the century, China implemented a radical shift in its economic policy. At the international level, during long years' negotiations aiming at resuming its position as an original contracting party of GATT and then entering the WTO as a new member, China became aware that the international multilateral trade system had its own inevitable weaknesses in organizational structure and operating mechanism.[14] Therefore Beijing diverted its sight to regional economic cooperation.

---

[14] The WTO's weaknesses were much studied by both Chinese scholars and foreign scholars, though expressed in various utterances. Their attention was paid mainly to WTO's weaknesses of: ①the dispute settlement mechanism; ②the anti-dumping rule and Section 201 of the US 1974 Trade Act; ③the Rule of Origin; and ④the double standards of products. For discussion of the weakness of the WTO dispute settlement mechanism, see Chang Jinglong, 'The Implementation Status and Real Defect of the Operating Institution of the WTO Dispute Settlement Body', in Li Qi, eds. *Xiamen University Law Review (Series 15)* (Xiamen: Xiamen University Press 2008), pp.157-200; Liu Gongwen, 'The Weakness of the Appellate of the WTO Dispute Settlement Mechanism and its Solutions', *Around Southeast Asia*, No. 2, 2003, pp. 72-76; Mao Yanqiong, *(The) Problems and Reforms of the WTO Dispute Settlement Mechanism* (unpublished doctoral dissertation) (East China University of Political science and Law/10276: Student Number/05209002), May 2008; Liu Hu, 'How to Deal with the WTO's weakness of the Dispute Settlement Mechanism', *Foreign Business,* October 2001, pp. 80-82. For discussion of the weakness of the anti-dumping rule and Section 201 of the US 1974 Trade Act, see Shaun Breslin, 'Reforming China's Embedded Socialist Compromise: China and the WTO', *Global Change, Peace and Security*, No. 15, 2003, pp.213-219; Liu Yajun, 'The Legislative Defect of the WTO Anti-dumping Rules and Related Reforms', *Journal of Gansu Institute of Political Science and Law*, Vol. 93, July 2007, pp. 128-133; Fan Ying, 'Exploring the WTO's Weakness of its Safeguards in the case of US's Using 'Section 201' to limit the Steel Importation', *Asia-Pacific Economic Review*, April 2002, pp. 13-16; Wang Chuanli and Bai Yan,' Analyzing the Defects of the WTO Anti-dumping Agreement in the Case of US-Japan Hot-rolled Steel Antidumping', *Journal of Henan Administrative Institute of Politics and Law*, No. 2, Vol. 77, 2003, pp. 111-117; Peng Meixiu, 'Suspicion on the WTO Anti-dumping Agreement', *Journal of Harbin University of Commerce*, NO. 6, Vol. 67, 2002, pp. 20-22; Cao Peizhong, Yang Xiaoyan and Liu Chengxiang, 'On the Reasons and Countermeasures for Anti-dumping Sanction to China', *Commercial Research*, No. 4, Vol. 312, 2005, pp. 21-24. For other supplementary information, see Xiao Wenhong, 'The Defects of WTO Anti-dumping Rules and Related Reform', *China's Foreign Trade (English*

Confident of China's success in entering the WTO in the near future and realizing the weaknesses of the WTO, Beijing expressed its good will to enhance economic cooperation with the AFTA at the 3rd China-ASEAN Summit in Manila in 1999. As a follow up to this Summit, experts from China and ASEAN were assembled to make up an expert group to investigate the possible negative impacts China's entry into the WTO would have on ASEAN and the possibility of enhancing economic cooperation between China and ASEAN. Holding the optimistic report the Expert Group submitted, Mr. Zhu Rongji, the former Premier, on behalf of the Government, officially proposed to build a China-ASEAN Free Trade Relationship at the 4th China-ASEAN Summit in Singapore in November 2000. Besides, he officially proposed to set up the CAFTA within ten years at the 5th China-ASEAN Summit in Brunei in 2001. After two years of negotiation, ASEAN and China signed the Framework Agreement on 4th November, 2002. This marked China and ASEAN's entry into a new stage of economic cooperation.

The Framework Agreement consisted of five sub agreements, the EHP (included in the Framework Agreement and effective on 1st January, 2004), the ATG (signed on 29th November, 2004 and effective on 1st January, 2005), the ADSM (signed on 29th November, 2004 and effective on 1st January, 2005), the ATS (signed on 14th January, 2007 and effective on 1st July, 2007) and the IA (signed on 15th August, 2009 and effective on 15th February, 2010).

These five sub agreements highlighted three features of China-ASEAN economic cooperation: the rules of the Framework Agreement were highly consistent with those of the international trade mechanism; both China and ASEAN showed great respect for domestic legislation and regulation; and both sides showed much flexibility to make some necessary concessions.

1.   Rules of the Framework Agreement were highly consistent with those of the international trade mechanism such as the WTO, the IMF and the World Bank, etc.. Based on the main principles of these international multilateral trade rules, both sides agreed to adjust, modify, or sometimes even dismantle some of their specific clauses and articles.

For example, Article 9 of the ATG stated that

---

version), No. 9, 2008, pp. 60-61; Zhao Minyan, 'On the Applied Shortage and Countermeasure of The Agricultural Products Agreement of WTO', *Journal of Anhui Vocational College of Police Officers*, No.8, Vol. 44, 2009, pp. 5-9; Li Juan, *Comparative Study of Special Safeguard Measures Under WTO Legal Framework: With the Focus on Special Safeguard Mechanism against Products from China* (Unpublished doctoral dissertation) (East China University of Political science and Law/10276: Student Number/03209012), August 2006; Liu Yu, 'Analyzing the 'Soft Law' Defects in WTO Rules-According to the Rules Concerning Less-developed Countries', *Journal of Changshu Institute of Technology (Philosophy and Social Science)*, No. 11, November 2007, pp. 52-55 and Han Long, 'On the WTO's Weakness of the Double Standards for the 'Same' Products and it Solution', *Journal of Henan Administrative Institute of Politics and Law*, No. 1, Vol. 70, 2002, pp. 86-90.

'In applying ACFTA safeguard measures, the Parties shall adopt the rules for the application of safeguard measures as provided under the WTO Agreement on Safeguards, with the exception of the quantitative restriction measures set out in Article 5, and Articles 9, 13 and 14 of the WTO Agreement on Safeguards. As such, all other provisions of the WTO Agreement on Safeguards shall, mutatis mutandis, be incorporated into and form an integral part of this Agreement.'

When trade disputes took place between two sides, the settlement mechanism would follow the main principles of the WTO and International Court of Justice. Article 3 of the ADSM clearly stated that

'Once the complaining party and the party complained against have appointed their respective arbitrators subject to paragraph 2, the parties concerned shall endeavour to agree on an additional arbitrator who shall serve as chair. If the parties concerned are unable to agree on the chair of the arbitral tribunal within 30 days after the date on which the last arbitrator has been appointed under paragraph 2, they shall request the Director-General of the World Trade Organization (WTO) to appoint the chair and such appointment shall be accepted by them. In the event that the Director-General is a national of one of the parties to the dispute, the Deputy Director-General or the officer next in seniority who is not a national of either party to the dispute shall be requested to appoint the chair. If one of the parties to the dispute is a non-WTO member, the parties to the dispute shall request the President of the International Court of Justice to appoint the chair and such appointment shall be accepted by them. In the event that the President is a national of one of the parties to the dispute, the Vice President or the officer next in seniority that is not a national of either party to the dispute shall be requested to appoint the chair.'

In ATS, Article 9 stated that

'The Parties note the multilateral negotiations pursuant to Article X of the (WTO) GATS (General Agreement on Trade in Services) on the question of

> *emergency safeguard measures based on the principle of non-discrimination';*
>
> *and it is ruled in Article 10 that 'Nothing in this Agreement shall affect the*
>
> *rights and obligations of any Party who is a member of the International*
>
> *Monetary Fund under the Articles of Agreement of the Fund*

Based on the international rules, China and ASEAN modified and sometimes even abandoned certain articles, in the specific case of the CAFTA. Just to give an example. As clearly stated by Article 14 in ATG:

> *Each of the ten ASEAN Member States agrees to recognise China as a full*
>
> *market economy and shall not apply, from the date of the signature of this*
>
> *Agreement, Sections 15 and 16 of the Protocol of Accession of the People's*
>
> *Republic of China to the WTO and Paragraph 242 of the Report of the Working*
>
> *Party on the Accession of China to WTO in relation to the trade between China*
>
> *and each of the ten ASEAN Member States.*

2.   Both China and ASEAN showed great respect for the domestic legislation and regulation of their counterparts. For example, when discussing the qualifications of contracting parties who were going to refuse to give some interests to certain non-contracting parties, the IA made it clear in the note to Article 15 that 'it is ruled by domestic laws and rules in Indonesia, Myanmar, the Philippines and Vietnam on who owns or manages the investment if he/she belongs to a non-contracting party'

3.   When negotiating, both China and ASEAN were willing to make some appropriate concessions, aiming at long-term economic and political goals. As far as China was concerned, it gave full consideration to ASEAN members who were developing at different economic stages. The Framework Agreement made frequent reference to 'different stages of economic development among ASEAN Member States and the need for flexibility' at various points[15]. Given the imbalance of economic development among ASEAN members, 'China shall accord Most-Favoured Nation (MFN) Treatment consistent with the WTO rules and disciplines to all the non-WTO ASEAN Member States upon the date of signature of this Agreement'(Article 9, the Framework Agreement) and different timetables for tariff reduction are applied in four new ASEAN members. In return, 'each of the ten ASEAN Member States agrees to recognize China as a full market economy' (Article 14, ATG); recognition which China had not been accorded within

---

[15] For instance, the exact terms and phrases 'different stages', 'special and differential treatment', and ''flexibility' can be found in Preamble, Article 2, 8, etc.

the WTO framework. This benefited all Chinese enterprises trading with or investing in ASEAN members. As an official from the Ministry of Commerce of China said:

> *'If (they) set up factories in ASEAN and exported products from ASEAN member countries to the markets in developed economies such as the US and EU, they were not limited to their quota distributed to China. Besides, even if they were obsessed in the anti-dumping cases, (they) were not going to be taxed according to the high rate based on the non-market economy. ASEAN's recognition of China's status as a full market economy not only provided Chinese enterprises with low tariff when exporting to the US or EU, and but also reduced their risk of anti-dumping charges from there.'[16]*

This was also part of the reason why Chinese enterprises chose ASEAN as the first investment destination after the Framework Agreement was endorsed and China's investment policy of 'going out' was implemented.

With economic exchanges increasing, progress was also made on the Sino-ASEAN diplomatic relationship. By releasing the 'Plan of Action to Implement the Joint Declaration on ASEAN-China Strategic Partnership for Peace and Prosperity' on 21st December, 2004, the Sino-ASEAN relationship was further upgraded to be a strategic partnership. Increasing economic exchanges, together with the upgrading of political and diplomatic relations, contributed significantly to the establishment of the CAFTA, which was declared complete on 1st January, 2010. 'ASEAN-China is the largest FTA in population size and includes 1.9 billion total people. It is the third largest FTA in economic size, with a cumulative GDP of US $5.8 trillion. And after the EU and the North American Free Trade Agreement, it is the third largest FTA in terms of total trade transacted. In 2008, ASEAN-China accounted for a combined US $4.3 trillion, or 13 percent of global trade (Pushpanathan, 2010).' Comparing the value data of China-ASEAN trade before and after 2001 in different dimensions, we are able to describe the Sino-ASEAN trade relationship as accurately as possible before and after 2001 in the second section. Based on the trade relations between China and ASEAN, we are also able to identify China's role in trade cooperation before and after 2001. This is discussed in details in the third section.

---

[16] Interview with a former official of the Ministry of Commerce of China, Nanning, China, 18 August, 2010

5.3   Bilateral Trade between China and ASEAN before and after 2001

Although there was lack of a clear regional economic cooperation policy during the 1990s, China slowly shifted the focus of its economic policy from multilateral trade cooperation at the international level to bilateral cooperation at the regional level in the 2000s, by negotiating, signing and implementing five sub agreements of the CAFTA with ASEAN one by one. China's shift of focus on economic cooperation had a far-reaching impact on trade exchanges between China and ASEAN, whose members were at different stages of economic development and had a variety of industrial structures. It made both sides endogenously and mutually complementary on trade structure. With five sub agreements completed, custom tariffs between China and ASEAN were reduced greatly; the trade value between two sides substantially increased; ASEAN, whether as a trade source or destination, ranked higher in China's imports and exports as an increasingly important partner for China.

5.3.1   GDP per Capita and Level Classification of Industry Structure

Table 5.1 GDP per Capita at Current Prices

GDP per Capita at Current Prices										
										in US dollars
Year	States									
	Brunei	Cambodia	China	Singapore	Indonesia	Laos	Malaysia	Myanmar	Philippines	Thailand	Viet Nam
1991	14,001	185	373	13,951	778	238	2,744	128	710	1,711	113
2001	16,429	307	1,050	20,996	771	304	3,903	162	899	1,834	410
2008	37,048	769	3,292	39,423	2,247	858	8,197	578	1,866	4,187	1,041

Source: United Nations Statistics Division (Compiled and computed by the author)

Data of GDP per capita and industrial structure in ASEAN members and China showed a gap in economic development between China and. As Table 5.1 shows, four levels can be classified in terms of the GDP per capita of China and ASEAN members in 1991. Among them, Brunei and Singapore constituted the first level, where the GDP per capita was more than 10,000 US dollars; Malaysia and Thailand made up the second level, where the GDP per capita was more than 1000 US dollars; Indonesia and the Philippines belonged to the third level, with the GDP per capita between 500 and 1000 US dollars; and the five remaining states, Cambodia, China, Laos Myanmar and Vietnam were at the bottom, with the GDP per capita below 500 US dollars. There was no fundamental change in the grouping of four levels in terms of the GDP per capita in 2001, although China was upgraded from the bottom to the second level after a ten-year fast economic leap. The reform and market opening in the late 1970s may be a good reason to explain this change. However, essential changes occurred in 2008. Only three levels can be clearly identified, among which Brunei and Singapore still remained at the first level with GDP per capita more than 30,000

US dollars; and the bottom level was made up of Cambodia, Laos, Myanmar and Vietnam, with GDP per capita below 1000 US dollars. As far as the second level is concerned, in addition to the original members of Malaysia, Thailand and China, another two new members, Indonesia and the Philippines, joined, resulting in GDP per capita in the second level of over 1000 US dollars. Three assessments can be made from the data in Table 5.1:

1.   ASEAN and China endeavoured to develop the domestic economies at a rapid pace during the two decades before and after 2001. Of special note is that rapid economic progress was made in China during the 1990s and in Indonesia and the Philippines during the 2000s;

2.   ASEAN and China were marching on the way to economic integration: four economic levels were integrated into three.

3.   On the way to economic integration, the existing gap on economic development was broadened rather than narrowed. In 1991, the GDP per capita of the first level was about 20 times that of the third level and this did not change fundamentally after the first decade; however, by 2008 after the second decade it was nearly 30 times that of the third level. The economic gap among ASEAN members seems to be somehow similar to that between East and West parts in China, which shows the common objective of narrowing the domestic gap for China and ASEAN through regional economic integration.

Among the four/three levels East Asian states comprised, three industries accounted for different proportions of GDP. The first level was characterised by depending mainly on the tertiary sector l. Singapore was a perfect example of the first level. According to statistics[17], the primary, secondary and tertiary sectors accounted respectively for about 0.1%, 34.7% and 65.2% of GDP at current prices in 1998. The proportion of the primary sector decreased to as little as 0.07% of GDP in 2008 and the tertiary sector increased as high as 72.53% of GDP, more than 6% the that 1998 level. Members in the second level were characterised by depending mainly on the secondary sector. Take China as an example. [18] Its primary, secondary and tertiary sectors accounted respectively for about 7%, 63% and 30% of GDP at current prices in 1991. In 2008, its proportion of the primary sector to GDP was 6%, nearly as much as that in 1991. Though there was a small decline in the proportion of the secondary sector (51%) and a slight rise in that of the tertiary sector (43%) in 2008, the fundamental structure of the GDP remained essentially unchanged. Moving on to the third level, it was characterised by depending mainly on the primary sector, as seen in Cambodia, Laos, and Myanmar. Based on statistics for Cambodia[19], the primary, secondary and tertiary

[17] Data for Singapore comes from *Singapore Yearbook of Statistics 2009*, Singapore Department of Statistics (Compiled and computed by the author)

[18] Data for China comes from *China Statistics Yearbook 2009*, National Bureau of Statistics of China (Compiled and computed by the author)

[19] Data for Cambodia comes from *Cambodia Statistical Yearbook 2006*, National Institute of Statistics, Cambodia (Compiled and computed by the author)

sectors accounted respectively for about 47%, 13% and 40% of GDP at current prices in 1993. In 2005, the proportion still remained generally similar, at 48%, 14% and 38% respectively. Laos and Myanmar maintained a roughly similar tendency to Cambodia. However, Vietnam [20] was an exception. The proportion of the primary sector to GDP remained virtually unchanged during the two decades since1990s; however, the proportion of the secondary sector continued to rise, from about 29% in 1995 to 38% in 2001 and then to 41% in 2007. This demonstrates that following integration with other East Asian economies, the domestic industry structure of Vietnam was upgraded. At risk of making an arbitrary judgment, we can argue that Vietnam probably should be the next member, most likely to join the second level of economy in East Asia. Upgrading the sector structure of the four new ASEAN members was also one of the goals of the Framework Agreement, as set out in Article 7 Clause 4: 'to adjust their economic structure and expand their trade and investment with China'. Data of GDP structure of ASEAN and China after 2001 showed that, to some extent, the Framework Agreement was successful, at least, in this respect.

Comparison of data on the GDP of East Asian economies demonstrates the possibility and feasibility of East Asian economic integration and also the golden opportunity for China to play an increasingly important role in providing impetus to integration as the third core promoter in East Asia after the Cold War. In addition, based on the data of GDP and industry structure of China and ASEAN, it is obviously that

> *'natural competition exists not only between China and ASEAN but also among*
> *ASEAN members, given their similarity in economic development levels and the*
> *industry structure. Therefore it does not make much sense to emphasize the*
> *competition between China and ASEAN'.[21]*

5.3.2   The Custom Tariff and Trade Value between China and ASEAN

Since the 1990s, the custom tariff of imports and exports between China and ASEAN remained at a high level due to lack of a preferential/free trade agreement between them. This was part of the reason why trade value did not see a sharp rise. Before the Framework Agreement was signed, more than 46% of Thai commodities were exported to China at a high tariff of over 20%. The corresponding values were 26.5%, 3.5% and 3.2% in Malaysia, Indonesia and the Philippines respectively. When the Framework Agreement came into effect after 2003, the custom tariff between China and ASEAN was reduced to a great extent.

---

[20] Data for Vietnam comes from Database of *General Statistics Office of Vietnam* (Compiled and computed by the author)

[21] Interview with the special assistant of Mr. Qian Qichen, the former Premier (the Chinese member of the China-ASEAN Eminent Persons Group (EPG) Nanjing, China, 23 April, 2010

China gave all ASEAN members MFN treatment, whether they had joined the WTO at that time or not.

According to Article 6 of the Framework Agreement, China and six original ASEAN members reduced the tariffs of those commodities whose tariff was less than 5% listed in Product Catalogue 1 to zero by 1st January, 2004; tariffs higher than 5% but less than 15% listed in Product Catalogue 2 to zero by 1st January, 2005; and tariffs higher than 15% listed in Product Catalogue 3 were reduced to zero by 1st January, 2006. For commodities transacted between China and the four new ASEAN members, flexibility on timetable was adopted. Different members had their own timetable for implementation of zero tariffs after discussion and agreement with China. For example, in Vietnam, tariffs higher than 30% listed in Product Catalogue 1 were reduced to zero no later than 1st January, 2008; while the date could be delayed to 1st January, 2009 for Laos and Myanmar, and it to 1st January, 2010 in Cambodia. In Vietnam, tariffs equal or higher than 15% but less than 30% listed on Product Catalogue 2 was ruled to reduce to zero by 1st January, 2008; while the date could be delayed to 1st January, 2009 for Laos and Myanmar, and to 1st January, 2010 for Cambodia. For commodities whose tariffs were lower than 5%, listed in Product Catalogue 3, the flexibility on implementation of zero tariffs was much more obvious. For Vietnam, the tariff was reduced to zero on 1st January, 2008, while it could still remain between 0-5% for Laos and Myanmar, before it was reduced to zero on 1st January, 2009. In Cambodia, it remained between 0-5% in January 2009, and reduced to zero by 1st January, 2010. China stood in a stark contrast with ASEAN and its four new members in particular; in that China did not enjoy the timetable flexibility it gave to ASEAN new members. In addition, China included all traded agricultural products in chapters at the 8/9 digit level (HS Code) in the EHP to phase out their tariffs while it agreed on some ASEAN members such as Cambodia, Laos, Malaysia, Vietnam having their own Exclusion List of products, whose tariffs would not be reduced as ruled by the EHP. The joint efforts taken by China and ASEAN on tariff phase-out led to a sharp rise in bilateral trade transactions between China and ASEAN from the 2000s.

As shown in Table 5.2, total trade value between China and ASEAN in 1997 was 22,901 million dollars. The low value can be attributed to the 1997-8 AFC, which heavily hit the newly industrializing economies in East Asia and China's lack of a clear regional policy on economic cooperation. Bilateral trade value saw a sharp rise in 2002, almost twice that in 1997, after the proposal of the CAFTA was put forth in 2001. It grew at a faster speed, arriving at 184,469 million dollars in 2007, after the ATG was signed in 2004. To summarize, it doubled during five years from 1997 to 2002; and it tripled during another five years from 2002 to 2007. Part of the reason for the miracle during the latter five years might be China's entry into the WTO and China's shifting attitude towards economic cooperation with ASEAN. The endorsement and implementation of ATG marked a substantive stage in bilateral economic cooperation between China and ASEAN (Rong & Yang, 2006) (Guo & Wu, 2007). Tariff reduction laid a good basis for trade promotion; measures for trade facilitation and gradual liberalization directly brought about not only a sharp rise in trade value between China and ASEAN in the 2000s, but also an expansion of ASEAN's proportion in

China's total trade value in Asia and in the world. In 1998, trade value between China and ASEAN accounted for about 12% of China's total trade value in Asia and 7% of that in the world. It rose slightly to 13% of China's trade value in Asia and 8% in the world in 2002. Although it continued to represent 8% of China's world trade in 2007, its share of China's trade value in Asia reached a relatively high proportion of 15%. This illustrates that China had much closer trade cooperation with ASEAN than other Asian partners. This was also one the goals of Framework Agreement: to enhance economic exchanges and to promote bilateral trade cooperation between China and ASEAN. The expanding bilateral trade value at least reflected, to some extent, the success of China's FTA strategy. Undoubtedly, the bilateral trade increase between China and ASEAN could not be attributed solely to the establishment of the CAFTA. China's entry into the WTO in late 2001 also made its contributions. However, the CAFTA was much more significant than the WTO accession, because most of the trade between China and ASEAN happened between ASEAN and provinces in West China, which was not the priority area for China's opening-up (as illustrated as a critical step when China entered the WTO).

Table 5.2 Total Trade Value between China and Main ASEAN Members

Total Trade Value between China and Main ASEAN Members in the 1990s and 2000s

in Million Dollars

	1995	1996	1997	1998	1999	2000	2001	2002	2003	2004	2005	2006	2007	2008	2009
Singapore	6,898	N/A	8,788	8,179	8,563	10,821	10,919	14,031	19,349	16,682	33,147	40,858	47,497	52,477	47,863
Malaysia	3,352	N/A	4,417	4,270	5,279	8,045	9,425	14,271	20,127	26,261	30,700	37,110	46,467	53,557	51,963
Thailand	3,362	N/A	3,515	3,672	4,216	6,624	7,051	8,557	12,655	17,342	21,811	27,726	34,699	41,293	38,204
Philippines	3,490	N/A	1,666	3,631	4,830	7,464	6,724	7,935	10,229	13,472	16,787	19,055	25,160	31,516	28,348
Indonesia	1,306	N/A	4,515	2,026	2,287	3,142	3,564	5,259	9,400	13,328	17,557	23,413	30,646	28,637	20,531
ASEAN-5	18,408		22,901	21,778	25,175	36,096	37,683	50,053	71,760	87,085	120,002	148,162	184,469	207,480	186,909

Note: ASEAN-5 includes Singapore, Malaysia, Thailand, Philippines and Indonesia

Source: UN COMTRADE Database. Data of 1997 comes from China Customs Statistics Yearbook 1998, General Administration of Customs of the People's Republic of China (Compiled and computed by the author)

N/A means data is not available.

96

With the expanding bilateral trade, ASEAN's position as an increasingly important trade partner of China was reinforced. Only Singapore, among ASEAN members, was listed in the top10 importing and exporting trade partners of China in 1999. Other ASEAN members had minimal trade with China in the 1990s. In the 2000s, ASEAN, as a whole, expanded its overall trade with China, encouraged by China's friendly policy on trade cooperation. ASEAN was the fifth trade partner of China, following Japan, U.S.A, European Union (EU) and Hong Kong in 2004, and it caught up with Hong Kong in 2008, ranking fourth as a trade partner of China. After the CAFTA was declared complete on 1st January, 2010, ASEAN became the third trade partner of China, based on Chinese Customs statistics for the first half year of 2010. In the meanwhile, China ranked third trade partner of ASEAN.

Based on the data in Table 5.2, we computed the data in Table 5.3, which reveals the real growth in trade between China and ASEAN in the late 1990s and 2000s. Beginning from the 1997-8 AFC and ending up with the 2008 global financial crisis, the late 1990s and 2000s saw a continuous growth of bilateral trade between China and ASEAN except in 1998 and 2009. In 1998 and 2009, bilateral trade between China and ASEAN decreased by 4.90% and 9.91% respectively, due to heavy attacks of the financial crisis. All other years, when bilateral trade increased, saw stable growth, which peaked in 2000 and 2003. Bilateral trade was enhanced and its real growth rushed at the unprecedented rate of 43.38% in 2000, when China initiatively proposed to set up a free trade area. It remained a rising tendency even within the context of global economic recession in 2001, and it grew at a similar growth rate after the Framework Agreement came into effect in 2003. From 2002 to 2007, bilateral trade between China and ASEAN kept increasing at an average growth rate of over 20% for six years. The tendency of bilateral trade was reflected not only in the value rise and growth rate of trade in goods between China and ASEAN but also in the structure change of traded goods. More details of types and quantities of trade in goods follow in the next section.

Table 5.3 Real Growth in Trade between China and ASEAN

Real Growth in Trade between China and ASEAN in late 1990s and 2000s											
										in percentage	
Period	1998	1999	2000	2001	2002	2003	2004	2005	2006	2007	2008	2009
Growth	-4.90	15.60	43.38	4.40	32.83	43.37	21.36	37.80	23.47	25.50	12.47	-9.91
Source: UN COMTRADE Database (Compiled and computed by the author)											

5.3.3   Trade Structure of Goods between China and ASEAN

Changes in trade between China and ASEAN before and after 2001 were not only reflected in a substantial value increase, but also in changes in types of goods traded. Table 5.4 supplies some numeric evidence of this change. According to UN COMTRADE Database, S1-6 Manufactured goods classified chiefly by material, ranked number one of the total value of China's exports to ASEAN-5 in 1991, followed by S1-3 Mineral fuels, lubricants and related materials and S1-7 Machinery and transport equipment. It ranked number two of China's imports from ASEAN, following S1-3 and followed by S1-2 Crude material, inedible, except fuels. S1-7 became the largest classification of China's trade with ASEAN in 2000. It occupied the first place in China's exports to ASEAN, followed by S1-6 and S1-8, and ranked the first of China's imports from ASEAN, followed by S1-5 and S1-3. S1-7 retained its ranking till 2009, when it still ranked the first largest value of China's export to ASEAN, followed by S1-8 and S1-6, and ranked the largest of China's imports from ASEAN, followed by S1-5 of Chemicals and S1-3. Great changes happened to S1-6, whose value was listed in the top three of both China's exports and imports; and whose value of China's exports gradually decreased, to number two in 2000 and number three in 2009. Figure 5.1 reveals that both exports and imports of 1-6 increased during the 1990s and 2000s. Export value increased from 968,781 thousand dollars in 1991 to 2,606,740 thousand dollars in 2000 and 13,252,270 thousand dollars in 2009, more than ten times the value in 1991. Import value of S1-6 also increased from 696,170 thousand dollars in 1991, to 2,565,239 thousand dollars in 2000 and 5,454,427 thousand dollars in 2009, over twice the value in 2000. However, as illustrated in

Figure 5.2 and Figure 5.3, although the export and import value of S1-6 increased, both of their proportion in China's total export and import declined. Its proportion of export declined from 24.1% in 1991 to 17.2% in 2000 and 8.4% in 2009, and its proportion of import declined from 18.3% in 1991 to 12.2% in 2000 and sharply to 3.3% in 2009. These changes illustrated that although China's demand for manufactured goods from ASEAN increased since 1990, its proportion in China's trade declined under competition from other imperative needs such as S1-7, as shown in Figure 5.4.

Table 5.4 Top3 Types of China's Exports to and Imports from ASEAN

Top3 Types of China's Exports and Imports to and from ASEAN in the 1990s and 2000s			
Period	Rank	Export	Import
1991	1	S1-6	S1-3
	2	S1-3	S1-6
	3	S1-7	S1-2
2000	1	S1-7	S1-7
	2	S1-6	S1-5
	3	S1-8	S1-3
2009	1	S1-7	S1-7
	2	S1-8	S1-5
	3	S1-6	S1-3

Source: UN COMTRADE Database (Compiled and computed by the author)

Note: Here, data on China is only limited to that of mainland China, excluding those of Hong Kong, Macao and Taiwan

As Figure 5.4 shows, both exports and imports of S1-7 of China remained at a low level in 1991, with exports of only 666,029 thousand dollars and imports of 439,919 thousand dollars. Both of them grew slowly in 2000 but surged in 2009.The exports value of S1-7 in 2009 reached as high as 44,255,741 thousand dollars, increasing by more than 66 times during two decades; and its imports soared to 54,817,712 thousand dollars, increasing to nearly 125 times the 1991 level. Part of the reason is the upgrading of China's domestic industry structure and growing demand for machinery and transport equipment from ASEAN during the 1990s and 2000s in order to meet the needs of its rapid industrialization. In accordance with total export and import value growth, the proportion of S1-7's trade value in total China's trade with ASEAN also enlarged. As Figure 5.5 and Figure 5.6 show, the proportions of both export and import of S1-7 reached over 40%, and it occupied almost half of China's total trade with ASEAN. Both figures soared by more than 50% in 2009, reaching a level unprecedented during the twenty years.

Figure 5.1 Trade value of S1-6 of China's Export and Import with ASEAN

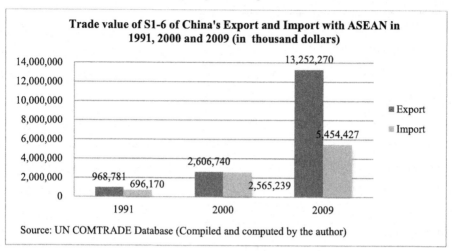

Figure 5.2 Share of S1-6 of China's Export with ASEAN in China's Total

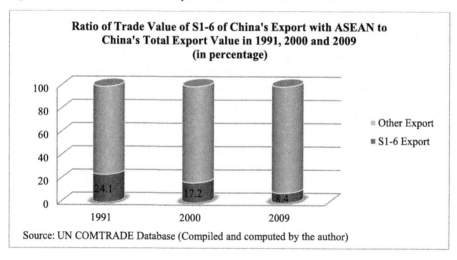

Figure 5.3 Share of S1-6 of China's Import with ASEAN in China's Total

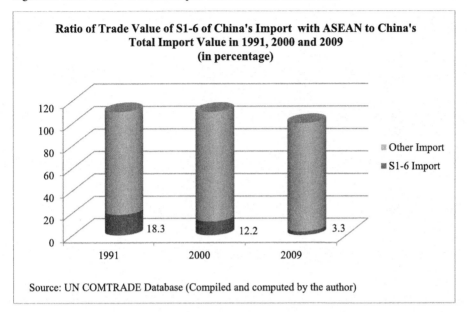

Ratio of Trade Value of S1-6 of China's Import with ASEAN to China's Total Import Value in 1991, 2000 and 2009 (in percentage)

Other Import
S1-6 Import

1991: 18.3
2000: 12.2
2009: 3.3

Source: UN COMTRADE Database (Compiled and computed by the author)

Figure 5.4 Trade Value of S1-7 of China's Export and Import with ASEAN

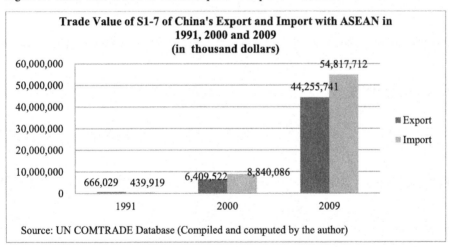

Trade Value of S1-7 of China's Export and Import with ASEAN in 1991, 2000 and 2009 (in thousand dollars)

54,817,712
44,255,741
8,840,086
6,409,522
666,029   439,919

Export
Import

1991   2000   2009

Source: UN COMTRADE Database (Compiled and computed by the author)

Figure 5.5 Share of S1-7 of China's Export with ASEAN in China's Total

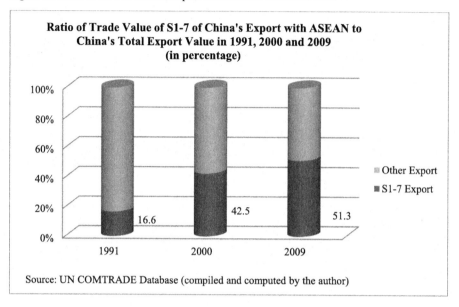

Source: UN COMTRADE Database (compiled and computed by the author)

Figure 5.6 Share of S1-7 of China's Import with ASEAN in China's Total

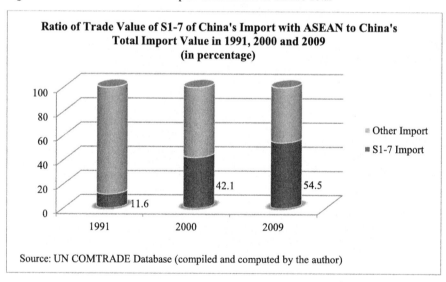

Source: UN COMTRADE Database (compiled and computed by the author)

In the meanwhile, China's trade value of S1-3 Mineral fuels, lubricants and related materials with ASEAN, together with other types of goods trade, reduced after agricultural trade was given the first priority in bilateral trade cooperation between China and ASEAN. The proportion of S1-3 in China's export value decreased sharply from 21.5% in 1991 to 7.5% in 2000 and then gradually to 5.1% in 2009; and its proportion in China's import value also declined from 28.2% in 1991 to 12.9% in 2000 and finally 10.7%

in 2009.

Here, it is absolutely necessary to take a look at the bilateral trade of S1-0, since it constituted the major part of bilateral agricultural trade between China and ASEAN after the EHP came into effect in 2004. As Table 5.5 shows, China's export value on S1-0 to ASEAN remained at the middle level among ten types of export goods whether in year 1991, 2000 or 2009; and China's import value on S1-0 ranked seventh of ten types of import goods during the two decades. However, Table 5.6 reveals it increased to a very great extent after 2003, although the total values of S1-0 were not particularly high. Take year 2004 as an example. China's import of S1-0 substantially increased by 86.02% over 2003 after the EHP was implemented in 2004. This was an unprecedented annual growth rate, which no other classifications of traded goods had ever achieved. In the meanwhile, China's export value of S1-0 had a small decline. This demonstrates that China imported much more goods of S1-0 from ASEAN than before and it did not export more of them to ASEAN. As a matter of fact, its export of S1-0 to ASEAN decreased by 7.53% in 2004, comparing to the previous year. This proves that ASEAN benefited more from the concession China made within the Framework Agreement, which will be discussed in detail in the next chapter. As shown in Table 5.6, although the export value of S1-0 still remained at a low level in 2004, its annual growth rate (86.02%) ranked the first among ten types of China's export goods; it was even much higher than that of S1-7 (37.02%), which had the biggest trade value between China and ASEAN.

Both China's export and import of S1-0 with ASEAN maintained on an ascending trajectory after the global economic crisis broke out in 2008. China's export of S1-0 increased by 19.47% in 2009, while its import increased by 30.90% in the same year. This made a sharp contrast with trade in other types of goods. Again, take S1-7 for example. China's export of S1-7 in 2009 decreased by 7.48% than in 2008 and its import decreased by 13.32% meanwhile, due to the severe impact of the economic crisis. The tremendous growth of S1-0's trade may be attributed, in the short term, to the implementation of EHP, and in the long term, to China's shift in its attitude toward economic cooperation with ASEAN and ASEAN's coordination with China's initiative of regional economic cooperation. The example of S1-0 shows that bilateral economic cooperation not only benefited both sides, but also helped them to fight against the negative impacts of the global economic crisis. Summarizing Table 5.5 and Table 5.6, we also find out an interesting phenomenon; although the trade value of S1-0 between China and ASEAN had never been among the important cooperative pillars before 2004, it really was after the Framework Agreement was agreed in 2002. Why did China and ASEAN choose such a humble field as one of the five priority cooperation areas between China and ASEAN? This will be discussed in detail in the next chapter.

Table 5.5 Trade of S1-0 between China and ASEAN in 1991, 2000 and 2009

Trade of S1-0 between China and ASEAN in 1991, 2000 and 2009						
	Export			Import		
Period	Value (in thousand dollars)	Proportion in total (%)	Rank of ten types of SITC	Value (in thousand dollars)	Proportion in total (%)	Rank of ten types of SITC
1991	541,194	13.5	4/10	181,927	4.8	7/10
2000	1,042,720	6.9	5/10	583,701	2.8	7/10
2009	3,613,649	2.1	5/10	2,435,506	2.4	7/10

Source: UN COMTRADE Database (compiled and computed by the author)

Table 5.6 China's Trade of S1-0 with ASEAN in the 2000s

China's Trade of S1-0 with ASEAN in the 2000s				
	Export		Import	
Period	Value (in million dollars)	Growth Rate (in percentage)	Value (in million dollars)	Growth Rate (in percentage)
2001	890		696	
2002	1,403	57.64%	576	-17.24%
2003	1,607	14.54%	658	14.24%
2004	1,486	-7.53%	1,224	86.02%
2005	1,674	12.65%	1,219	-0.41%
2006	2,175	29.93%	1,622	33.06%
2007	2,820	29.66%	1,854	14.30%
2008	3,025	7.27%	1,861	0.38%
2009	3,614	19.47%	2,436	30.90%

Source: UN COMTRADE Database (compiled and computed by the author)

5.4 Trade Relationship between China and ASEAN before and after 2001

As complex interdependence theorists asserted that it was the relative gains rather than joint gains or joint less that was the focus (Keohane & Nye, 1989, p. 10) when an interdependent relationship was analysed. Therefore, when the Sino-ASEAN relationship on trade is analysed, the problem whether the trade relationship is competitive or mutually complementary was highlighted. Actually, it had attracted most politicians' and researchers' attention. When Dr. Surin Pistuwan, the general secretary of the ASEAN Secretariat, was interviewed by a Chinese journalist on 8th October 2009, he summarized the Sino-ASEAN economic relationship with a simple sentence: the two sides were mutually complementary in economy (Pitsuwan, 2010, p. 15). Mr. Long Yongtu, the former Vice Minister of MOFTEC and the chief negotiating representative for China's WTO accession negotiations, also confirmed the mutual economic complementarity between China and ASEAN and foresaw an extensive potential for bilateral trade cooperation (Long, 26 April, 2002) before the Framework Agreement was signed. When Mr. Gao Hucheng, the Vice Minister of MOC of China also underlined the mutual complementarity between China and ASEAN in their resources and industrial structure, although both ASEAN and China were developing economies (Gao, 2010, p. 21).

In contrast with politicians' confirmation of the mutual complementarity between China and ASEAN, there was not an agreement on this issue in academia. Most researchers agreed that the Sino-ASEAN relationship on trade was not only competitive, but also mutually complementary (Jia & Li, 1997, pp. 21-26) (Zhou, July 2003, pp. 56-59) (Song, 2005, pp. 87-91) (Zhang, July 2009, pp. 116-118,125). Yet, some researchers argued that it was more competitive than mutually complementary (Wong & Chan, May/June 2003, p. 507) (Zhang & Xu, November 2003, p. 85); moreover, 'the export competition between China and ASEAN would be chronic (Shi, 2003, p. 53)'. On the contrary, it was argued by some other researchers that the mutual complementarity was much greater than the competition (Li & Huang, 2005, p. 11) (Wang, 2004, p. 63) (Xue, March 2007, p. 29). Some researchers further asserted that the relationship was more mutually complementary between China, who was on the second level of East Asian industry structure and those ASEAN members who were on other levels, but it was more competitive between China and the ASEAN countries on the same level of industry structure, which was embodied in the third market (Wang Q. , 2004, p. 10).

Some analysis was made of Sino-ASEAN trade relationship on the basis of countries. 'The highest mutual complementarity in trade existed between China and Singapore (Wang & Zeng, 2008, p. 23)' and 'the highest competitiveness existed between China and Thailand (Wang Q. , 2004, p. 7)'. Also, some studies were made on Sino-ASEAN trade relationship on the basis of various industrial products, among which three kinds of products, were classified as primary products, capital-intensive and technology-intensive products, and labour intensive products, were classified. A conclusion was drawn that 'China and ASEAN had their own advantages on trade in primary products, therefore mutual complementarity existed between them'; 'both complementarity and competition existed on trade in capital-intensive and technology-intensive products; and 'China had more advantage than five ASEAN members on trade in labour-intensive products' (Xue, March 2007, p. 30).

In a word, many efforts have been made by researchers to investigate Sino-ASEAN trade relationships from different aspects. However, most of the literature focused on Sino-ASEAN trade relationships for a certain year or several years in the late 1990s or early 2000s. No efforts were made to look into the tendency of the mutual complementarity or competition between China and ASEAN during the whole of the 1990s and the 2000s. As a matter of fact, no substantial changes happened to them during the two decades; therefore it is not too difficult to examine the tendency of the mutual complementarity or competition between China and ASEAN. In addition, no specific classifications based on the SITC were chosen as special cases in order that the advantage of China or ASEAN on trade in any specific classification could be investigated. In consideration of these two points, three classifications of traded goods, based on the SITC, are chosen as examples here in order that the advantage of China or ASEAN could be explored. Among the three classifications, S1-6 is chosen because it had the largest trade value of export from ASEAN to China generally during the whole 1990s; S1-7 is chosen because it was the counterpart of S1-6 during the 2000s; and finally S1-0 is chosen because it was given the first priority[22] on the agenda of economic cooperation between China and ASEAN after the Framework Agreement was endorsed.

Aiming at ensuring the data integrity, the years 1991, 1995 and 2000 are chosen for the 1990s; while 2001, 2005 and 2009 are chosen for the 2000s. It is important to note that, the American market is the biggest

---

[22] There are five priority areas for economic cooperation between China and ASEAN, which are respectively the agriculture, information and communication, human resource development, mutual investment and Mekong River development.

single export market for both China and ASEAN outside East Asia. For this reason, the advantages of S1-6, S1-7 and S1-0 of both China and ASEAN in the American market are explored.

When the advantage of specific classification is analysed, the RCA Index is applied. It is the ratio of the proportion of the export value of a specific classification in the total value of a certain country to the proportion of its total export value in the total export value in the world. The RCA equation is expressed as follows:

$$RCAX_{ij} = (X_{ij}/X_i) / (X_{aj}/X_a),$$

in which,

X_{ij} = the export value of the product j from country i in the American market;

X_i = the total value of exports from country i to the American market;

X_{aj} = the total value of the specific products exported to the American market; and

X_a = the total value of exports in the American market.

When the RCA is bigger than 1, product j of country i has the comparative advantage; and when RCA is less than 1, then the product j of country i has disadvantage. Table 5.7 reveals the separate advantage of S1-6 Manufactured Goods of China and ASEAN-5 in American market in the 1990s and 2000s. China's RCA of S1-6 generally maintained first place in the 1990s, with Indonesia, Thailand, Malaysia, the Philippines and Singapore following in a descending order. China's RCA of 1.59 was much more that of Indonesia (1.202), who ranked next to China, and it was nearly ten times of that of Singapore (0.122) at the bottom. Moreover, the same ranking occurred in 1995. This illustrates that China had comparative advantage on trade in S1-6 in the American market from 1990 to 1995. However, the order was broken in 2000, when Indonesia's RCA caught up with that of China, ranking the first. Behind followed China, Thailand, Malaysia, the Philippines and Singapore in a descending order. This reflects that Indonesia had a big advantage in S1-6 at the end of the 1990s that China had had almost during the whole decade. Singapore was the one whose export of S1-6 had no advantage at all in the American market. In the 2000s, ranking of RCA among China and ASEAN-5 maintained a similar trend with that in the second half of the 1990s. Radical changes took place in 2005, when China returned to the first place with the highest comparative advantage of 1.177. In the meanwhile, Indonesia's RCA went down to less than 1, followed successively by Thailand (0.937), the Philippines (0.361), Malaysia (0.255) and Singapore (0.079). The same tendency was repeated in year 2009. In summary, during the whole 1990s and 2000s, only China and Indonesia had comparative advantage in exports of S1-6 in the American market. This is reasonable given their industrial structure; the secondary sector constituted more than one third GDP, the manufacturing industry was well developed and manufacturing had more advantages.

Table 5.7 RCA of S1-6 of China and ASEAN in the 1990s and 2000s

RCA of S1-6 of China and ASEAN in the 1990s and 2000s						
Period	China	Indonesia	Malaysia	Philippines	Singapore	Thailand
1991	1.591	1.202	0.365	0.325	0.122	0.942
1995	1.002	1.000	0.236	0.219	0.066	0.747
2000	1.116	1.272	0.263	0.206	0.094	0.909
2001	1.149	1.220	0.271	0.248	0.097	0.888
2005	1.177	0.924	0.255	0.361	0.079	0.937
2009	1.189	1.088	0.273	0.245	0.104	0.982

Source: UN COMTRADE Database (Compiled and computed by the author)

Table 5.8 reveals the RCA of S1-7 Machinery and Transport Equipment of China and ASEAN-5 in the American market. The RCA of the six countries can be classified into two levels in 1991. In the first level, Singapore and Malaysia had RCA of over 1, which showed their advantage of S1-7 in the American market. The other four countries, the Philippines, Thailand, China and Indonesia, followed in the second level, and all had RCA less than 1. No Changes in level occurred in 1995. However, it happened in year 2000 when the Philippines joined the first level, with RCA of S1-7 of 1.517. Table 5.8 reveals that ASEAN, compared with China, had more comparative advantage in S1-7 Machinery and Transport Equipment in 1990s and this was maintained till the first half of the 2000s. Then, China and the Philippines joined the first level in 2005. So far, only Indonesia lacked comparative advantage in S1-7 export among ASEAN-5; and all other four countries had advantages. Adding the fact that China had the biggest total export and import value of S1-7 with ASEAN during the 2000s, one can say that China and ASEAN were mutually complementary and competitive. As far as complementarity is concerned, China exported a large volume of S1-7 from ASEAN in 1990s and 2000s and ASEAN also exported a large number of S1-7 to China. As far as competition is concerned, Singapore had the biggest comparative advantage in the American market and China's advantage of S1-7 export on American market was gradually increasing over time.

Table 5.8 RCA of S1-7 of China and ASEAN in the 1990s and 2000s

RCA of S1-7 of China and ASEAN in the 1990s and 2000s						
Period	China	Indonesia	Malaysia	Philippines	Singapore	Thailand
1991	0.255	0.089	1.472	0.733	1.813	0.678
1995	0.523	0.219	1.576	0.456	1.875	0.768
2000	0.725	0.286	1.677	1.517	1.907	0.900
2001	0.772	0.249	1.723	1.445	1.904	0.855
2005	1.175	0.274	2.086	1.405	2.010	1.029
2009	1.307	0.293	1.879	1.725	2.102	1.116

Source: UN COMTRADE Database (Compiled and computed by the author)

Table 5.9 RCA of S1-0 of China and ASEAN in the 1990s and 2000s

RCA of S1-0 of China and ASEAN in the 1990s and 2000s						
	China	Indonesia	Malaysia	Philippines	Singapore	Thailand
1991	1.130	2.375	0.461	2.420	0.349	4.293
1995	0.569	1.876	0.129	1.239	0.223	4.130
2000	0.538	2.523	0.135	0.869	0.218	4.520
2001	0.518	2.460	0.145	0.927	0.182	4.275
2005	0.469	3.379	0.359	1.477	0.167	4.140
2009	0.465	3.441	0.608	1.730	0.197	4.678

Source: UN COMTRADE Database (Compiled and computed by the author)

Table 5.9 reveals the RCA of export of S1-0 of Food and Live Animals among China and ASEAN-5 in the American market. In 1991, four countries Thailand, the Philippines, Indonesia and China, had the RCA of S1-0 more than 1. This demonstrates that these four countries had comparative advantage in S1-7 exports. Great changes happened in 1995 when China dropped from the first level (where RCA is over 1) with its RCA only reaching 0.569. The situation continued to deteriorate in 2001 when the Philippines also dropped out of the first level with its RCA of 0.869. This means that China and the Philippines lost their comparative advantage on S1-0 export in the American market in the first and second half of the 1990s respectively. The year 2005 saw a change when the Philippines returned to the first level, with its RCA of S1-0 export in the American market going back to 1.477, much higher than that in 2000 and 2001. Then the general tendency remained stable until 2009. During the two decades, when RCA of S1-0 is analysed, Thailand, who maintained the highest comparative advantage on S1-0 export in the American market, is worthy of more attention. Thailand's RCA was 4.193 in 1991, 4.130 in 1995 and 4.520 in 2000, which drew a very large gap with those countries that lagged behind it. Besides, its RCA in the 2000s was 4.275 in 2001, 4.140 in 2005 and 4.678 in 2009, which not only inherited the advantage tendency of the previous decade, but also further widened the gap with other countries. Moreover, Thailand agreed with China to implement a zero tariff on vegetables and fruit from 1st October, 2003, which promoted bilateral trade in S1-0 between them. This also sent a signal that China, who had an obvious *disadvantage*, was cooperating on S1-0 with Thailand, who had the highest comparative advantage. The conclusion in section two asserts that trade in S1-0 had never, ever, been among the most important cooperative areas between China and ASEAN before 2004. Given the conclusion, it was an interesting phenomenon that China actively chose S1-0 Food and Live Animals, whose goods constituted the major part of the agriculture products, as the first priority cooperation area with ASEAN. This will be analysed in more details in the next chapter, when the author goes on to discuss China's motives for changing its attitudes toward economic cooperation with ASEAN and regional economic integration in East Asia.

6 China's Role in Investment Cooperation with ASEAN before and after 2001

6.1   Introduction

This chapter explores China's role in investment cooperation with ASEAN before and after 2001 by describing Beijing's investment policy in the 1980s, 1990s and 2000s, analysing Sino-ASEAN investment relations and addressing whether China crowded out ASEAN's FDI after its accession to the WTO. To do this, there are three sections in this chapter. The first describes Beijing's investment policy before and after 2001. The second section offers an analysis of Sino-ASEAN investment relations in the 1990s and 2000s by presenting China's inward investment from ASEAN and China's outward investment to ASEAN. The third section addresses the 'FDI Crowd-out' issue by taking the United States and Japan as the FDI sources for China and ASEAN and comparing their distribution to China and ASEAN after 2001.

After it implemented economic reform and opening up policy in the late 1970s, Beijing focused predominantly on attracting as much foreign investment as it could in order to support its needs for rapid economic growth domestically (Shi, August 2006, p. 11). Beijing opened coastal cities and regions step by step to attract foreign investment in the 1980s, when the main sources of the foreign investment were Hong Kong/Macao, and some developed economies such as the United States, Japan and some European countries. In the 1990s, Beijing followed a 'bringing in' strategy and further opened inland and western cities in order to continue attracting foreign investment as much as possible, albeit, this time, from main sources where overseas Chinese abounded, such as Hong Kong, Taiwan and Southeast Asia plus some developed countries such as the United States, Western Europe and so on. However, this time not only east China but also the western part became the destinations for FDI. When it came to the 2000s, Beijing paid much attention to encouraging Chinese enterprises to invest outwards, making ASEAN one of its first priority destinations; meanwhile it continued to attract foreign investment to both East and West China. That ASEAN was one of the main sources of China's foreign investment in the 1990s and became the first priority destination of China's outward investment in the 2000s highlighted ASEAN's significance as a critical investment cooperation partner for Beijing. In the meanwhile, China turned itself from a net investment recipient of ASEAN in the 1980s and 1990s to a key investment source in the 2000s, which reflected the changes of Sino-ASEAN investment relations during the three decades.

However, ASEAN had many doubts about whether China would divert ASEAN's FDI from the world in general and from the developed countries in particular on the eve of Beijing's accession to the WTO. In order to remove those doubts and realize the win-win objectives of co-current economic growth for China and ASEAN, Beijing signed the IA within the framework of the CAFTA on 15th August, 2008 with ASEAN, based on those rough measures of investment cooperation included in the Framework Agreement in 2002. Close research on the investment flows between China and ASEAN suggests that ASEAN benefited from China's investment not only before but also after China's accession to the WTO because of those measures of investment cooperation; China's shifting investment policy and the subsequent changes of Sino-ASEAN investment relations.

All the data, whether originally quoted or computed by the author, are collected from:

1.   Official database, e.g. OECD Database, UN COMTRADE Database, Asian Development Bank (ADB) Database, etc.

2.   Annual official statistics yearbooks, e.g. China Statistical Yearbook (1991-2009), China Customs

Statistics Yearbook (1991-2009) , ASEAN Statistical Yearbook (2003-2008) and so on.

3.   Some other reliable data sources such as the official website of the Statistics Bureau of China

Of note is that 2001 is used as the dividing line to analyse Beijing's investment policy and analyse the Sino-ASEAN investment relations, as in the Chapter Four. As a matter of fact, it was at the turn of the century that China's investment policy went through a radical change. It was in year 2000 that China launched the programme of 'Greater Western Development (GWD)', calling on more domestic and foreign investment to go west. As a result, West China progressively became another attractive destination for foreign investment. This partly diversified the distribution of China's foreign investment. Moreover, it was in 2000 that Beijing implemented the strategy of 'going out' by encouraging Chinese enterprises to invest outward, and gave ASEAN the first priority as a competitive investment destination. This actually added another dimension of investing outwards to the whole picture of Beijing's investment policy to the original dimension of attracting inward foreign investment to China; besides it confirmed ASEAN's status as the main destination of China's outward investment. In addition, it was in 2001 that China entered the WTO and officially proposed to set up the CAFTA to promote trade and investment cooperation between Chin and ASEAN. China's WTO-accession marked a new historic stage in China's 'open door' policy; and China's initiative of the CAFTA illustrated that China's focus of economic policy (including investment policy) diverted to the regional level from the international level. On the other hand, China's WTO accession in 2001 caused worries among ASEAN members about whether China would crowd out ASEAN's FDI flows from the developed economies. Therefore, Beijing's investment policy is described in two subsections, for the 1980s-1900s and the 2000s; and Sino-ASEAN investment relations are analysed in the 1990s and 2000s. The issue whether China crowded out ASEAN's FDI is explored after 2001, when China entered the WTO in consideration of the possible impact of China's accession to the WTO on ASEAN's FDI flows.

In the second section, where Sino-ASEAN investment relations are analysed, the ten ASEAN members are divided into two groups, the first made up of five old members (Indonesia, Malaysia, the Philippines, Singapore, and Thailand; hereafter ASEAN-5) and the other made up of five new members (Brunei, Cambodia, Laos, Myanmar and Vietnam; hereafter BCLMV). This is because ASEAN-5 were expected to be one of the main sources for China's foreign investment in the 1980s and 1990s and the BCLMV were the new investment destinations for China in the 2000s. To ensure the data's exactness and reduce the possibility of a sharp increase in certain data, data for the five new ASEAN members are also collected even though they did not officially join the ASEAN in the first half of the 1990s.

In the third section, where the 'FDI crowd-out' problem is addressed, the direct foreign investment from the United States and Japan to China and ASEAN respectively is analysed because the United States is the biggest single source country for both China and ASEAN outside the East Asian region and Japan is the biggest source inside the region.[23] In addition, the Inward FDI Performance Index is adopted to check how well the inward FDI of China and ASEAN after 2001 performed in accordance with their GDP. If ASEAN's index performed worse after 2001 than before, its inward FDI from the US and Japan dropped and this happened to have causality with China's competitive performance; then it can be argued that China crowded out ASEAN's FDI after 2001. If this did not happen, then China should not take the

---

[23] Actually, Hong Kong was the biggest source of FDI inflows into China while the Europe Union (EU) was the biggest source of FDI inflows into ASEAN from 2001 to 2008. However, given that EU makes up of many European nations, which adds the difficulties in data statistics, and that Hong Kong is a Special Administrative Region (SAR) subordinate to China, both EU and Hong Kong are beyond the scope of discussion here.

responsibility for the decline of ASEAN's FDI after its accession to the WTO.

6.2 Beijing's Investment Policy from the 1980s onward

As asserted by complex interdependence theorist, if the interdependence theory was applied to studies of the policy of a nation under interdependent conditions, the comparative analysis of the domestic policy of the particular nations must be investigated (Keohane & Nye, 1989, p. 223). Therefore, before analysing Sino-ASEAN investment relationship, it is necessary to conduct comparative studies of China's investment policy before and after 2001.

China focused its investment policy predominantly on attracting FDI flows to meet the needs of rapid domestic economic growth and reform after announcing the 'open door' policy in 1978. Beijing tentatively opened some economic zones and coastal cities in the eastern region to attract foreign investments mainly from where overseas Chinese abounded during the 1980s. Driven by the dynamic momentum in the 1980s, Beijing went on to open inland cities in West and Middle China step by step in order to attract foreign investments mainly from such developed economies as the United States, Western Europe and Japan during the 1990s. In the meantime, there was a small amount of outward investment from China going to Hong Kong, Southeast Asia etc. in the form of contracted projects, labour cooperation, and design consultation and so on. The 2000s witnessed a tremendous change in China's investment policy. Beijing attached much emphasis to outward investment by implementing the strategy of 'going out'. The 'bringing in' strategy with a view to attracting foreign investments implemented in the 1980s and 1990s; and the 'going out' strategy with a view to encouraging outward investments in the 2000s constituted the two components of China's overall investment policy. China increased its outward FDI flows to an astonishingly high level in no time, by encouraging Chinese enterprises to invest directly in Hong Kong, ASEAN, the US and so forth. China attracted FDI of 53,504 million US dollars from the world and invested outward FDI of 33,222 million dollars to the world in 2003. The inward FDI flows into China stood at 90,032 million dollars, increasing at an annual average growth rate of 11.4% in 2009 and total China's FDI flows added up to as high as 245,755 million dollars in 2009, increasing at an annual growth rate of 107%. In other words, Beijing's outward FDI increased year by year and it doubled every year over the year before during 203-2009. This section explores the evolution of Beijing's investment policy before and after 2001 so as to analyse Sino-ASEAN investment relations in the second section, lay a basis for the 'crowd-out' issue in the third section and to ultimately identify China's role in investment cooperation with ASEAN at the end.

6.2.1 Beijing's Investment Policy before 2001

A plethora of literature reports studies on Beijing's investment policy in terms of its steps, measures, relevant laws and regulations (Buckley, Clegg, Cross, & Tan, Spring 2005, pp. 7-8) (Fung, Iizaka, & Tong, June 2002, pp. 1-14) (Das, 2007, pp. 285-301). In general, the 1980s was the bourgeoning period for Beijing's investment policy; while the 1990s witnessed the harvest and in the meanwhile, China pushed the policy to a climax and began an adjusting period in the second half of the decade.

As to the direction Beijing's investment policy focused on during the 1980s and 1990s, it was inward foreign investment that Beijing emphasized. Attracting and utilizing foreign investment was seen as one of the basic elements of China's 'open door' policy. The objective then was to manage to attract as much investment as possible in order to meet the needs for rapid domestic economic growth and reform. In the immediate wake of the 'open door' policy, China's economy was completely underdeveloped. Attracting foreign investment to help China's economy grow was given the first priority on the agenda of Beijing's investment policy. Beijing opened four special economic zones (SEZs, Shen Zhen, Zhu Hai, Shan Tou, Xia Men, 1980), fourteen coastal cities[24] (1984), three deltas (the Yangtze River Delta, the Pearl River Delta and South Fujian area, 1985), two peninsulas (the East Liaoning Peninsula and the Shandong Peninsula, 1988) and Shanghai's Pudong New Area (1990) as the flagship SEZ in succession in 1980s in order to attract foreign investment. Seeing the benefits of the growing foreign investment to the coastal open cities and regions, Beijing went on to open five inland cities along the Yangtze River[25] (1992), seventeen inland capital cities[26], and many border cities.[27] These opened cities and regions, in a geographical sequence from the south to the north, from the east to the middle and the west in China, attracted most of the foreign investment in the 1980s and 1990s. This was reflected in the total inward investment values in various provinces. Take 1989 and 1999 as examples. According to statistics from various provinces in China, the total actually utilized FDI of all provinces added up to 5,844.82 million US dollars, with Southeast China[28] accounting for 46.89%, East China (excluding Southeast China)[29] for 23.92%, West China[30] for 8.35% and others for 0.80% in 1989. Besides, actually utilized FDI of all provinces in 1999 stood at 39,934.82 million dollars, with Southeast China making up of 30.40%, East China (excluding Southeast China) of 42.60%, West China of 4.44% and others of 22.56%. This revealed that there was an imbalance in foreign investment between East China and West China. West China was weak in competitiveness for attracting foreign investment, although inland and western cities were also opened in the 1990s. This constituted part of the reason why Beijing implemented a 'greater western development (GWD)' strategy in the 2000s.

With respect to the main sources of China's foreign investment in the 1980s, Beijing opened its coastal cities to attract foreign investment from geographically adjacent Hong Kong, Macao and Southeast Asian regions, where overseas Chinese abounded. Many of China's original opened SEZs were geographically adjacent to Hong Kong, Macao and Southeast Asia; therefore they were opened on purpose to attract foreign investment mainly from the three sources. For instant, Shenzhen, as one of the four opened SEZs in 1980, was geographically located to the north of the Deep Bay/Shenzhen Bay while Hong Kong was at the south of the Bay. Xiamen, another one of the four opened SEZs, was only separated by the Taiwan Strait from Taiwan. Hainan, the fifth SEZ opened later in 1988, is also geographically adjacent to Southeast Asia across the sea. Zhuhai was located adjacent to Macao. Overseas Chinese were willing to invest in mainland China not only because of the geographical proximity, but also of the cultural convergence and even of family ties (Chen, 2007, p. 41). However, ASEAN did not become one of the main sources for China's inward foreign investment, due to the lagging economy of ASEAN in Southeast Asia. In the 1980s, apart from the adjacent investment sources such as Hong Kong and Macao, some developed economies such as Japan, the United States and some European countries were the main sources for China. For example, foreign investment from Japan (39.9%), Hong Kong and Macao (21.7%), the United States (5.6%) and Federal Republic of Germany (4.7%) added up to more than 70% of China's total inward foreign investment in 1986; while in comparison, ASEAN accounted for only 1.04%[31]. With the

---

[24] Da Lian, Qin Huangdao, Tian Jin, Yan Tai, Qing Dai, Lian Yungang, Nan Tong, Shang Hai, Ning Bo, Wen Zhou, Guang Zhou, Fu Zhou, Zhan Jiang, Bei Hai
[25] Wu Hu, Jiu Jiang, Yue Yang, Wu Han and Chong Qing
[26] He Fei, Nan Chang, Chang Sha, Cheng Du, Zheng Zhou, Tai Yuan, Xi An, Lan Zhou, Yin Chuan, Xi Ning, Urumchi, Gui Yang, Kun Ming, Nan Ning, Ha Erbin, Chang Chun and Hohehot
[27] Hei He, Sui Fenhe, Hui Chun, Man Zhouli, Erenhot, Yi Ning, Bo Le, Ta Cheng, Pu Lan, Zhang Mu, Rui Li, Wan Ding, He Kou, Ping Xiang and Dong Xing
[28] Southeast China refers to Guangdong and Hainan Provinces
[29] East China refers to Shang Hai, Jiang Su, Zhe Jiang, An Hui, Fu Jian, Jiang Xi and Shan Dong
[30] West China refers to Chong Qing, Si Chuan, Yun Nan, Gui Zhou, Tibet and Guang Xi in Southwest China and Shaan Xi, Gan Su, Qing Hai, Ning Xia and Xin Jiang in Northwest China
[31] Data comes from National Bureau of Statistics of China, *China Statistical Yearbook 1986* (Beijing: China Statistical

deepening of the 'open door' policy in the 1990s, besides Hong Kong, the United States and Japan, Taiwan joined the main sources of foreign investment to China. In addition, ASEAN enlarged to cover all the ten members in Southeast Asia and was accorded the full acceptance of the world community as an increasingly independent economic and political entity in the 1990s. ASEAN, therefore, became one of the main sources of China's inward foreign investment in the 1990s. In 1999, over 70% of China's total foreign investment came from Hong Kong (41%), the United States (9.95%), ASEAN (7.75%), Japan (7.22%) and Taiwan (6.5%)[32].

Pertaining to the structure of China's inward foreign investment, it was made up of three elements: foreign loans, FDI and other investment. Among them, foreign loans made up over 50% of the total foreign investment in the 1980s and vanished during the 1990s with the rapid economic growth of China. In comparison, FDI constituted the major part of the total foreign investment in the 1990s. Other investment (outward investment) was nominal in comparison. Again, take 1989 and 1999 as examples. In 1989, China's actually utilized foreign investment was 10,059.15 million dollars, with 6,285.7 dollars from foreign loans (62.49%), 3,392.57 million dollars from FDI (33.73%) and 380.88 million dollars from other investment (3.78%)[33]. In 1999, China attracted total foreign investment of 42,446.96 million dollars, of which none was foreign loans, 95% was FDI and the remaining 5% was other investment[34]. This reveals that FDI took the place of foreign loans in the 1980s and became the main means of China's inward investment in the 1990s.

In regard to the sectors foreign investment entered, most of the foreign investment entered the industry and the sectors of real estate, public utilities and services in the mid 1990s, when data were available for the first time. Over 80% of China's total utilized foreign investment of 73,276.42 million dollars was distributed into industry (68.9%) and the sectors of real estate, public utilities and services (17.54%) in 1996[35]. Foreign investment further focused on manufacturing, real estate and social services in the late 1990s. The year 1999 is a good case in point. Among China's total actually utilized foreign investment of 40,318.71 million dollars in 1999, the manufacturing sector accounted for 56.06%, the real estate sector for 13.86% and the social services sector for 6.33%. In other words, these three sectors accounted for nearly 80% of China's foreign investment[36].

6.2.2 Beijing's Investment Policy after 2001

Chinese people's income was substantially increased after two decades of 'reform and opening up'. The annual household income per capita in rural areas was 133.6 RMB in 1978, which increased to 2,253.4

Publishing House 1987) (Compiled and computed by the author)

[32] Data comes from National Bureau of Statistics of China, *China Statistical Yearbook 1999* (Beijing: China Statistics Press 2000) (Compiled and computed by the author)

[33] Data comes from National Bureau of Statistics of China, *China Statistical Yearbook 1989* (Beijing: China Statistical Publishing House 1990) (Compiled and computed by the author)

[34] Data comes from National Bureau of Statistics of China, *China Statistical Yearbook 1999* (Beijing: China Statistics Press 2000) (Compiled and computed by the author)

[35] Data comes from National Bureau of Statistics of China, *China Statistical Yearbook 1996* (Beijing: China Statistics Press 1997) (Compiled and computed by the author)

[36] Data comes from National Bureau of Statistics of China, *China Statistical Yearbook 1999* (Beijing: China Statistics Press 2000) (Compiled and computed by the author)

RMB in 2000; and the annual household income per capita in urban areas was 343.4 RMB in 1978, which grew to 6280.0 RMB in 2000. Besides, given China's highest saving rate in the world, China's average ratio of saving rate to the Gross National Product (GNP) reached 37% during the reform era (post-1978), exceeding that of the US (13.5%-18.4% from 1990 to 2007) and Japan (average at 28.8% from 1990-2002) by substantial margins. As a result of a high saving rate and a rapid economic growth, China achieved substantial domestic savings. Moreover, China accumulated a huge amount of foreign exchange reserves after two decades of 'bringing in' investment policy. China had 154.675 billion US dollars of foreign exchange reserves by 1999. Both high national savings and the huge foreign exchange reserves laid a solid basis for China's outward investment policy. In addition, China did not devalue RMB during the 1997-8 AFC, while its neighbours in Southeast devalued their currencies. This made a regional context in favour of China's outward FDI flows to ASEAN, because devaluation in the value of the recipient country's currency stimulates the inflows of FDI (Xing & Wan, 2006, pp. 420-421). Finally, Beijing's Central government gave special attention to the 'going out' policy at the 16th CPC National Congress. The 16th National Congress report asserted that the implementation of the strategy of 'going out' was an important measure taken in the new stage of opening up and it pointed out that '(China) should encourage and help relatively competitive enterprises with various forms of ownership to invest abroad in order to increase export of goods and labour services and bring about a number of strong multinational enterprises and brand names'.

Investment cooperation became one of the five priority cooperation areas between China and ASEAN with the endorsement of the Framework Agreement in 2002. The Framework Agreement included some rough regulations about bilateral investment promotion and facilitation. On 15th August 2009, China and ASEAN endorsed the IA, which included more detailed regulations about the objectives, treatments, measures of bilateral investment cooperation. Three features were embodied in the IA: it showed great respect for those rules of the international multilateral institutions such as the IMF, the WTO and etc.; the main content focused on national treatment, MFN treatment and fair and equitable investment treatment; and investment promotion and facilitation were the main measures to enhance bilateral investment cooperation.

1.   The IA showed great respect for the rules of international multilateral mechanisms, such as the WTO, the IMF and the World Bank. Based on the main principles of these multilateral rules, both sides of ASEAN and China agreed to adjust, or sometimes even dismantle some of their specific clauses and articles.

For example, it was stated clearly in Clause 5 of the Article 10, that

> *'Nothing in this Agreement shall affect the rights and obligations of the Parties as members of the IMF under the Articles of Agreement of the IMF, including the use of exchange actions which are in conformity with the Articles of Agreement of the IMF.'*

In Clause 6 of Article 8, it was ruled that

> *'This article shall not apply to the issuance of compulsory licenses granted to intellectual property rights in accordance with the Agreement on Trade-Related Aspects of Intellectual Property Rights in Annex 1C to the WTO Agreement.'*

2. National treatment, MFN treatment and fair and equitable investment treatment were designed to be the three main contents of bilateral investment cooperation between ASEAN and China. In accordance with Articles 4 and 5, national treatment and MFN treatment were supplied by ASEAN and China to those enterprises investing in each other. According to Article 7, 'each Party shall accord to investments of investors of another Party fair and equitable treatment and full protection and security'.

3. Investment promotion and facilitation were the main measures to enhance bilateral investment cooperation between ASEAN and China, which were included in Articles 20 and 21. Investment promotions were ruled as measures in order to promote the awareness of China-ASEAN as an investment area. Investment promotions covered:

> '1. increasing China-ASEAN investment; 2. organizing investment promotion activities; 3. promoting business matching events; 4. organizing and supporting the organization of various briefings and seminars on investment opportunities and on investment laws, regulations and policies; and 5. conducting information exchanges on other issues of mutual concern relating to investment promotion and facilitation'

Article 21 ruled the measures of investment facilitation.

> '1. creating the necessary environment for all forms of investment; 2. simplifying procedures for investment applications and approvals; 3. promoting dissemination of investment information, including investment rules, regulations, policies and procedures; and 4. establishing one-stop investment centres in the respective host Parties to provide assistance and advisory services to the business sectors including facilitation of operating licenses and permits. '

ASEAN was chosen by Chinese enterprises as one of the key areas (Morck, Yeung, & Zhao, 2008, p. 337) and most of the time, even the first destination of investment (Wu, 2006, p. 41) (Shi, August 2006, p. 33) (Yu & Wang, 2004, p. 12) (Huang, 2009, p. 21), with the endorsement of the Framework Agreement and the IA. More and more Chinese enterprises invested in ASEAN, which improved the bilateral investment relations between China and ASEAN. The next section goes into details.

In addition to implementing the strategy of 'going out', Beijing did not ignore another part of its investment policy −'bringing in'. Beijing promised to 'attract more foreign direct investment and use it more effectively and open the service sector to the outside world step by step' at the 16th CPC National Congress in 1997. However, the 2000s distinguished from the 1990s not only because the service sector was opened and the strategy of 'going out' was implemented, but also because the western part of China was chosen as a potential investment destination, besides East China. As mentioned earlier, the GWD programme was also launched in the 2000s. Beijing's Central government planned to 'vigorously improve the soft investment environment' in the western region (The State Council of PRC, 2000) in order to attract more foreign investment to support the local economic growth. Many preferential measures were taken to help to attract foreign investment. For example, 'Enterprise income tax could be reduced to 15% for Chinese enterprises and foreign enterprises established in West China and engaged in nationally encouraged industries from 2001 to 2010 (The Ministry of Finance, State Administration of Taxation, and General Administration of Customs of PRC, 2001)'. Investment cooperation between China and ASEAN was greatly enhanced with the strategic support of foreign investment in China and China's outward investment. Section Two discusses this in more detail.

6.3   Sino-ASEAN Investment Relations

China turned itself from a net recipient of ASEAN's FDI in the 1990s into a FDI investment exporter for ASEAN in the 2000s, based on studies in the Chapter Three. This chapter analyses the Sino-ASEAN investment relations in further details from two aspects: China's inward investment from ASEAN and China's outward investment to ASEAN.

6.3.1   China's Inward Investment from ASEAN

China's inward investment from ASEAN increased during the 1990s and 2000s, guided by China's investment strategy of 'bringing in'. Generally, China attracted ASEAN's investment through three means: foreign loans, FDI and other investment. Among them, other investment accounted for more than foreign loans and FDI at the very outset of the 1990s. With the substantial increase in ASEAN's outward FDI flows into China, the proportion of FDI exceeded that of other investment and became the key means of ASEAN's outward investment to China in the 1990s. Table 6.1 shows clearly ASEAN's total investment in China by ASEAN-5 and BCLMV from 1991 to 2008. Except in 1992 and 1993 when ASEAN invested foreign loans of 17.22 and 183 million dollars respectively in China, ASEAN did not make loans to China during the 1990s and 2000s. FDI remained the most important means for ASEAN to invest in China during the 1990s and 2000s. Take 1992, 2000 and 2008 as examples. In 1992, ASEAN-5 invested in China through foreign loans of 17.22 million dollars, FDI and other investment of 271.64 million dollars; BCLMV invested in China through FDI and other investment of 9.43 million dollars. In 2000, no ASEAN members made loans to China. ASEAN-5 invested in China through FDI of 2,836.71 million dollars and other investment of 0.43 million dollars; BCLMV invested in China through FDI of 7.87 million dollars without any other investment. In 2008, FDI and other investment of ASEAN-5 in China stood respectively at 5,105.58 and 15.72 million dollars; and those of BCLMV stood respectively at 355.41 and zero million dollars. The data reveals that FDI was the most important means of investment in China whether for ASEAN-5 or for BCLMV in the 1990s and 2000s, although they used to invest more of other investment compared to FDI at the very outset of the 1990s. Flows through the means of other investment were only supplementary to FDI, accounting for a very small proportion of the total investments in the 2000s.

Data on investment from ASEAN-5 and BCLMV also reveals that ASEAN-5, in comparison with BCLMV, was the main source of China when its proportion of total ASEAN's investment in China became increasingly large in the 1990s and 2000s. Computing the investment on the basis of the data in the Table 6.1, we know that in 1992, investment from ASEAN-5 accounted for 97% of total ASEAN investment in China while BCLMV accounted only for the remaining 3%. In 2000, ASEAN-5 accounted for 99% and BCLMV for the remaining 1%. However, BCLMV's proportion began to increase in 2003. ASEAN-5's proportion dropped to 93% in 2008 when BCLMV's proportion increased to 7%. This indicates that BLCMV's capability of investing outwards was greatly improved after the completion of AFTA in 2003.

As displayed in Table 6.1, the ten ASEAN members' investment in China remained a very low proportion of China's total inward investment from the world, which illustrates that ASEAN, as a whole, was not the main source for China's inward investment in the 1980s. In the 1990s, ASEAN's proportion of total China's investment kept growing from 0.8% in 1991 to the historic high of 8.88% in 1998. ASEAN's proportion fluctuated slightly between 4.75% and 6.01% in the 2000s due to the fact that many ASEAN members' economies were severely trampled by the 1997-8 AFC. Therefore, ASEAN was not among China's main sources of foreign investment in the 2000s, when tax heavens such as Hong Kong and the Virgin Island and the developed economies such as the United States, some European countries and Japan were the main sources for China. In terms of the falling trend, it is foreseeable that in the future, ASEAN is unlikely to become one of the main sources for China's foreign investment.

Table 6.1 ASENA's Investment Inflows into China, 1991-2008

ASENA's Investment Inflows into China, 1991-2008

Flows: in million US dollars; Share: in percentage

Year	ASEAN-5's Investment Inflows into China				BCLMV's Investment Inflows into China				Total	Total China's Inward Investment Flows	ASEAN's Share
	Foreign Loans	FDI	Other Investment	Subtotal	Foreign Loans	FDI	Other Investment	Subtotal			
1991		39.61	52.92	92.53		0	0.00	0.00	92.53	11,554.17	0.80
1992	17.22	271.64		288.86		0	9.43	9.43	298.29	19,202.33	1.55
1993	183.00	1,005.84		1,188.84		0	11.61	11.61	1,200.45	38,959.72	3.08
1994		1,871.57		1,871.57		0	18.54	18.54	1,890.11	43,212.84	4.37
1995		2,625.26		2,625.26		0	28.30	28.30	2,653.56	48,132.69	5.51
1996		3,184.34		3,184.34		0	9.47	9.47	3,193.81	54,804.16	5.83
1997		3,223.85	0.55	3,224.40		0	10.15	10.15	3,234.55	45,970.34	7.04
1998		4,198.08	0.08	4,198.16	0.80	0	25.10	25.90	4,224.06	47,557.49	8.88
1999		3,274.97	0.05	3,275.02	0.00	0	13.80	13.80	3,288.82	42,446.96	7.75
2000		2,836.71	0.43	2,837.14	0.00	0	7.87	7.87	2,845.01	49,356.27	5.76
2001		2,969.77	3.39	2,973.16	0.00	0	14.08	14.08	2,987.24	49,672.12	6.01
2002		3,200.42	2.14	3,202.56	0.00	0	55.52	55.52	3,258.08	55,011.09	5.92
2003		2,853.09	5.48	2,858.57	2.75	0	72.34	75.09	2,933.66	56,140.15	5.23
2004		2,909.62	3.57	2,913.19	0.00	0	130.91	130.91	3,044.10	64,072.98	4.75
2005		2,937.27	12.65	2,949.92	0.10	0	168.16	168.26	3,118.18	63,804.97	4.89
2006		3,033.78	9.54	3,043.32	0.00	0	317.35	317.35	3,360.67	67,075.72	5.01
2007		4,001.03	7.68	4,008.71	0.00	0	390.21	390.21	4,398.92	78,339.41	5.62
2008		5,105.58	15.72	5,121.30	0.00	0	355.41	355.41	5,476.71	95,253.37	5.75

Source: China Statistical Yearbook (1992-2009) (Beijing: China Statistical Publishing House/China Statistics Press 1992-2009) (Compiled and computed by the author)

6.3.2   China's Outward Investment to ASEAN

China realized outward investment to AESAN through two means; one was outward economic cooperation, constituting by contracted projects, labour cooperation and design consultation, the other was outward FDI. China made little FDI to ASEAN in the 1990s and outward economic cooperation was the key means for China's outward investment. After the 'going out' strategy was implemented by the central government in 2000, more FDI flowed to ASEAN from China. However, the annual flows of FDI from China to ASAEN still remained at a very low level, though growing at a fast speed. Outward economic cooperation, therefore, was the key means for China's outward investment in the 1990s and 2000s. Table 6.2 and Table 6.3 supply some statistical evidence for this.

Table 6.2 displays the annual flows of China's outward economic cooperation with ASEAN from 1998 to 2008, and Table 6.3 shows the annual flows of China's FDI in ASEAN from 2003 to 2009. Take 1998, 2003 and 2008 as examples. China's outward investment in ASEAN reached 2,310.36 million dollars of outward economic cooperation without statistics of FDI in 1998. China released the first statistical bulletin of China's outward FDI in 2003, when the FDI flows were 87.37 million dollars while the outward cooperation flows 730.54 million dollars, much more than the former. The former rose up to 2,484.35 million dollars in 2008, at an average annual growth rate of 548.69%, while the latter rose to 3,299.89 million dollars, at an average annual growth rate of 70.3%. It is foreseeable that given the dynamic momentum and rapidly growing speed, FDI flows are likely to exceed the outward cooperation flows and become the key means for China's outward investment with ASEAN in the near future. Of special note is that China's FDI did not rise at such a fast rate during 2003-2007. In 2007, the FDI flows stood at 968.08 million dollars. However, embracing the promising hope of the IA negotiations between China and ASEAN, China's FDI flows in 2008 sharply increased to 2,484.35 million dollars, and in 2009 it retained the fierce momentum with the virtual endorsement of IA and rose to 2,698.1 million dollars. At such a growth rate, China's FDI flows to ASEAN should definitely exceed that of China's outward economic cooperation with AESAN after 2010.

It has not been a long time since China released its first outward FDI bulletin in 2003; therefore, many specific data regarding to who the investors were and what kind of investment Chinese investors made in ASEAN were not available. According to China's Statistical Bulletin 2003, 'State-owned large and medium-sized enterprises held a dominating part (in China's outward FDI in the world), and the private enterprises was newly emerging (The Ministry of Commerce of People's Republic of China, National Bureau of Statistics of PRC, and State Administration of Foreign Exchange, 2003, p. 12)' shortly after the implementation of the 'going out' strategy. Things changed in 2008, when state-owned enterprises (SOEs) accounted for 16.1% of China's total outward FDI in the world, SOE-based restructuring enterprises for 50.2% and private enterprises for 9.4%.[37] If this trend had happened to China's outward FDI in ASEAN, then SOE-based restructuring enterprises would have become the main enterprises that invested FDI in ASEAN. Regarding to the entry mode of China's outward FDI in ASEAN, according to China's Statistical Bulletin, 96% of Chinese investing enterprises chose to set up subsidiary company or affiliates in the world in 2008 and the remaining 4% chose associated company. If this trend had happened to ASEAN, then most of the China's investing enterprises would have chosen to set up subsidiary company or affiliates in ASEAN.

---

[37] Data comes from The Ministry of Commerce of People's Republic of China, National Bureau of Statistics of PRC, and State Administration of Foreign Exchange, *'2008 Statistical Bulletin of China's Outward Foreign Direct Investment'* (Beijing: China Statistical Publishing House 2003), p. 22

In terms of the three forms of China's outward investment cooperation with ASEAN, contracted projects continued to account for the biggest proportion in both ASEAN-5 and BCLMV. Table 6.2 shows some evidence for this. Take 1998 and 2008 as examples. China invested ASEAN-5 of 1,478.15 million dollars in 1998, with 1,084.37 million dollars of contracted projects, 393.59 million dollars of labour cooperation and 0.19 million dollars of design consultation. Besides, China invested 832.21 million dollars to BCLMV in 1998, with 752.07 million dollars of contracted projects, 77.01 million dollars of labour cooperation and 3.13 million dollars of design consultation. Contracted projects accounted for the biggest proportion both for ASEAN-5 and for BCLMV. This trend continues to the present. This was partly because of Chinese abundant and cheap labour, which set up a solid basis for China's labour exports to ASEAN. In addition, China's technical development also supported this trend by backing up the contracted projects with advanced technology. These two factors contributed significantly to the increase of labour cooperation and design consultation. As another result of China's abundant and cheap labour, China's labour cooperation with ASEAN increased. China's labour cooperation with ASEAN-5 and BCLMV were 393.59 and 77.01 million dollars respectively in 1998, which grew to 569.99 and 56.77 million dollars in 2008. As another result of China's relatively advanced technology in comparison with BCLMV, China's outward investment in the form of design consultation increased during the 1990s and 2000s. It was 3.13 million dollars in 1998, and grew up to 51.18 million dollars in 2008, or nearly at the similar level of labour cooperation of 56.77 million dollars in 2008. Compared with 2008, data for 2007 seemed more supportive to the argument. Design consultation exceeded labour cooperation by a substantial margin, with the former at 79.14 million dollars and the latter at 48.48 million dollars. In the meanwhile, China's design consultation in ASEAN-5 increased as well. This demonstrates a feature of China's outward investment in ASEAN, who focused on the labour-intensive cooperation in the 1990s gradually diverted to the technology-intensive sectors, particularly in BCLMV. However, given China's current technology and the weak basis for bilateral design consultation, it cannot exceed the contracted projects and become the biggest form of China's outward investment in ASEAN in a near future.

Table 6.2 China's Outward Economic Cooperation with ASEAN-5 and BCLMV

China's Outward Economic Cooperation with ASEAN-5 and BCLMV, 1998-2008

Flows: in million US dollars; Share: in percentage

Year	Flows Value into ASEAN-5				Flows Value into BCLMV				Total	China's Total Outward Investment	ASEAN's Share
	Contracted Project	Labor Cooperation	Design Consultation	Subtotal	Contracted Project	Labor Cooperation	Design Consultation	Subtotal			
1998	1,084.37	393.59	0.19	1,478.15	752.07	77.01	3.13	832.21	2,310.36	11,773.23	19.62
1999	805.41	548.89	10.80	1,365.10	372.98	45.80	5.59	424.37	1,789.47	11,234.58	15.93
2000	887.66	608.21	1.40	1,497.27	364.61	58.87	4.22	427.70	1,924.97	11,325.36	17.00
2001	791.75	725.65	0.28	1,517.68	482.15	72.03	23.49	577.67	2,095.35	12,139.31	17.26
2002	1,007.63	601.37	0.60	1,609.60	629.73	55.15	11.49	696.37	2,305.97	14,352.22	16.07
2003	1,091.48	475.28	0.76	1,567.52	669.53	52.08	8.93	730.54	2,298.06	17,233.93	13.33
2004	1,425.39	501.03	6.16	1,932.58	806.99	36.79	18.53	862.31	2,794.89	21,368.98	13.08
2005	1,997.92	441.20	7.16	2,446.28	864.01	28.98	9.96	902.95	3,349.23	26,776.05	12.51
2006	2,786.15	451.29	15.37	3,252.81	1,089.18	45.68	14.86	1,149.72	4,402.53	35,694.97	12.33
2007	3,689.43	477.80	12.82	4,180.05	1,919.29	48.48	79.14	2,046.91	6,226.96	47,899.53	13.00
2008	5,190.89	569.99	43.80	5,804.68	3,191.94	56.77	51.18	3,299.89	9,104.57	65,116.30	13.98

Source: China Statistical Yearbook (2000-2009) (Beijing: China Statistical Publishing House/China Statistics Press 1999-2009) (Compiled and computed by the author)

Table 6.3 China's Outward FDI Flows in ASEAN-5 and BCLMV, 2003-2008

China's Outward FDI Flows in ASEAN-5 and BCLMV, 2003-2008					
Flows: in million US dollars; Share: in percentage					
Year	China's Outward FDI into ASEAN-5	China's Outward FDI into BCLMV	Subtotal into ASEAN	China's Total Outward FDI	Share
2003	83.82	3.55	87.37	2,854.65	3.06
2004	141.54	54.02	195.56	5,497.99	3.56
2005	98.17	59.54	157.71	12,261.17	1.29
2006	221.74	114.01	335.75	17,633.97	1.90
2007	544.91	423.17	968.08	26,506.09	3.65
2008	1,838.52	645.83	2,484.35	55,907.17	4.44
2009	1,784.13	913.97	2,698.10	56,528.99	4.77

Source: 2009 Statistical Bulletin of China's Outward Foreign Direct Investment (Beijing: China Statistics Press 2009) (Compiled and computed by the author)

In comparison of ASEAN-5 and BCLMV, the former was the main destination of China's outward investment. Table 6.2 and Table 6.3 provide some statistical illustration for this. As to China's outward investment cooperation, ASEAN-5 accounted for 64% in 1998, which grew to 69% in 2003 and fell back to 64% in 2008; BCLMV's proportion, following a contrary trend, dropped to 31% in 2003 from 36% in 1998 and returned to 36% at % in 2008. As to FDI flows, ASEAN-5 made up of 95% of China's total FDI in ASEAN in 2003, a historic high, which dropped to 74% in 2008 and 66% in 2009. Correspondingly, BCLMV's proportion rose from 4% in 1998 to 25% in 2008 and 33% in 2009. Based on the numerical evidence, it is hard for BCLMV's proportion of China's outward *investment cooperation* (in form of projected labour, design consultation) in ASEAN to catch up with that of ASEAN-5. However, given such a growing rate of FDI, there is a high possibility that BCLMV's proportion of China's *outward FDI* in ASEAN will exceed that of ASEAN-5 in the next decade.

ASEAN, as a whole, became a major destination for China with China's increasing outward investment to both ASEAN-5 and BCLMV. As to China's economic cooperation with the world, ASEAN was the biggest economic entity, receiving 19.62% of China's total outward economic cooperation in 1998. ASEAN became the second biggest destination in 2003, accounting for 13.33%, next to Hong Kong with16.5 %. ASEAN returned to the first place as an investment destination for China's outward economic cooperation in 2008, with a proportion of 13.98%, followed by Algeria with 5%, Sudan with 4% and Hong Kong with 4%. This reveals that China's outward economic cooperation with Africa was increasing as well; Africa tended to be the second biggest investment destination for China's outward economic cooperation. As to China's outward FDI, ASAEN was not a main destination; in the early 2000s, ASEAN accounted for 3.06% of China's total FDI in 2003, following many countries/regions such as Hong Kong (40.2%), the Cayman Islands (28.26%), the Virgin Islands (7.34%), Korea (5.39%) and so on. There was s slight rise of ASEAN's proportion of China's total FDI in 2008, when it grew to 4.44% and ASEAN became the second biggest destination for China's FDI, following Hong Kong (69.16%) and followed by the Virgin Islands (3.76%) and Cayman Islands of (2.72%) and so forth. This illustrates there was a great potential for ASEAN to attract more outward FDI from China.

In sum, regarding China's inward investment, ASEAN was not a main source for it. Regarding China's outward investment, ASEAN was the biggest destination of China's outward economic cooperation and the second biggest destination of China's outward FDI so far. Comparing China's economic cooperation in ASEAN and China's outward FDI in ASEAN, it is foreseeable that the latter will exceed the former in the near future. Comparing ASEAN-5 and BCLMV, the latter is expected to exceed the former in receiving China's FDI flows.

6.4   FDI Crowd-out Issue

As complex interdependence theorists asserted that it was the relative gains rather than joint gains or joint less that was the focus (Keohane & Nye, 1989, p. 10) when an interdependent relationship was analysed. Therefore, when analysing the Sino-ASEAN investment relationship, we also pay attention to the issue that whether China crowded out ASEAN's FDI from developed countries in the West after China's accession to the WTO in 2001. As a matter of fact, it was a hotly debated problem at the academia at the turn of the century. The debate originated before China's accession to the WTO in 2001 and became more intense after the accession. ASEAN officials insisted that with respect to the FDI flows, 'there (was) almost a one-to-one correlation. ASEAN (had) lost and China (had) gained' (Kazmin, McNulty, & William, 13 October, 2003). A plethora of literature exists on this 'FDI crowd-out' issue. However, there is no general agreement in academia about it.

The Japan External Trade Organization (JETRO) (Xing & Wan, 2006, p. 419), the Japan Bank for International Cooperation (JBIC) (McKibbin & Woo, 2003, pp. 12-15) and the Asian Development Bank Institute (ADBI) (Oxford Analytical, 19 January, 2005, p. 1) all made surveys about the 'FDI crowd-out' issue before China's accession to the WTO. They unanimously predicted that China's WTO membership would encourage producers to take China in precedence over ASEAN as their investment destination; and as a result, more FDI would flow to China instead of ASEAN. The prediction coincided with the studies of some research institutes such as the Oxford Analytica, which assumed 'Beijing (was) attracting a rising share of foreign direct investment (FDI) in Asian; indeed, pressure from Chinese competition (was) cited as part of the reason for the meltdown in Southeast Asian economies in the 1997-98 East Asia economic crisis (Oxford Analytical, 08 January, 2001, p. 1).' Besides, such a prediction was justified by empirical studies Warwick J. McKibbin and Wing Thye Woo conducted after China's accession to the WTO. Their studies concluded that 'there would be diversion of FDI to China, especially from its East and Southeast Asian neighbours (McKibbin & Woo, 2004, p. 9)'. ASEAN did not perform as well in attracting FDI flows as previously in the 2000s, which was attributed to the competition from China after its accession to the WTO. According to McKibbin and Woo,

> 'as the Asian financial crisis was over by early 2000, the changes in the frequency of identification and ranking of the ASEAN-4 (Indonesia, Malaysia, the Philippines and Thailand) economies on the list of profitable FDI locations between 2000 and 2001 could therefore justifiably be attributed to the WTO-created improvement in China's reliability as an international supplier (McKibbin & Woo, 2003, p. 13)'.

Although many people asserted that 'FDI flows (diverted) from ASEAN to China (Chen H. , 2008, p. 36)', they understated its implications on ASEAN. It was agreed that 'the diversion of FDI flows to China (did) not necessarily pose a threat to ASEAN members (Zhu, 2005, p. 7)'.

However, some scholars made contrary assertions. They argued that FDI diversion did not happen. After China's accession to the WTO, 'the country's dynamic economic growth (would) propel overseas investment in the ASEAN countries, rather than divert FDI from the ASEAN nations (Wong & Chan, 2003, p. 278)'. Particularly after the endorsement of the Framework Agreement in 2002 and the Investment Agreement in 2008 between China and ASEAN, some argued that 'the liberal investment agreement (would) greatly promote mutual investment between China and ASEAN (Chen H. , January 2006, p. 9)'. It was admitted that there was a growth of FDI in China, yet 'increasing FDI in China is not at the expense of the Asian economics but, if anything, they benefit from it (Das, 2007, p. 298).' After all, 'there was no obvious evidence that the rise of China has squeezed out the FDI inflows to ASEAN (Wong, Zou, & Zeng, 2006, p. 9)'. It was also admitted that there was a decline of FDI in ASEAN, yet 'the Asian Financial Crisis, rather than China, has been primarily responsible for the decrease in ASEAN-5's inward FDI flows (Wu,

Siaw, Sia, & Keong, 2002, p. 110)'.

Many reasons were sought to explain why China's FDI increased while ASEAN's FDI decreased and why China did not crowd out ASEAN's FDI. It was insisted that part of the reason for the decline of ASEAN's FDI was the substantial drop of the intra-regional FDI (Buckley, Clegg, Cross, & Tan, Spring 2005, pp. 26-27). It was deemed by some scholars that China did not divert ASEAN's FDI flows because 'ASEANS's FDI flow was mainly from the US and the Europe while China's FDI flow was mainly from the Asian region (Qin, February-March 2007, p. 6) (Tang, 2002, p. 54)'. In addition, 'the political instability in ASEAN members, to some extent, played a negative role in attracting FDI flows.'[38]

To sum up, there was no agreement on whether ASEAN's FDI flows diverted to China and whether China crowded out ASEAN's FDI after its accession to the WTO. In addition, due to lack of an a generally approved method to measure the causality between China's WTO-accession and the decline of ASEAN's FDI flows, some scholars had to admit that 'the interactions (between China's WTO-accession and ASEAN's FDI flows) (were) complex and the outcome - for China as well as for the Southeast Asian countries – (was) far from clear (Buckley, Clegg, Cross, & Tan, Spring 2005, p. 15)'.

The 'FDI crowd-out' issue has two levels: first, did ASEAN's FDI decrease while China's FDI was increasing after China's accession to the WTO? Second, if it happened, was China responsible for ASEAN's FDI decline? The analysis, firstly, investigates whether there was some time when China's FDI from the investment sources was increasing while ASEAN's FDI from the same sources was decreasing after China's accession to the WTO. Moreover, it explores whether there was causality between China's increase and ASEAN's decrease. If there was, then the conclusion that China crowded out ASEAN's FDI flows after China's accession to the WTO makes sense. If there was not, then the probable reasons are investigated. The United States and Japan are taken as examples of the investment sources due to the great significance of their FDI to China and ASEAN. The United States was the biggest single source of China and ASEAN's FDI outside of the East Asian region in the 2000s apart from such tax haven as the Virgin Islands; Japan was the counterpart of the US inside the region apart from Hong Kong. Therefore, the United States and Japan are chosen to check whether their FDI flows into ASEAN were crowded out by China after its entry into the WTO.

Table 6.4 shows the value and share of China and ASEAN's FDI in total American outward FDI from 2001 to 2009. If there is some time when ASEAN's share dropped and China's share increased at the same time; moreover the former happened as a direct result of the latter, then there is a high possibility that China crowded out ASEAN's FDI from the source of the United States after China's accession to the WTO. As

---

[38] Interview with a director of the China Association of Southeast Asian Studies (CASAS), Nanjing, China, 18 June, 2010

shown in Table 6.4, there are only two years, 2004 and 2008, when China's share grew while ASEAN's share dropped. During other years, ASEAN's share grew synchronously when China's grew and *vice versa;* ASEAN's share dropped synchronously when China's share dropped and *vice versa*. Then, the issue whether China crowded out ASEAN's share in American outward FDI in these two years of 2004 and 2008 matters. Two factors add difficulties in analysing the causality between the former and the latter. The one is that 2004 and 2008 were years away from China's accession to the WTO; therefore, it is hard to judge whether ASEAN's declining share directly resulted from China's accession. The other factor relates to where the competition comes from. It is hard to judge where the competition comes from inside or outside Asia because data on Asia's share in the US's total outward FDI are not available. Therefore, the causality between ASEAN's declining share and China's rising share is unclear.

Figure 6.1 draws a curve according to the share in Table 6.4 in order to make it clearer and more understandable. As displayed in

Figure 6.1, there is a similar change of ASEAN's share in American total outward FDI flows in accordance with China's share except in 2004 and 2008. However, there might be another issue worthy of attention. According to the ASEAN Statistical Yearbook 2008, ASEAN received 4,384.4 million dollars of FDI flows from the US in 2004, which was much more than the 1,298 million dollars according to the OECD database. The same problem happens in 2008, when ASEAN received 34,866 million dollars, based on ASEAN statistics, also much more than the 11,794 million dollars claimed in OECD statistics. Computation based on ASEAN's data does not show the decline of ASEAN's share in US's total outward FDI flows. It seems the statistical data from OECD gave this impression. However, the OECD is still a reliable source for the 'FDI crowd-out' issue because there was no data on the US's total outward FDI flows in ASEAN's statistical yearbooks. In light of the unclear discussion on this 'FDI crowd-out' issue with the US as an example, we introduce Japan, which was the biggest single FDI source inside East Asian region for both China and ASEAN, as another example.

Table 6.4 American Outward FDI Flows into ASEAN and China, 2001-2009

American Outward FDI Flows into ASEAN and China, 2001-2009

Value: in million US dollars; Share: in percentage

	2001		2002		2003		2004		2005		2006		2007		2008		2009	
	Value	Share	Value	Share	Value	Share	Value	Share	Value	Share	Value	Share	Value	Share	Value	Share	Value	Share
World Total	124,873	100	134,946	100	129,352	100	294,905	100	15,369	100	224,220	100	393,518	100	330,491	100	248,074	100
ASEAN	8,851	7.09	680	0.50	5,228	4.04	1,298	0.44	5,947	38.69	10,239	4.57	17,859	4.54	11,794	3.57	8,840	3.56
China	1,912	1.53	875	0.65	1,273	0.98	4,499	1.53	1,955	12.72	4,226	1.88	5,243	1.33	15,839	4.79	-6,997	-2.82

Source: data extracted on 04 Nov 2010 14:50 UTC (GMT) from OECD.Stat (Compiled and computed by the author)

Note: Hong Kong and Macau's FDI are not included due to part lack of the data.

Figure 6.1 Share of China and ASEAN in the US's Outward FDI Flows, 2001-2009

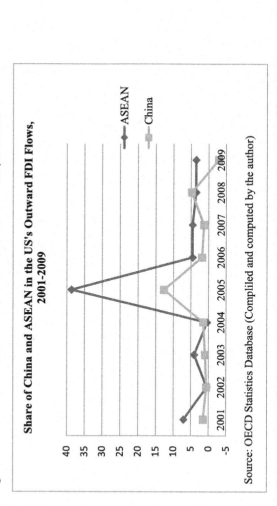

Share of China and ASEAN in the US's Outward FDI Flows, 2001-2009

Source: OECD Statistics Database (Compiled and computed by the author)

Table 6.5 Japanese Outward FDI Flows into ASEAN and China, 2001-2009

Japanese Outward FDI Flows into ASEAN and China, 2001-2009

Value: in million US dollars; Share: in percentage

	2001		2002		2003		2004		2005		2006		2007		2008		2009	
	Value	Share	Value	Share	Value	Share	Value	Share	Value	Share	Value	Share	Value	Share	Value	Share	Value	Share
Japanese Total Outward FDI Flows	32,554	100	35,268	100	35,187	100	35,332	100	45,831	100	50,244	100	73,546	100	127,981	100	74,699	100
Asia, total	n/a	n/a	n/a	n/a	n/a	n/a	9,335	26.42	16,894	36.86	17,456	34.74	20,376	27.70	24,146	18.87	21,308	28.52
Asia, excluding Near and Middle East and OECD	5,803	17.83	4,794	13.59	5,962	16.94	8,491	24.03	14,545	31.74	15,695	31.24	18,109	24.62	20,634	16.12	19,688	26.36
ASEAN	3,430	10.54	2,105	5.97	2,201	6.26	2,744	7.77	5,065	11.05	6,953	13.84	7,786	10.59	6,304	4.93	7,040	9.42
China	1,483	4.56	1,718	4.87	3,065	8.71	4,539	12.85	6,596	14.39	6,164	12.27	6,203	8.43	6,480	5.06	6,938	9.29

Source: Data extracted on 04 Nov 2010 15:20 UTC (GMT) from OECD.Stat (Compiled and computed by the author)

Note: Hong Kong and Macao's FDI are not included due to partially missing data.

Figure 6. 2 Share of Asia, China and ASEAN in Japanese Outward FDI Flows

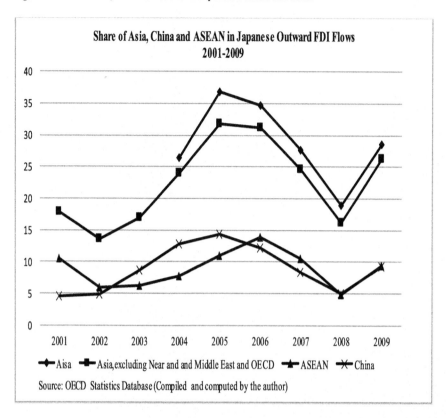

Japan is the biggest source inside the East Asian region apart from such tax havens as Hong Kong. Table 6.5 and Figure 6. **2** give us some ideas about the share and the trend of ASEAN and China's FDI from Japan. As shown in Table 6.5, ASEAN's FDI value from Japan dropped in 2002 to 2,105 million dollars from 3,430 million dollars in 2001. During the following five years from 2003 to 2007, ASEAN saw a steady increase in FDI flows from Japan, which reached a historic high of 7,786 million dollars in 2007. ASEAN's share of total Japanese FDI flows dropped as a result of the 2008 global financial crisis and the subsequent FDI shrinking in the world. With respect to China, its FDI flows from Japan saw a steady increase from 2001 to 2009, except in 2006 when there was a slight decline. Of special note, China's FDI from Japan increased during the 2008 global financial crisis (although its share dropped a little), which illustrates those Japanese producers had strong confidence in China's economic vitality, even within the general context of the global financial crisis in 2008.

Figure 6. 2 displays a more graphic picture of ASEAN and China and Asia's share in Japanese outward FDI from 2001 to 2009. Generally, the decade can be divided into three periods. During the first period from 2002 to 2005, all Asian countries', some Asia countries' (excluding Near and Middle East and OECD), China and ASEAN's share in Japanese outward FDI all increased. In comparison, China's share grew at a larger extent than ASEAN's. During the second period from 2006 to 2008, all four destinations' shares dropped, and China's dropped to a larger extent than ASEAN's. They all rose during the last period from 2008 to 2009. The trend of these three periods suggests that both ASEAN and China's share in Japanese outward FDI changed in exact accordance with Asia's, where there were some changes as a result of Japan's shifting distribution of FDI in the world. However, two periods, 2001-2002 and 2005-2006 are distinct from the generally paralleling trend.

During the period from 2001 to 2002, China's share rose while ASEAN's share dropped; during 2005 to 2006, China's share dropped while ASEAN's share rose. The latter period naturally does not illustrate the issue that China crowded out ASEAN's share. The former period, however, shows the possibility that China's increase was at the expense of ASEAN's decrease. So far, the first level of the 'FDI crowd-out' issue has emerged: China's share rose while ASEAN's share dropped in 2002 shortly after China's accession to the WTO. Then, the next step is to investigate the causality between China' increase and ASEAN's decrease. Analysis investigates whether China's rising share in 2002 directly resulted in the decline of ASEAN's share in 2002. If it did, then there is a great possibility that China crowded out ASEAN's share of FDI from Japan in the immediate wake of China's entry into the WTO. However, the 'crowd-out' effect is limited to 2002 because both China and ASEAN saw an identical rising/dropping trend after 2002.

Figure 6. 2 also shows two curves of the share of all Asian countries in total Japanese outward FDI flows and the share of some Asian countries (excluding the Near and Middle East and OECD) in exact parallel, which indicates that little competition from countries of Near and Middle and OECD in Asia needs to be taken into consideration. The reasonable inference is that there is a high likelihood that other Asian countries including China (albeit apart from the Near and Middle East and OECD), crowded out ASEAN's share of Japanese FDI flows in 2002.

Figure 6.3 presents the distribution of the Japanese outward FDI in Asia[39] in 2001 and 2002. As displayed, ASEAN, Hong Kong, China, India, Taiwan and other countries added up to account for all the share of Japanese outward FDI flows in Asia. ASEAN accounted for 59% of Japanese outward FDI flows in Asia in 2001, but its share dropped by 15% to 44% in 2002. Moreover, the share of Hong Kong also dropped by 1% in 2002 compared to 2001. In contrast to ASEAN and Hong Kong's declining share, China's share saw an increase, which grew from 25% in 2001 to 36% in 2002. At the same time, the share of India and Taiwan also increased; the former grew from 3% in 2001 to 6% in 2002, and the latter grew from 6% to 8%. Thus, China, India and Taiwan jointly occupied the lost share of ASEAN and Hong Kong in 2002; and China made up the biggest part among the three economies.

---

[39] Hereafter in this section, Asia specifically refers to those Asian countries, excluding Near and Middle East and OECD.

Figure 6.3 The Distribution of Japanese Outward FDI Flows in Asia, 2001 and 2002

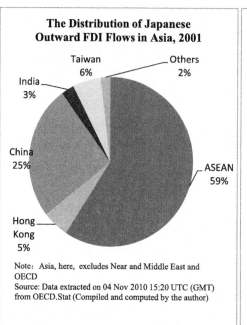

The Distribution of Japanese Outward FDI Flows in Asia, 2001

Taiwan 6%
Others 2%
India 3%
China 25%
ASEAN 59%
Hong Kong 5%

Note: Asia, here, excludes Near and Middle East and OECD
Source: Data extracted on 04 Nov 2010 15:20 UTC (GMT) from OECD.Stat (Compiled and computed by the author)

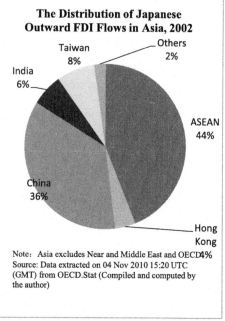

The Distribution of Japanese Outward FDI Flows in Asia, 2002

Taiwan 8%
Others 2%
India 6%
ASEAN 44%
China 36%
Hong Kong 4%

Note: Asia excludes Near and Middle East and OECD
Source: Data extracted on 04 Nov 2010 15:20 UTC (GMT) from OECD.Stat (Compiled and computed by the author)

Several reasons can be offered for this phenomenon. First, China and India belong to the 'BRICs (Brazil, Russia, India and China)' group, whose dynamic economies attracted Japanese investors. Similarly, Taiwan belongs to the 'NIEs' in East Asia, whose economies also set a good basis for attracting FDI. More importantly, China and Taiwan shared something in common, which was that both of them entered the WTO. China entered the WTO on 11 November, 2001 and Taiwan on 1 January, 2002. China and Taiwan's entry into the WTO in late 2001 and early 2002 obviously reinforced their status as competitive investment destinations by attracting more FDI flows. This might be the most important part of the reason for the 'FDI crowd-out' issue. This could be the more critical factor for them to increase their share in total Japanese outward FDI, and account for the share ASEAN lost. Besides, China is distinguished from Taiwan by accounting for the biggest part of ASEAN's lost share in 2002; it occupied 11% of ASEAN's lost share of 15%. Taiwan occupied another 2%. Therefore, it is absolutely reasonable to argue that both China and Taiwan crowded out ASEAN's share of FDI from Japan in 2002 because of their accession to the WTO and China should take most of the responsibility. *Inter alia*, China's accession to the WTO in 2001 played the critical role in accounting for the most part of ASEAN's lost share. Apart from 2002, ASEAN's share grew when China's grew and *vice versa*; ASEAN's share dropped when China's dropped and *vice versa*. This indicates the increasing interdependence of investment between China and ASEAN, in interdependence theorists' words.

However, the internal reasons for ASEAN's decreased FDI in 2002 cannot be ignored. ASEAN did not pay adequate attention to attract extra-regional FDI in 2002 because its focus was fully placed on promoting intra-regional FDI flows in ASEAN. As well known, 2002 was the last year before the AFTAwas declared at the very outset of 2003. ASEAN made the final push to complete the AFTA in 2002 by taking measures to encourage intra-regional FDI flows within ASEAN *per se*. Comparing data in 2001, 2002, and 2003, Table 6.6 provides some numeric evidence for this. ASEAN attracted 2,526.50 million US dollars of intra-regional FDI in 2001, accounting for 12.2% of total FDI flows and attracted 18,103.90 million US dollars of extra-regional FDI, accounting for 87.7%. In 2002, ASEAN's intra-regional FDI saw a substantial rise to 3,812.90 million dollars, accounting for 21.4% of total FDI flows of that year. Correspondingly, the share of extra-regional FDI dropped significantly. Actually 2002 saw a historic high of intra-regional FDI since 1995; and also saw a historic low of extra-regional FDI since 1995. In 2003, the shares of intra-regional FDI (11.2%) and extra-regional FDI (88.8%) both returned to the previous level of year 2001. This numeric evidence clearly illustrates that ASEAN encouraged more intra-regional FDI in 2002 and correspondingly paid less attention to attract extra-regional FDI. A similar trend happened to ASEAN'S FDI from Japan in 2001, 2002 and 2003. ASEAN's FDI from Japan in 2002 decreased by17.4% compared to 2001, and returned to the level of 2001 in 2003. ASEAN's less attention paid to the extra-regional FDI from the world in general and to the FDI from Japan in particular was the internal reason for the decrease of ASEAN's FDI from Japan in 2002. Therefore, ASEAN's loss of some of its share of Japanese FDI in 2002 was not only the result of China's entry into the WTO, but also a result of the greater attention ASEAN gave to intra-regional FDI and less attention to extra-regional FDI.

Table 6.6 ASEAN's Intra-regional and Extra-regional FDI flows in 2001, 2002 and 2003

ASEAN's Intra-regional and Extra-regional FDI flows in 2001, 2002 and 2003				
			Flows: in million US dollars, Share: in percentage	
Year	Intra-regional FDI Flows	Share	Extra-regional FDI flows	Share
2001	2,526.50	12.2	18,103.90	87.8
2002	3,812.90	21.4	13,974.40	78.6
2003	2,702.00	11.2	21,364.70	88.8

Source: ASEAN Statistical Yearboook 2008 (Compiled and computed by the author)

In order to further measure the performance of ASEAN and China in attracting inward FDI and ultimately evaluate China's role in investment cooperation with ASEAN, the UNCTAD Inward FDI Performance Index (UNCTAD, 2002) is utilized. 'The Inward FDI Performance Index is the ratio of a country's share in global FDI flows to its share in global GDP. Countries with an index value of one receive FDI exactly in line with their relative economic size. Countries with an index value greater than one attract more FDI may be expected on the basis of relative GDP (UNCTAD, 2002, p. 37).' As shown in Table 6.7, the Inward FDI Performance Index of ASEAN and China after 2001 are available. Given the unstable FDI flows to ASEAN and China, three years are taken at an average. ASEAN is divided into two groups of ASEAN-5 (Indonesia, Malaysia, the Philippines, Singapore and Thailand) and BCLMV (Brunei, Cambodia, Laos,

133

Myanmar and Vietnam) based on the huge difference in investment environment among the ten ASEAN members.

As shown by Table 6.7, the China, ASEAN-5 and BCLMV's indexes are greater than one, which suggests a dynamic and competitive performance of their inward FDI. During 2001-2003, the Western developed economies, led by the US, performed worse in their capability of attracting global FDI due to the great economic recession. The developing economies, led by China and ASEAN, performed strongly in their competitiveness in attracting inward FDI based on the decades' rapid economic growth in 1990s. During 2004-2006, both China and BCLMV's indexes decreased, indicating their gradual loss of comparative advantage because the developed economies recovered from the great economic recession at the very beginning of the first decade of the 21st century. China's index decreased from 2.11 during 2001-2003 to 1.97 during 2004-2007; and BCLMV's dropped from 3.17 to 1.63. Distinguishing from their neighbours, ASEAN-5 performs somehow better during 2004-2007 than in 2001-2003, with its index growing slightly from 2.01 to 2.16. Among the five ASEAN-5 members, Singapore contributed a lot to the better performance of ASEAN-5. Actually Singapore ranked the first in the world in the inward FDI Performance Index during 1988-1990. It performed a relatively poorly during 1998-1990, ranking 18th in the world, due to the heavy attack of the 1997-8 AFC. All five ASEAN-5 members performed better after surviving the economic crisis, although they did not return to the previous level during 1988-1990. During 2007-2009, another wave of global financial crisis, originating from the US, plagued the global economy, which Asian developing economies could not escape. Hit by the global financial crisis in 2008, both China and ASEAN-5 performed worse. China and ASEAN-5's index respectively dropped to 1.27 and 1.19, both at a historic low. On the contrary, BCLMV performed much better than during 2004-2007. More and more FDI of the BCLMV came from China based on the preferential and facilitating measures of bilateral investment.

No one doubts the fact that the preferential measures in the Framework Agreement and the IA contributed greatly to enhancing BCLMV's competitiveness in attracting inward FDI. However, China itself performed worse in the end of the 2000s than at the beginning. China's index during 2007-2009 dropped equally to the previous level of 1.2 during 1998-2000 according to the statistics from the 2002 World Investment Report. This suggests that China obtained less FDI relative to its increasing economic size. In further words, China had no capability to compete ASEAN's performance of attracting inward FDI during the 2000s. During the first half of the 2000s, China's Inward FDI Performance lagged far behind that of ASEAN-5; during the second half of the 2000s, it lagged far behind that of BCLMV. Part of the reason could be because China diverted its focus on attracting inward investment to encouragement of outward investment, which changed China's role in investment cooperation from a net recipient of investment from ASEAN to a potential investment exporter, mainly to ASEAN, at a regional level.

As a result of China's worse performance in the 2000s, there is a great possibility that the overall performance of East and Southeast Asia, whose index are respectively 1.73 and 1.2 on a decreasing track during 1988-1990 and 1998-2000 will continue to decline. If this is the case, the overall competitiveness of East and Southeast Asia in attracting FDI will be reduced. This will definitely play a negative role in East Asian integration, where most of the markets are made up of the developing economies. On the other hand, China has more opportunities to play a critical role in East Asian integration with respect to investment cooperation, in consideration of its excellent performance in investing outward in ASEAN and of the fact that most East Asian participants are hungry for inward investment to realize a relatively rapid economic growth.

Table 6.7 UNCTAD Inward FDI Performance Index of China, ASEAN-5 and BCLMV

UNCTAD Inward FDI Performance Index of China, ASEAN-5 and BCLMV, 2001-2003, 2004-2006 and 2007-2009			
	2001-2003	2004-2006	2007-2009
China	2.11	1.97	1.27
ASEAN-5	2.01	2.16	1.19
BCLMV	3.17	1.63	2.05

Source: UNCTAD Stat Database (Compiled and computed by the author)

7 China's Motives for Shifting its Attitude towards Economic Cooperation with ASEAN[40]

This chapter explores the motives that prompted China to shift its attitude towards economic cooperation with ASEAN and that towards regional economic integration in East Asia. As analysed in Chapter Four, in the second half of the 1980s and the 1990s, China was preoccupied with resuming its position as an original contracting party of the GATT first and then the multilateral negotiations to enter the WTO. In 2001, China officially proposed to set up the CAFTA, through which China turned itself from a bystander of regional economic cooperation to a proactive player. During the 2000s, China focused on the establishment of the CAFTA, which took ten years to complete. As stated in Chapter Five, in the 1980s and 1990s, China made extensive efforts to attract foreign investment by opening up four special economic zones, fourteen coastal cities, four coastal economic zones and thirteen border cities, six cities along the Yangtze River and eighteen inland provincial capital cities. At the same time, however, when the decision to establish the CAFTA was made, Beijing domestically implemented the investment policy of 'going out' by encouraging Chinese enterprises to invest outside of China. This turned China from an attractive investment destination to a potential investment source for its neighbouring economic partners in general and for ASEAN in particular. The motives behind China's shifting its attitudes towards economic cooperation with ASEAN and that towards regional economic integration in East Asia are addressed in this chapter.

This shift in attitude took place within a general context of radical changes at the international and regional level. At the international level, the Cold War ended in 1991, and the bipolarity era faded away into history. In the economic field, China was striving to enter the WTO where the Uruguay round negotiations proceeded slowly. At the regional level, the regional economic integration in Western Europe and North America was ascendant while in East Asia, most countries were heavily attacked by the 1997-8 AFC. It is within the general context at the international and regional level that China shifted its attitudes towards East Asian economic integration. Hence, China's outward-oriented motives were explored by a plethora of scholarly works. In terms of economic benefits, 'one immediate reason for China's offer of the CAFTA is its economic competition with ASEAN that could intensify following its entry into the WTO (Sheng, 2003, p. 6).' Moreover, also 'the CAFTA is to protect against economic shocks in the globalization (Sheng, 2003, p. 17).' More importantly, the regional FTA is 'a complementary platform to the WTO for gaining market

---

[40] The author is sponsored in the chapter by the 'Shanghai Pujiang Program 2013' (13PJC104). She gratefully acknowledges a number of government/non-government officials in Nanjing, Nanning and Beijing, China for their granting interviews. Their valuable time and shining perspectives are highly appreciated.

access in view of the slow progress of the multilateral negotiations (Jiang, 2010, p. 251).' In terms of political benefits, Beijing initiated the regional trade arrangements in order to 'cultivate goodwill among China's important neighbours, maintain peace and security (Wang, 2005, p. 43)', and 'pre-empt other powers' dominance of Asia' as well as to 'defuse American influence in the region (Greenwald, 2006, p. 197)'. Effectively, the China-initiated regional economic cooperation between China and ASEAN was intended to 'help achieve China's major foreign policy objectives of prompting multilateralism in global affairs, fostering East Asian cooperation, and enhancing the role of China in East Asia and the wider Asia Pacific (Song & Li, 2002, p. 31) (Cai, 2003, p. 397)' and ultimately this would help 'accelerate the emergence of a tripartite world between NAFTA, EU and East Asian groups (Kuik, 2005, p. 118)'.

However, the motives for outward-orientation did not give us the full picture. If the initiated economic cooperation in East Asia was part of China's economic diplomacy, then the domestic economy and politics must be explored. As asserted by interdependence theorists, if the interdependence theory was applied to studies of the policy of a nation under interdependent conditions, the domestic structures and politics of the particular nations must be investigated (Keohane & Nye, 1989, p. 223). According to Hugo Restall, 'in every country domestic politics is the key to understanding foreign policy, in China the dynamic is especially important (Restall, June 2007, p. 72)'. The domestic politics in China, therefore, must be investigated in order to understand China's shifting attitudes towards regional cooperation/integration. When China shifted its attitudes towards regional cooperation at the turn of the century, two problems arose domestically in China. One was the growing disparity of development between East and West China. The other is the increasing gap between urban and rural areas. Both problems were rooted in the ongoing economic reform and opening up of China. After decades of reform and opening up, provinces in East China became more developed than before. This increased the development gap between them and those provinces in West China. Meanwhile, the income of the urban people grew to a large extent due to the reform which resulted in increasing income gap between them and those people in rural areas. These two problems will threaten the CPC's rule in China if not addressed appropriately. Therefore, narrowing the gaps between East and West China and that between the urban and the rural was given high priority in the CPC's agenda. In order to solve the problems at home, Beijing took the initiative in launching economic cooperation with ASEAN and regional integration in East Asia. Geographically, ASEAN is located adjacent to West China and particularly Southwest China. The CAFTA between China and ASEAN was anticipated to provide more chances for Southwest China, where provinces seemed to have been forgotten by Beijing's central government during the early years of reform and opening up (Rong L. , 2010, p. 37). Furthermore, agriculture in ASEAN and China were complementary in terms of the different types of agricultural products, different harvest timing and different levels of mechanization in China and ASEAN. This would contribute significantly to developing Chinese agriculture, increasing peasants' income and constructing a new countryside in China (Hu & Lu, 2009, p. 15).

Based on the general context at the international, regional and domestic level, the chapter summarizes three key motives of China's shifting its attitudes towards economic cooperation with ASEAN and that towards East Asia economic integration. First and foremost, China's regional diplomacy asserted that the surrounding stability was a *sine qua non* to China's economic development at home and underlined ASEAN's great significance for China, due to its strategic geographical location, the large numbers of overseas Chinese living in ASEAN countries and ASEAN's wealthy experience in regional economic cooperation, which China lacked. Moreover, in consideration of the geographical proximity between Southwest China and ASEAN, the economic cooperation between China and ASEAN was expected to develop Southwest China in particular and West China in general economically, in order to reduce the disparity between West China and East China. In addition, due to the mutual complementarity in agriculture between China and ASEAN, economic cooperation, with agriculture designated first among the five priority areas, was anticipated to offset, to some extent, the negative impacts of China's entry into the WTO and to narrow the existing urban-rural gap. This chapter is organized into four sections. The first three sections address each of the most important motives for China's shifting attitudes towards regional economic cooperation one by one. The fourth makes some concluding remarks.

7.1 The CAFTA and China's Grand Strategy

China's grand strategy was the fundamental factor for its shifting attitude towards economic cooperation with ASEAN and towards regional economic integration in East Asia. China's grand foreign strategy had two parts: the political part and the economic part. The political part placed emphasis on building good political relations with the surrounding countries while the economic part focused on exploring regional markets in surrounding countries. China's strategic choice of promoting economic cooperation with ASEAN, based on the good political relations of two sides, exactly and concretely demonstrated China's grand strategy.

7.1.1 China's Political Grand Strategy

In terms of the political strategy, China's regional diplomacy (周边外交) underlined the significance of the surrounding countries on China's stability and development. China achieved tremendous economic development after the reform and opening up in late 1970s. This, on the one hand, improved people's living standard and reinforced the comprehensive national strength, and on the other hand, stirred the 'China threat' in the world and in Southeast Asia in particular. Beijing adjusted its diplomatic strategy and adopted regional diplomacy in an effort to alleviate the fear of China's peaceful rise and clarify the confusion as to China's benign intention. President Jiang Zemin stressed in his speech at the 15th CPC National Congress in 1997 that 'in carrying out the socialist modernization programme, we need a long-term peaceful international environment, and above all, we need to maintain good relations with the surrounding countries (Jiang Z. , 1997)'. From then on, China's regional diplomacy was virtually launched. In the same speech, President Jiang proposed 'a new security concept (NSC) featuring mutual trust, mutual benefit, equality and coordination' to take economic security as an important part of national security and take the stability of periphery as a *sine qua non* of China's domestic economic development. President Jiang Zemin further put forth the guideline of the regional diplomacy in his speech at the 16th CPC National Congress in 2002, by clearly stating that 'we will continue to cement our friendly ties with our neighbours and persist in building a good-neighbourly relationship and partnership with them (Jiang Z. , 2002)'. Premier Wen Jiabao completed China's regional diplomacy by indicating a concrete policy with regard to ASEAN. Premier Wen delivered a speech at the ASEAN Business & Investment Summit in October 2003, where he articulated the policy of China's regional diplomacy. According to him,

> *'It is an important component of China's own development strategy to build an amicable, tranquil and prosperous neighbourhood in the region. To build an amicable neighbourhood means adherence to the Chinese philosophy which emphasizes benevolence, good neighbourliness and harmony. To build a tranquil neighbourhood is to actively maintain peace and stability in the region, to consistently enhance mutual trust through dialogue and cooperation, and to settle disputes through peaceful negotiations, thus creating a peaceful, tranquil and stable regional environment for Asia's development. To build a prosperous neighbourhood is to step up mutually beneficial cooperation with the neighbouring countries, deepen regional and sub-regional cooperation, and vigorously facilitate economic integration in the region, thus achieving common development with other Asian countries (Wen, 2003)'.*

China's regional diplomacy, constituting the NSC, the guideline and the policy, in some sense, expressed China's willingness to share its economic achievements with its neighbours; it also boosted the priority of the surrounding countries in East Asia on the agenda of China's diplomacy. China diverted its sight from great powers in the west to the surrounding countries in the region of East Asia, following a policy of the regional diplomacy and looked for economic cooperation partners at the regional level in East Asia. ASEAN, which, as a (sub)regional entity, had restored or newly built good relations between its members and China in the 1990s, attracted China's attention.

'After China and ASEAN members established diplomatic relations in 1990s, two sides had been in a hostile state. That China exported revolutions to ASEAN had a negative implication (on bilateral relations). Now China changed the grand strategy, assuming that a stable surrounding environment was conducive to China's development. ASEAN exactly belongs to the surrounding area of China; the new security concept endows ASEAN with special significance, which is the radical reason why China chose to cooperate with ASEAN.'[41]

7.1.2   China's Economic Grand Strategy

In terms of economic strategy, to enter the WTO was the first step for China to explore the world market. However, China's status as a full market economy was not recognized by most members of the WTO until fifteen years later (2015). As a result, China did not have full access to the world market. In the meanwhile, the regional free trade areas (FTAs) in West Europe and North America were burgeoning when China negotiated to enter the WTO. China belonged to the few countries remaining in the world, who were not members of any regional free trade areas in the 1990s. The world market was not as opened to China as expected and the worries of exclusion from the regional FTAs diverted China's focus of economic strategy on regional economic cooperation in East Asia.

'China encountered two changes after its entry into the WTO. The one was the fifteen years' limitation. The world market was not completely opened to China. The other was that China found lots of regional FTAs were springing up in the world. China could not completely enjoy the preferential treatment brought by its entry into the WTO only through multilateral free trade (at the regional level in East Asia). China became aware that it must establish the regional FTAs at the regional level. However, China could not do anything to establish the FTAs before its entry into the WTO. China, therefore, focused on its entry into the WTO in the 1990s. Now to establish the regional FTAs was seen as the second

---

[41] Interview with the special assistant of China-Qian Qichen (the former vice Premier of China and the Chinese member of the China-ASEAN Eminent Persons Group), Nanjing, China, 23 April, 2010.

step of China's economic strategy after it entered the WTO. The surrounding

countries became the first choice for China to set up regional FTAs'.[42]

In the 1990s, China's embracing the WTO aroused great worries in Southeast Asia. On the one hand, ASEAN was worried that cheap Chinese products would pose challenges to ASEAN after China's entry into the WTO, given China's strengthened status as a stable international products supplier; on the other hand, they were worried that the FDI flows would divert from ASEAN into China given the great attraction of China as a potential investment destination. Within such a context at the international and the regional level, China took the initiative in proposing to establish the CAFTA and enhance economic cooperation with ASEAN so as to eliminate fear of the 'China threat' because of China's rising and to erase ASEAN's worries because of China's entry into the WTO. To summarize, China's grand political strategy underlined the significance of the stable surrounding countries for China's stability and development while China's grand economic strategy diverted its focus on multilateral economic cooperation at the international level to regional FTAs. These were the fundamental motives for China's proposal of the CAFTA in particular and for China's shifting attitude towards regional economic cooperation in East Asia in general.

7.1.3   ASEAN's significance for Beijing

ASEAN, as a historic economic partner of China, is of geopolitical and geoeconomic significance in China's grand political and economic strategy. Above all, ASEAN, 'geographically located inter-continental, assumes one of the most important strategic hubs in the world's geopolitical layout, and is of important strategic significance for China (Lu, 2009, p. 58).' Ten ASEAN members are located between two continents-Asia and Oceania, segmenting the Indian Ocean and the Pacific Ocean. The Malacca Straits is the throat of the marine traffic going through the Indian Ocean to the Pacific Ocean, which is compared to the 'the Gibraltar of the East'. Through the Malacca Straits, goods originally produced in West Europe, Africa, the Middle East and even South Asia go to East Asia by marine traffic. The Malacca Straits is a marine crossroad that connects Southeast and South Asian, West Africa and East Asia. ASEAN members located in Southeast Asia and the Malacca Straits, are of strategic significance for China's trade.

Moreover, a large number of overseas Chinese live in ASEAN, most of whom are engaged in business and more importantly, are willing to trade with/invest in China. According to statistics, there are approximately 10 million Chinese in Indonesia, or 5% of its total population; 6 million in Malaysia, or 40% of its total

---

[42] Interview with the leader of the ASEAN-China Expert Group on Economic Cooperation (EGEC), Beijing, China, 9 July, 2010

population; and 3 million in Singapore, or more than 90% of its total population. Totally, there live more than 25 million overseas Chinese in ASEAN, who are holding a massive capital of over 200 billion U.S. dollars, tantamount to be 60-80% of local business values or 50% of foreign trade values (Zhang, 2003, p. 38). The overseas Chinese there are happy to work with China for trade and investment activities due to the historic culture and ethic relations (Li, 1999, p. 6).

Thirdly, 'Southeast Asia, rich in natural resources, has a great potential for development (Lu, 2009, p. 58)', which attracted many Chinese enterprises, such as High-tech Materials Co., Ltd. Tungsten, China Nonferrous Metal Mining Group Co., Ltd. and Aluminium Corporation of China, to go and invest there. This formed the second round of the 'South Seas gold rush'. 'However, obvious changes happened between the two rounds of the 'South Seas gold rush'. The first round (during the 17th and 18th centuries) was nongovernmental, spontaneous and purely labours' investment, while the second was planned, organized, step-by-step investment with a careful analysis of pre-certification and a careful decision-making. Governmental participation and encouragement characterized the second round of the gold rush.'[43] The Chinese government encouraged Chinese enterprises to go to ASEAN to invest in the areas of natural resources with the support of the 'going out' strategy. This investment brought ASEAN not only capital, but also labour, with a view to promoting local modernization in ASEAN. On the other hand, it 'helped China's efforts to acquire much needed energy and raw resources (Kuik, 2005, p. 110)'. In Chapter Four, the data of S1-3 of Mineral Fuels Lubricants & Related Materials reveals that China had not imported more minerals in the 2000s than in the 1990s. As shown in Chapter Five, China invested more in minerals. This is part of the reason why China chose ASEAN as a partner for regional economic cooperation. 'China's strong economic growth needed the support of market and sources in ASEAN. Given its geographical conditions, ASEAN was taken for granted to be the one China needed.'[44]

Last, but not least, ASEAN was sophisticated in experience of regional economic cooperation, which happens to be what China lacked. ASEAN made the decision to set up the AFTA in 1992. All ASEAN members committed themselves to (sub)regional economic cooperation and the eventual establishment of the AFTA, which took them ten years to complete on 1st January, 2003. During the ten years, both ASEAN as a whole and its members individually accumulated rich experience in (sub)regional economic cooperation and learned many lessons as well. In comparison, economic cooperation between/among partners at the regional level was totally new to China, although it had been reforming and opening up for over two decades. Its lack of experience in regional economic cooperation undermined China's confidence

---

[43] Interview with an official of the China-ASEAN Business and Investment Summit Secretariat, Nanning, Guangxi, China, 19 August, 2010

[44] Interview with an associate professor from Institute of South and Southeast Asian Studies, CICIR, Beijing, 6 July, 2010

in economic cooperation with its neighbours. ASEAN, with rich experience in regional economic cooperation, exactly compensated China's weakness, which promised a rosy prospect for bilateral economic cooperation between them.

7.1.4 Comprehensive Cooperation between China and ASEAN

Besides the economic fields, cooperation between China and ASEAN is laid out in various fields, such as politics and security. Economically, Beijing proposed to set up CAFTA in 2001. In 2002, the Framework Agreement was endorsed. Its sub agreements on trade in goods and service, the dispute settlement mechanism and investment agreement were also signed one by one. On 1st January, 2010, the CAFTA was declared complete. 'The establishment of a FTA between ASEAN and China create(ed) an economic region with 1.7 million consumers, a regional GDP of about US $ 2 trillion and total trade estimated at US $ 1.23 trillion (The EGEC, 2001, p. 2).' It is currently the biggest regional FTA in the world.

Politically, China established, resumed and repaired its relationship with each ASEAN member in the 1990s after the cold war ended. China joined the Treaty of Amity and Cooperation (TAC) in 2003, making itself the first great power to do so. The bilateral political relationship between China and ASEAN was upgraded to be a strategic partnership by releasing the '*Joint Declaration on Strategic Partnership for Peace and Prosperity*' in 2003. China and ASEAN released a joint statement, '*Towards an Enhanced ASEAN-China Strategic Partnership*', at the 15th anniversary of bilateral partnership in 2006, which suggested another big move in bilateral political relations between China and ASEAN. China sent an ambassador to ASEAN in 2008, setting up a formal diplomatic relationship with ASEAN as a whole. Currently, ASEAN was one of the most important partners for China in the world.

As far as security is concerned, China and ASEAN worked together to address the security issue of the territorial disputes among China and some ASEAN members. That the Spratly Islands were claimed by four countries (China, Malaysia, the Philippines and Vietnam) and five parties (four countries plus Taiwan) was a good case for this. The dispute was rooted so deeply in history that no country unilaterally could solve it. Beijing took into consideration the far-reaching significance of dealing with it properly, for China's domestic political stability and economic development. They thought a peaceful solution was the best choice for all parties. Therefore, Deng Xiaoping proposed 'shelving the disputes and seeking joint development' in the 1980s, which constituted the main principle of solving the territorial dispute and led to the signing of the '*Declaration on the Code of Conduct on the South China Sea*' in 2002. It was acceptable for every concerned party and constituted a legal framework to solve the territorial dispute in the region. Following the declaration, no serious territorial disputes occurred though small ones continued. Successful response to the security problem in South China Sea provided Beijing with solid basis to develop the domestic economy single-mindedly.

In sum, China's regional diplomacy assumed the stability of the surrounding environment, including ASEAN in Southeast Asia, was *a sine qua non* to China's economic development domestically. China's economic strategy highlighted ASEAN's significance as a regional economic partner. ASEAN is geographically inter-continental and the Malacca Straits is one of the most important marine traffic routes for China, both of which empower ASEAN with geo-political and geo-economic significance for China. Besides, a great number of overseas Chinese live in ASEAN, who undertake business in local ASEAN countries and are willing to trade with/invest in China. More important is that the wealthy experience ASEAN accumulated in regional economic cooperation during the ten years of the establishment of the AFTA happens to be what China lacked. The economic cooperation between China and ASEAN could in the short term erase ASEAN's worries of China's entry into the WTO, and in the long term diminish the 'China threat' brought about by China's economic rise. According to an official of Ministry of Foreign Affairs, China,

> *'The point and the essence of China's grand strategy are to share Chinese interest with other nations in order to receive a kind response from outside world. Even though the CAFTA (agreement) has some tough articles, the large part of it is beneficial to China. That Beijing was sure about the potential benefits from the establishment of the CAFTA also contributed to China's shifting attitude toward the economic cooperation with ASEAN.'*[45]

7.2   The CAFTA and Southwest China

Domestically, China was preoccupied with two great problems, on which Beijing has dwelled on after the policy of reform and opening up was implemented in late 1970s. Besides, as the policy went into depth, the two problems deteriorated. One of the problems was the developing gap between East China and West China (including the southwest and northwest parts). The other was the urban-rural disparity (this problem is addressed in the third section of the chapter). According to the report of the EGEC, the increased regional disparity and growing gaps in the income level of different groups of the population are two of the most serious social problems arising from the development process; the acceleration of liberalization and competition arising from China's implementation of its WTO commitments may make those problems worse (The EGEC, 2001, p. 17). Therefore, the prospect of economic cooperation with ASEAN was a good solution for these two problems. Here, special attention was given to the first problem by addressing the benefits of economic cooperation between China and ASEAN for Southwest China.

---

[45] Interview with an official of the Ministry of Foreign Affairs of the PRC, Beijing, China, 24 July 2010

The twelve provinces/regions[46] in West China have 6.9 million square kilometres of land area, or 71.5% of the whole land of China with 364.5 million of population, or 28.7% of the total population of China. West China is the relatively underdeveloped part in terms of economic and social development, in that East China was planned as the pioneer and priority area of China's reform and opening up. After two decades of reform and opening up, the GDP of West China was 1,824 billion RMB, about 17.1% of China's total GDP in 2001; the total trade value was 16.8 billion US dollars, only accounting for 3.3% of that of all China; the yearly disposal income of urban residents in West China is 6,169 RMB, slightly lower than the national average of 6,859 RMB and the net income of rural residents per capita is 1,755 RMB, nearly 40% lower than the national average of 2,366 RMB. [47] As one part of West China, Southwest municipality/provinces/regions[48] also seemed to have been forgotten during the early years of China's reform and opening-up and their development lagged far behind that of their eastern counterparts.

7.2.1 Central and Local Governments' Measures to Develop Southwest Part by Economic Cooperation with ASEAN

In order to develop West China, Chinese leaders had great hope of economic cooperation between China and ASEAN. In 1999, Mr. Zhu Rongji, the former Premier, delivered a speech titled 'China and Asia in the new century' in Singapore. He reiterated that 'China welcome(d) ASEAN entrepreneurs to engage in trade and investment activities in particular in West China (Li & Kang, 2002, p. 24)'. Chinese leaders advocated enhanced economic cooperation between ASEAN and West China in the hope that this could help develop West China in general and Southwest China in particular, and would ultimately alleviate the disparity between West China and East China. In the view of Beijing's central government, two geographically favourable factors support the hope. Firstly, ASEAN members are geographically adjacent to the municipality/provinces/regions of Southwest China, which covers Guangxi Zhuang Autonomous Region, Yunnan Province, Guizhou Province, Sichuan Province, Xizang Autonomous Region (Tibet) and Chongqing Municipality. Further, the whole area of Southwest China is where the land transports routes and marine traffic artery for trade exchanges between China and ASEAN are. Yunnan and Guangxi are two

---

[46] According to the State Council of China, 'Implementing Suggestions on Certain Policies and Measures of Great Western Development' (No.6, 2000), West China includes 12 provinces/regions such as Chongqing Municipality, Sichuan province, Guizhou Province, Yunnan Province, Xizang Autonomous Region (Tibet), Shaanxi Province, Gansu Province, Ningxia Hui Autonomous Region, Qinghai Province, Xinjiang Uygur Autonomous Region, Inner Mongolia Autonomous Region and Guangxi Zhuang Autonomous Region.

[47] Data comes from National Bureau of Statistics of China, China Statistical Yearbook 2002 (Beijing: China Statistics Press 2002)

[48] Southwest China covers six municipality/provinces/regions such as Chongqing Municipality, Sichuan province, Guizhou Province, Yunnan Province, Xizang Autonomous Region (Tibet), and Guangxi Zhuang Autonomous Region

good cases in points. As to Yunnan, it shares a 4061-kilometre land border with Myanmar in the west, Laos and Vietnam in the south. Guangxi shares a 637-kilometres land border with Vietnam and it has about 1500 kilometres of continental coastline. Geographical proximity and long coastlines facing the Southeast Asian countries result in Southwest China's natural geographical advantage, which facilitates economic exchanges with ASEAN members.

Aside from the central government's efforts to develop Southwest China by proposing the CAFTA at the central level, local governments in Southwest China introduced various measures to encourage cooperation with ASEAN members at the provincial level. Sichuan, which had extensive exchanges on trade and investment with Singapore in the early 1990s, collaborated with Singapore to establish the 'Sichuan-Singapore Trade and Investment Committee' in 1996 in an effort to further enhance the trade and investment cooperation between the two sides. Yunnan, which also took ASEAN as the main partner of economic cooperation, put forward the idea of constructing an 'international channel' so as to link Yunnan and Southeast Asian countries via a transport connection. Sichuan organized a task force to explore the great potential of the ASEAN markets in 2002. Guangxi placed much emphasis on economic cooperation with ASEAN as well, particularly after the first China-ASEAN Expo was held in Guangxi in 2004. Guangxi's proposal of PBG Economic Cooperation in 2006 was responded positively from the central government, and then was approved in 2007. The local government of Guizhou put it clearly in the *'Guizhou Provincial Government Work Report 2007'*, that it 'supports those qualified enterprises to 'go out' and to participate in the international competition by enhancing the economic and technical cooperation with African and *ASEAN* countries, promoting market development and contracting projects and exporting labour service'. Local enterprises in Chongqing were encouraged by the provincial government to 'seize the big market of the CAFTA' in *'Chongqing Municipal Government Work Report 2007'*. In contrast with the piecemeal measures provincial governments took, Beijing's decision to set up the CAFTA at the central level made a dramatic step forward to enhance the economic cooperation between Southwest China and ASEAN members. With the joint efforts of the central and local governments, Southwest China benefited significantly from the enhanced economic cooperation with ASEAN members.

7.2.2   The CAFTA Benefited Southwest China

Firstly, as a direct outcome of the CAFTA, Southwest China increased its trade and investment exchanges with ASEAN. On the one hand, as a big market of trade and an investment destination of investment, Southwest China attracted more import trade and FDI flows from ASEAN. Guangxi was a good case in point. As displayed in Table 7.1, the trade value of Guangxi's imported goods from ASEAN increased at a steady speed year by year, from 129.39 million dollars in 2000 to 364.9 million dollars in 2004 and then 1,174.29 million dollars in 2007. Within less than a decade, the value increased nearly ten times. In the meanwhile, Guangxi's FDI from ASEAN also saw a fluctuating growth from 2000 to 2007. In 2000,

Guangxi's FDI value from ASEAN was 6.09 million dollars, which soared to 34.88 million dollars after two years' decline in 2001 and 2002. It added up to 46.74 million dollars in 2007, after another three years continuous decline in 2004, 2005 and 2006. In all, Guangxi attracted increasing FDI from ASEAN from 2000 to 2007 although the FDI value from ASEAN was not steadily increasing year by year. This happened, on the one side, because the FDI flows were not stable, and on the other side, because Guangxi faced competition for ASEAN's FDI flows from East China in general and Guangdong in particular. 'In terms of the net trade values with ASEAN and the FDI inflows values from ASEAN, Guangxi stands at a medium level of the whole country (of China). Although Guangxi makes great progress in enhancing trade cooperation with ASEAN and in attracting FDI flows from ASEAN, it can never compare with those relatively developed provinces in eastern coastal areas'.[49] Comparing Guangxi's FDI inflows from ASEAN with that of Guangdong, a province geographically next to Guangxi and not far from ASEAN, we found that Guangdong accounted for a much higher proportion of China's overall FDI inflows from ASAEN. In 2000, Guangdong attracted 505.22 million dollars of FDI inflows from ASEAN, accounting for nearly 18% of China's total while Guangxi accounted for only 0.2%. Guangdong's proportion in China's FDI inflows from ASEAN peaked in 2003, when it attracted more than 60% of China's total FDI inflows from ASEAN. Then its proportion began to drop, and finally decreased to 12% in 2007. In the meanwhile, Guangxi's proportion kept growing after 2000, albeit at a gradual pace and it stood at 1% in 2007. At the risk of oversimplification, East China's proportion in China's overall FDI inflows from ASEAN, represented in Guangdong's case, was decreasing while West China's proportion, represented in Guangxi's case was gradually increasing. During the first wave of decline of Guangxi's FDI from ASEAN in 2001 and 2002, provinces in East China attracted most of the FDI inflows from ASEAN. In 2003, Guangxi's status as the bridgehead of Sino-ASEAN economic cooperation was confirmed and the local government made greater efforts to attract foreign investment from ASEAN. This resulted in a rapid increase of Guangxi's FDI from ASEAN in 2003. However, the second wave of decline of Guangxi's FDI from ASEAN in 2004, 2005 and 2006 reveals that Southwest China, facing competition from East China, where local provinces had more sophisticated experience in attracting foreign investment, had to adjust and improve its investment environment to fight for more investment. Because East China's proportion in China's overall FDI inflows from ASEAN saw a significant decline during these years, it is safe to say that West China will have a positive, albeit gradual and fluctuating increase in attracting FDI inflows from ASEAN.

On the other hand, as a traditional trade partner and an emerging investment source, Southwest China exported more goods to ASEAN and invested there by signing overseas contracted projects in ASEAN. Also shown by Table 7.1 the value of Guangxi's exported goods to ASEAN increased steadily from 310.11 million dollars in 2000 to 636.2 million dollars in 2004 and then substantially to 1,734.17 million dollars in

---

[49] Interview with a senior official of the Guangxi Provincial Department of Commerce, Nanning, Guangxi, 18 August, 2010

2007. In contrast with the steady increasing tendency of Guangxi' exported value to ASEAN, its overseas contracted projects did not see a clearly increasing tendency. They fluctuated. In 2000, their value was 6.99 million dollars, and soared to a historic high of 33.68 million dollars in 2003. Then it gradually decreased in 2004 and 2005, and finally ended up in zero in 2006 and 2007. The historic high in the value of Guangxi's overseas contracted project in ASEAN happened at the same time as the rush of Guangxi's FDI from ASEAN, for the same reason that Guangxi's status as the bridgehead in Sino-ASEAN economic cooperation was well placed in 2003. However, the declining tendency of Guangxi's overseas contracted projects reveals that such projects were no longer a key approach for the investment cooperation between China and ASEAN. As analyzed in Chapter Five, China's outward FDI flows to ASEAN took the place of overseas contracted investment and became the key investment approach between two sides. In this respect, Guangxi's case conformed to the policy and measures of the central government.[50]

Similar increasing trade and investment cooperation to that between Guangxi and ASEAN happened in other provinces in West China. As can be seen in Table 7.2, the total value of Sichuan's imports and exports with ASEAN increased steadily from 274.56 million dollars in 2000 to 634.47 million in 2003 and then finally to 1,364.85 million dollars in 2007. Yunnan and Chongqing maintained an increasing trend from 2000 to 2007 as well. Of note is that Yunnan and Chongqing's total value of imports and export with ASEAN slightly declined in 2002. This was consistent with the general trend of Sino-ASEAN trade exchanges in 2002. With a view to the final push and the completion of AFTA in 2002, ASEAN took various measures to enhance intra-regional trade, which resulted in a corresponding decline of the total trade value between China and ASEAN. In consideration of the great economic recession in the world, 2001 even saw a historic low of the total trade value between China and ASEAN. As to Southwest China, this was reflected in 2002 by a slight decline of trade value between them and ASEAN.

In sum, except Tibet and Guizhou, for which data of their trade values with ASEAN is not available in their provincial statistical yearbooks, all provinces/regions in Southwest China promoted economic cooperation with ASEAN with more trade and FDI flows from ASEAN. This benefited from three factors. One was China's entry into the WTO, which stood for a new stage of China's opening up; the others were the establishment of the CAFTA and the GWD programme. In comparison, the latter two factors contributed more than the former did. It was East China, instead of West China, which benefited more from China's entry into the WTO because East China was the priority area of China's opening up. The GWD benefited the whole of West China, including the Southwest part. The establishment of the CAFTA benefited Southwest China particularly because of the natural advantages of Southwest China. In the long term, the enhanced economic cooperation between provinces in Southwest China and ASEAN is bound to

---

[50] Because most of China's outward foreign direct investment are operated by state-owned enterprises (SOEs) at the central level, Guangxi's outward FDI flows to ASEAN is not available.

help develop Southwest China and narrow the gap between it and East China.

Table 7.1 Trade and Investment Exchanges of Guangxi with ASEAN

Trade and Investment Exchanges of Guangxi with ASEAN 2000-2007

	Trade Value (in millon US dollars)			Investment Value (in million US dollars)		
	Export	Import	Total	FDI from ASEAN	Value of Overseas Contracted Projects in ASEAN	Total
2000	310.11	129.39	439.5	6.09	6.99	13.08
2001	259.14	159.91	419.05	3.45	5.72	9.17
2002	442.38	184.88	627.26	5.17	7.19	12.36
2003	552.35	273.84	826.19	34.88	33.68	68.56
2004	636.2	364.9	1,001.10	20.17	18.37	38.54
2005	830.59	393.44	1,224.03	26.53	4.12	30.65
2006	984.74	841.95	1,826.69	18.29	0	18.29
2007	1,734.17	1,174.29	2,908.46	46.74	0	46.74

Source: Guangxi Zhuang Autonomous Region Bureau of Statistics (eds.), Guangxi Statistical Yearbook 2001, 2002, 2003, 2004, 2005, 2006, 2007, 2008 (Beijing: China Statistics Press 2001, 2002, 2003, 2004, 2005, 2006, 2007, 2008) (Compiled and computed by the author)

Secondly, as an indirect outcome, the economic cooperation between Southwest China and ASEAN and the correspondingly intensified competitions facilitated resources reallocation and optimal industrial restructuring in Southwest China. 'Southwest China and ASEAN are not only mutually complementary but also competitive in trade structure. Both sides are able to benefit from this kind of benign competition, which facilitates the resources integration and industrial restructure through cooperation. If they could find out where are their own advantages and play to their strengths, they are able to benefit.'[51] As analysed in Chapter Four, the third section addressed the complementarity and competitiveness between China and ASEAN, based on the comparative advantage index of three types of goods S1-6 of Manufactured Goods, S1-7 Machinery and Transport Equipment and S1-0 Food and Live Animals. The index demonstrates that competitiveness dominated S1-6 in favour of China; while mutual complementarity dominated S1-7 and S1-0 where ASEAN had more comparative advantage. The bilateral economic cooperation between China and ASEAN intensified the competition, which led to resources reallocation in favour of the side that had the comparative advantage. In addition, the competition resulted indirectly in upgrading the industrial structure in provinces in Southwest China. Take Guangxi as an example. In 2003, primary, secondary and tertiary industry respectively accounted for 23.4%, 34.9% and 41.8% of the provincial GDP, which

---

[51] Interview with a scholar at Institute of Southeast Asian Studies, Guangxi Academy of Social Science, Nanning, Guangxi, 16 August, 2010

changed to 20.3%, 42.3% and 37.4% in 2008. The proportion of secondary industry had an obvious growth. Therefore, the bilateral economic cooperation between Southwest China and ASEAN resulted, on the one hand, in prompting enterprises to 'improve competitiveness to survive the market competition'; on the other hand, in 'survival of the fittest by labour division restructures and industrial restructure in Southwest China and ASEAN (Mang, June 2003, p. 7).'

Finally, local residents' income in Southwest China was increased owing to the economic cooperation between Southwest China and ASEAN. The increasing trade and investment exchanges between Southwest China and ASEAN supplied more job vacancies for local residents in Southwest China. Local workers could not only survive the lay-off crisis due to domestic reform all over China, but also were likely to increase their income. Local peasants in Southwest China also increased their income by exporting more agricultural products to ASEAN. Driven by the income increase in Southwest China, people's income in the whole of West China also increased correspondingly. In 2008, yearly disposable income of urban residents in West China grew to 12,971 RMB, nearly twice that in 2001. At a similar growth rate, the net income of rural residents per capita increased from 1,755 RMB in 2001 to 3,518 RMB in 2008.

In the short term, Southwest China increased its trade and investment exchanges with ASEAN, upgraded its industrial structure and increased local residents' income by economic cooperation between China and ASEAN. 'It is particularly after 2004, when the Framework Agreement took effect that Guangxi and other provinces in Southwest China develop much better than people anticipate. People's income grows at a significant extent and their living quality is substantially improved.'[52] As part of West China, the economic development of Southwest China contributed to increasing the overall economy of the whole West China and narrowing the disparity between the West and East parts of China.

In the long term, the CAFTA benefited Southwest China in terms of social development. The economic development in Southwest China set up a solid basis for national union. There exist plenty of minorities in Southwest China. As a matter of fact, Guangxi is the region/province who has the biggest population of minorities in China. Guangxi and Southwest China's economic development contributes significantly to unifying the minorities in China. In addition, Southwest China is located at the border of China in the southwest. Its development contributed to stabilizing the border so that the central government is able to concentrate on domestic economic development. As Alice D. Ba stated clearly, the economic cooperation between China and ASEAN is going to 'help stimulate development and growth in China's southern and western provinces, where much of China's minority population lives, and where development has lagged that along the eastern seaboard (Ba, 2003, p. 624)'.

It is important to emphasize that it does not make sense to attribute all the achievements of Southwest

---

[52] Interview with a senior official at Bureau of China-ASEAN Expo, Nanning, Guangxi, 20 August, 2010

development to the economic cooperation between China and ASEAN or the completion of the CAFTA. *Inter alia*, another factor that should not be ignored is the strategy of the GWD Beijing implemented in 2000 and the general context of China's entry into the WTO in 2001. According to the GWD programme, many preferential measures were taken in respect of trade and investment promotion, e.g. the 17% tax example for all enterprises investing in West China. These measures, together with the preferential programme within the CAFTA, jointly worked within the general context of the WTO framework to attract more trade and investments from ASEAN in Southwest China. In terms of the timetable, the CAFTA and the GWD programme synchronized. The former was planned for completion within ten years, beginning from 2001; the first ground of the latter was planned to attain the initial achievements also within ten years beginning from 2001. The former was virtually established in year 2010; and the second stage of the latter also began in 2010. In terms of the geographical location, ASEAN members share a common border with Southwest China. While the implementation of the CAFTA benefited whole China, it especially benefited the local economies in Southwest China. The establishment of the CAFTA and the GWD programme were compared to 'two gears meshing each other (Li & Kang, 2002, p. 26)'. The meshing space was geographical Southwest China. Two events jointly worked and helped to develop Southwest China together.

Table 7.2 Trade Exchanges of Sichuan, Yunnan and Chongqing with ASEAN

Trade Exchanges of Sichuan, Yunnan and Chongqing with ASEAN 2000-2007 (in million US dollars)

	Sichuan			Yunnan			Chongqing			Total of Three provinces/municipality
	Export	Import	Total by year	Export	Import	Total by year	Export	Import	Total by year	
2000	193.16	81.40	274.56	523.98	104.80	628.78	432.58	8.61	441.19	2,247.87
2001	218.59	67.54	286.13	624.86	198.82	823.68	503.81	12.74	516.55	2,736.17
2002	345.15	109.37	454.52	564.79	143.73	708.52	336.04	13.74	349.78	2,675.86
2003	418.92	215.55	634.47	n/a	n/a	771.30	379.83	30.19	410.02	2,450.26
2004	527.53	163.87	691.40	n/a	n/a	962.04	457.81	34.48	492.29	2,837.13
2005	663.20	113.37	776.57	n/a	n/a	1,090.54	366.25	33.16	399.41	3,043.09
2006	622.85	201.76	824.61	1,641.92	532.58	2,174.50	481.03	71.21	552.24	6,550.46
2007	997.58	367.27	1,364.85	2,175.11	803.69	2,978.80	645.17	83.18	728.35	9,415.65

Source: Sichuan Bureau of Statistics (eds.), Sichuan Statistical Yearbook 2001, 2002, 2003, 2004, 2005, 2006, 2007, 2008 (Beijing: China Statistics Press 2001, 2002, 2003, 2004, 2005, 2006, 2007, 2008) ; Yunnan Province Bureau of Statistics (eds.), Yunnan Statistical Yearbook 2001, 2002, 2003, 2007, 2008 (Beijing: China Statistics Press 2001, 2002, 2003, 2004,2005, 2006, 2007, 2008) ; and Chongqing Bureau of Statistics (eds.), Chongqing Statistical Yearbook 2001, 2002, 2003, 2004, 2005, 2006, 2007, 2008 (Beijing: China Statistics Press 2001, 2002, 2003, 2004, 2005, 2006, 2007, 2008) (Compiled and computed by the author)

7.3   The CAFTA and Agricultural Sector Development in China

China is the greatest agricultural country in the world, where there are some 800 million peasants, or nearly 60% of the total population; the rural area accounts for approximately 60% of the whole land and the agricultural sector is of strategic significance as the foundation for the national economy. Although the agricultural sector does not make up a high proportion of China's GDP, its development relates to Chinese people's livelihood. Beijing put agricultural development at the top of its agenda for decades and released the agriculture-related 'No. 1 Document' on 1st January in most of the years from 1982 onward[53]. Beijing gave special attention to the three agricultural problems- peasants, the rural area, and agricultural industry, whose significance was reflected in the 'No. 1 Document' particularly after 2003. Besides, China is a major agricultural trading country. China imported 52.17 billion U.S. dollars and exported 39.21 billion U.S. dollars of agricultural products, the total trading value of agricultural products adding up to 91.38 billion dollars in 2009. With such a huge trading value of agricultural products, China made itself the fourth largest agricultural trading nation in the world.

China's agricultural sector suffered a tremendous impact from its accession to the WTO in 2001.[54] 'China agreed to binding on all tariffs and to reduce them from an average of 31.5 to 17.4 per cent over the 1990–2005 period. Such a large tariff cut exceeded all expectations. China also committed to eliminating export subsidies and increasing the volume of tariff-rate quotas, which are two-tier tariffs (Das, 2007, p. 388)'. China's commitments on the agricultural sector within the framework of the WTO posed serious challenges to China's agricultural industry, peasants and rural area. This, to some extent, intensified the three agricultural problems in China in 2003, two years after China's WTO accession. China's agricultural industry was not ready to compete with its counterparts in the developed countries given its small scale, low productivity, and poor industrialization, etc.. China's agricultural products did not have an easy access to the markets of the developed countries due to the technical barriers (Jia, 2002, pp. 3-4). The negative impact of China's accession to the WTO on domestic agriculture gradually appeared after 2001. China had a trade deficit of agricultural products for the first time in 2004, after having enjoyed ten years of trade surplus from 1993 to 2003. The deficit continued to rise after 2004. It was 4.88 billion US dollars in 2004, and soared to 12.96 billion in 2009, or doubled the level of five years previously. In addition, China's accession to the WTO had another negative influence on farmers' income. A great many exotic agricultural products rushed into the Chinese market after China's entry into the WTO, which resulted in a reduction of production in China's agricultural sector. Correspondingly, farmers' income reduced. According to Shaun Breslin, 'as a result of WTO entry, rural farmers on marginal land resulted in greater poverty (Shaun, 2003, p. 229)'. In West China, where the agricultural sector was more heavily attacked by China's commitment to the WTO than East China (Ma & Sun, 20002, p. 50), many peasants went bankrupt and they had to migrate to east

[53] Beijing released the 'No. 1 Document' concerning the agricultural sector, the rural area and peasants from 1982 to 1986 and from 2004 onward.
[54] A plethora of Chinese-language sources pay attention to the challenges China's entry into the WTO brought to the domestic agriculture. To just list a few. Jia Daming, 'How does China's Agriculture Face the Clashes and Challenges after China's Entry into the WTO', *Science and Technology Review*, No. 10, 2002, pp. 3-6; Li Keshuang, 'The Challenge and Countermeasure of China's Agricultural Products Trade in the Period of Transition Under the WTO', *Modern Agricultural Science*, No. 5, 2008; Huang Jikun, 'Reassess the Impact of China's Entry into the WTO on Its Agriculture', *Industrial Economics Research*, No. 1, 2002; Xing Shuqing, 'Influence of China's Entry into the WTO on the Sustainable Development of China's Agriculture and Countermeasures', *Journal of Liaoning University (Philosophy and Social Science Edition)*, No. 3, 2007; Sun Haichao, 'Reflections on increase of Farmers' Income', *Shaanxi Finance*, No. 1, 2002, pp. 43-44; Cheng Ruiqiao, 'The Effect on China Agriculture of Joining the WTO', *Journal of Anyang Teachers College*, No. 4, 2002; Yang Xiuzhi, 'The Influence and Countermeasures of China's Agriculture Entering the WTO', *The Northern Forum*, No. 5, 2001; and Lv Yuhua, 'The Impact of Joining the WTO on Chinese Peasants' Income', *Science, Economy and Society*, Vol. 20, No. 3, 2002, pp. 36-39.

China to find temporary jobs. These migrant workers competed for job positions with urban workers and some of the urban workers were laid off, which ultimately threatened the social stability. Besides, on the other side, the exodus of young and strong peasants from the rural area further dimmed the prospects of China's agricultural industry. As Yao Min asserted, the agricultural liberalization within the framework of the WTO probably gave rise to the recession of China's agriculture sector, given the weakness of Chinese agriculture (Yao, 2003, p. 14). The former Premier Zhu Rongji openly admitted at the fifth ASEAN+3 Summit in 2001, that he was most worried about agriculture and 'adjustments would be most difficult in the rural sector (Cheng, 2003, p. 218)' after China entered the WTO.

7.3.1   Mutual Complementarity in Agriculture between China and ASEAN

Given those suffers China's agriculture had from the WTO accession, to enhance the agricultural cooperation with ASEAN might well have been an expedient solution for China. It proved to be a great thinking, particularly in consideration of the mutually complementary relationship of the agricultural trade between two sides. The mutual complementation dominated bilateral agricultural cooperation between China and ASEAN[55], although there was competition as well (Rong & Yang, 2006, p. 45). First and foremost,

> *'China and ASEAN are mutually complementary in varieties of the agricultural products. The climate difference, deriving from the different geographical altitude location of China and ASEAN, leads to the different harvest seasons and various agricultural products. Speaking of some same products, the two sides are mutually complementary given the different varieties and different harvest seasons. In simple words, China has most of the agricultural products that ASEAN needs to import while ASEAN has most that China needs to import. This results in mutual needs and markets. Thus the mutual complementation comes into being.'[56]*

---

[55] Most scholars, who conducted studies on the competitiveness and complementarity of the agricultural trades between China and ASEAN, agreed that complementarity was more predominant than competitiveness. See Zhang Jianzhong, 'Empirical Analysis on Agricultural Products Trading Relationship of Guangxi and ASEAN', *Around Southeast Asia*, No. 6, 2009, pp. 41-45; Sun Lin and Li Yueyun, 'An Analysis on Trade and Competitive Relations of Agricultural Products between China and the Main Countries of ASEAN', *World Economy Study*, No. 8, 2003, pp. 81-85; Wang Can, 'The Complementary Analysis of China-ASEAN Agricultural Products Trade', *Future and Development*, Vol. 30, No. 4, 2009, pp. 34-36, p.44; Zhou Xuechun, 'China-ASEAN Agricultural Cooperation Progress and Impact Analysis', *Agricultural Economy*, No. 1, 2007, pp.27-28; Chen Qianheng and Lv Zhiwang, 'The Current Situation and Prospect of Agricultural Cooperation between China and ASEAN', *Southeast Asian Studies*, No. 4, 2009, pp. 46-50; and Chen Li, 'The Influence and Countermeasures of Establishing China-ASEAN Free Trade Zone (Area) on the Export of Chinese Agricultural Products', *Journal of Yunnan University of Finance and Economics*, No. 5, Vol. 23, October 2007, pp. 79-83; Feng Xiaoming, 'China and ASEAN Can Share the Prosperity Together-Interview with Zhang Yunling, Director, Institute of Asia-Pacific, CASS', *China and World Economy*, No. 2002, p.5; Sun Lin and Li Yueyun, 'An Analysis on Trade and Competitive Relations of Agricultural Products between China and the Main Countries of ASEAN', *World Economy Study*, No. 8, 2003, p. 85; Sun Lin, 'Relationship of Agricultural Trade Competition between China and ASEAN, *Journal of International Trade*, No. 11, 2005, pp.71-75; Hu Chao and Lu Jianghai, 'The Analysis of Agricultural Goods Development between China and ASEAN', *Collected Essays on Finance and Economics*, No. 4, Vol. 145, July 2009, pp. 25-27.
[56] Interview with a senior official of China-ASEAN Chamber of Agricultural Commerce (CACAC), Nanning, Guangxi, 20 August, 2010

ASEAN members are all geographically located in Southeast Asia, where the tropical climate is suitable for tropical agricultural products such as vegetable grease, tropical fruits and tropical cereal etc. Most parts of China are located in the northern temperate zone, where the climate is suitable for temperate agricultural products such as temperate fruits and grain. China and ASEAN abound in different agricultural products due to their different geographical location and the subsequent different climate. This provides an extensive basis for bilateral trade exchanges and leads to a mutually complementary trading structure between the two sides.

ASEAN had a comparative advantage in land-intensive agricultural products given its small population with relatively large land area while China had comparative advantage in labour-intensive agricultural products, given the big population and cheap labour there (Qiu, Yang, & Huang, 2007, p. 57) (Tang, 2008, p. 5) (Liu, Huang, & Wang, 2006, pp. 35-38). China imported land-intensive products, in which ASEAN had advantages while ASEAN imported lots of labour-intensive products, in which China had advantages. This contributed to 'the mutual complementaity in terms of the agricultural trading structure (Geng, 2009, p. 59)' for the two sides. Although China had a deficit of trade in overall agricultural products with ASEAN, it had an increasing surplus of trade in the labour-intensive agricultural products. China had a trade surplus of 170 million US dollars in labour-intensive products with ASEAN in 2001, which increased to 630 million dollars in 2005. On the other hand, ASEAN had growing export values of land-intensive agricultural products with China. ASEAN exported 1,490 million dollars of land-intensive agricultural products to China in 2001, which grew to 3,950 million dollars in 2005. Both China and ASEAN exploited their respective advantages in agricultural products when trading with each other in agricultural goods. This led to a complementary trading structure of agriculture between the two sides.

In addition, China and ASEAN had mutual complementation in terms of agricultural mechanization and technological management (Wang C. , 2009, p. 36). There was a low degree of agricultural mechanization in four new ASEAN members, Vietnam, Laos, Cambodia and Myanmar. In contrast, China has obvious advantages on agricultural machinery and technology management. 'Both China and ASEAN are agricultural countries. In terms of agricultural mechanization and technological management, China is more sophisticated than ASEAN. Therefore, agricultural cooperation is more welcomed by ASEAN than in any other field.'[57]

Given the mutual complementarity in agricultural products, trading structure and agricultural mechanization and technological management, China and ASEAN agreed to designate the agricultural sector as one of the five priority cooperation areas at the 5th China-ASEAN Leaders Summit in November 2001 in Bandar Seri Begawan, Brunei. Besides, China and ASEAN endorsed the 'Memorandum of Understanding on Agricultural Cooperation (2002-2006)' at the 6th China-ASEAN Leaders Summit in Phnom Penh, Cambodia in November 2002. In addition, both sides agreed to implement the EHP to reduce the tariffs of more than 500 classifications of agricultural products 2003 before the Framework Agreement took actual effect. They endorsed the new 'Memorandum of Understanding on Agricultural Cooperation (2007-2011)' in a further effort to ensure a basis of understanding for bilateral economic cooperation on agriculture. These measures by the two sides benefited bilateral agricultural trade and domestic agricultural development in China and ASEAN.

The tariffs of most of the traded agricultural products were rapidly reduced to zero and bilateral agricultural trade saw a great increase after the Framework Agreement was signed in 2002. China and

---

[57] Interview with a senior official at the China-ASEAN Chamber of Agricultural Commerce in Nanning, Guangxi, 20 August, 2010

Thailand reduced the tariff of all included fruits and vegetables traded between them to zero in 1st October, 2003, according to the rules of the Agreement on Accelerated Tariff Elimination (AATE) subordinate to the EHP. Besides, China and the six old ASEAN members reduced the tariffs of all agricultural products included in EHP to zero in January 2006. China and the four new ASEAN members reduced the tariff of traded goods included in the EHP to zero in January 2010. Thus, the tariffs of all agricultural products, excluding the sensitive and exceptional classifications, were reduced to zero with the completion of the CAFTA on 1st January, 2010. This contributed to a great increase in the bilateral trade value of the agricultural products. The total trade in agricultural products between China and ASEAN reached approximately 6 billion U.S. dollars in 2002, and soared to 13.92 billion dollars in 2009, more than twice that in 2002. The substantially increasing bilateral trade value of agricultural products improved their status as major trading partners in agriculture. So far, ASEAN was the fourth biggest agricultural partner of China, following the US, Japan and EU. China was the second biggest agricultural partner of ASEAN and had considerable potential to be the first one in the near future.

7.3.2   The CAFTA Benefited China's Agriculture

ASEAN benefited from the bilateral agricultural cooperation. ASEAN significantly increased its exports volume of agricultural products to China and enjoyed a great deal of trade surplus in them. ASEAN obtained much more agricultural investment from Chinese companies, which were strongly encouraged by the central government to invest in ASEAN with the 'going out' strategy. ASEAN member countries upgraded their agricultural technology and improved their administrative standards by introducing them from China. In addition, net importing countries of the agricultural products, such as Singapore and Brunei, enjoyed a wider variety of agricultural products at a cheaper price though, when Chinese agricultural products flooded into their markets.

More importantly, China benefited from the bilateral agricultural cooperation in a strategic sense. On the one hand, China found another big market for Chinese agricultural products, apart from those in the western developed countries and found a potential investment destination for Chinese agriculture-related companies. Chinese exports of agricultural products encountered unprecedented technical barriers after China entered the WTO. According to statistics from the Ministry of Commerce of China, 90% of China's exporters of agricultural products were negatively influenced by foreign technical barriers and they suffered a loss of 9 billion U.S. dollars every year as a result of exporting goods that did not conform to the technical standard to Western markets. In contrast, ASEAN partners seldom operated technical barriers against China's agricultural exporters. 'The CAFTA opened a door for Chinese agricultural products by exploring another extensive market of ASEAN, within the context of numerous technical barriers on the international market (Xiao & Hu, 2006, p. 20).' According to statistics from the Nanning (China-ASEAN) Commodity Exchange (NCCE),

> *'the trade in agricultural products between China and ASEAN accounted for over 50% of total trades through the NCCE after the NCCE was established in 2006. Besides, the share is getting bigger every year; the rising trend of the trade in agricultural products is likely to maintain in the future because of China's great needs for agricultural products in general and food supplies in particular. There is a large population in China, albeit with a relatively small land. China's need for the food supplies are always the biggest one. Therefore, China imported a large quantity of food supplies from ASEAN. Some food*

supplies such as the rice from Thailand and Vietnam as well as starch from ASEAN are popularly welcomed (by Chinese people). Hence, the NCCE designated the trade in agricultural products as its main part.' [58]

In the meanwhile, ASEAN members hardly launched any protectionist measures of the agricultural trade against China, in contrast with the 707 cases of anti-dumping, countervailing and safeguard measures launched by the main importers of Chinese agricultural products in the West from the 1980s onward. This secured barrier-free access to the ASEAN market for Chinese agricultural exporters. In terms of investment, China benefited by taking ASEAN as a new investment destination of China's agriculture-related enterprises. China gave a considerably high priority to ASEAN among the investment destinations and encouraged Chinese enterprises to invest more in ASEAN, following the strategy of 'going out' implemented in 2000. As a result, most Chinese agriculture-related enterprises saw ASEAN as the first area of investment and went to ASEAN to invest.

On the other hand, the bilateral agricultural cooperation between China and ASAN strengthened ASEAN members' dependence on Chinese agricultural markets (Zhou, 2007, p. 28); and the cost of destroying the reliance increased to an unsustainable extent with the expanding and deepening of the bilateral cooperation, in interdependence theorist' words. Malaysia, Indonesia and Thailand are the first three biggest traders of Chinese agricultural products among ASEAN members. The agricultural trade value between the three members and China accounted for over 90% of the total trade value between China and ASEAN. For this reason, Malaysia, Indonesia and Thailand, are taken as examples here. Table 7.3 reveals the total values of the agricultural products of Malaysia, Indonesia and Thailand with the world and China's share in it, which suggests the increasing dependence of ASEAN on China's agricultural markets and sources. As to Malaysia, it exported 418 million dollars of agricultural products to China in 2001, or 7.86% of all its agricultural exports to the world. Its agricultural exports to China accounted for 17.42% of all the agricultural exports in 2009, about ten percent more than that in 2001. As to Indonesia, both its export and import share of China increased in 2009, among which the former increased from 3.37% in 2001 to 10.95% in 2009 and the latter grew from 9.73% in 2001 to 11. 65%. A similar trend happened in Thailand. Thailand exported 389 million dollars of agricultural products to China in 2001, or 3.89% of all its agricultural exports to the world, which rose to 5.7% in 2009. Thailand imported 123 million dollars worth of agricultural products from China in 2001, or 4.45% of all its agricultural imports, which grew to 9.90% in 2009, twice the level of 2001. Except for Malaysia's import trade value with China which declined a little, these three countries' trade value of agricultural products with China rose to varying degrees. China's agricultural products accounted for a bigger proportion in ASEAN's markets. ASEAN increasingly placed more dependence on Chinese agricultural products and China's agricultural market. This, more or less, alleviated China's worries about its agricultural exports and domestic agricultural development, which had been depressed by China's entry into the WTO.

---

[58] Interview with a senior official of the Nanning (China-ASEAN) Commodity Exchange, Nanning, Guangxi, China, 17 August, 2010

Table 7.3 Malaysia, Indonesia and Thailand's Agricultural Trade with World and China

		Malaysia			Indonesia			Thailand		
Malaysia, Indonesia and Thailand's Agricultural Trade with the World and China										
Year	Flows	Total Value (in million dollars) with the World	with China	Share	Total Value (in million dollars) with the World	with China	Share	Total Value (in million dollars) with the World	with China	Share
2001	Import	3,676	381	**10.35%**	2,771	270	**9.73%**	2,757	123	**4.45%**
	Export	5,320	418	**7.86%**	4,991	168	**3.37%**	9,990	389	**3.89%**
2009	Import	9,618	847	**8.81%**	7,827	912	**11.65%**	6,363	630	**9.90%**
	Export	17,601	3,066	**17.42%**	19,970	2,186	**10.95%**	22,111	1,258	**5.70%**

Source: UN COMTRADE Database and the UN Food and Agriculture Organization (FAO) countrySTAT Databse (compiled and computed by the author)

Notes: The agricultural products here only includes those types of S1-0 of Food and Live Animal, S1-1 of Beverage and Tobacco and S1-4 of Animal and Vegetable Oils Fats and Waxes.

The emphasis on the benefits the bilateral agricultural cooperation between China and ASEAN brought to China is not to deny the potential and real negative impacts on China's agriculture in general and agricultural development in southern China in particular. Southern provinces in China and ASEAN members had great similarity in their agricultural products, due to their similar geographical locations and similar climate. This intensified the competition in agricultural products and in particular posed severe challenges for the agriculture in Hainan province in Southeast China and Guangxi region in Southwest China. Two factors, however, eased people's fear over this issue. On the one hand, the agriculture in Hainan and Guangxi did not account for a high proportion of the trade in agricultural products of China as a whole; on the other hand, the central government in Beijing and local governments in Hainan and Guangxi took active measures to fight against the negative implications. For example, Hainan's banana production did not suffer a crushing defeat, despite the severe competition of Philippine's bananas. A major reason was that China Customs continued to collect the 17% of value-added tax on imported agricultural products, although China did give up the 10% custom tariff, strictly following the Framework Agreement. 'This value-added tax (played) a critical part in protecting the banana production in Hainan from the onslaught of the Philippines (Liao & Xia, 2008, p. 5)'. As to Guangxi, the local fruits were heavily shocked by imported fruits, particularly from Vietnam. 'On the one side, given the poor fruit processing industry in Vietnam, Guangxi is able to develop the processing industry to deeply process the fruits imported to Guangxi from Vietnam. On the other side, Guangxi is likely to act as the transition connection for trades by transporting the imported fruits to the whole of China. The trade in service with ASEAN is also a new economic growth source for Guangxi'.[59] Both Hainan and Guangxi found ways to fight against the impact on their agriculture by ASEAN.

As a matter of fact, a few ministries/commissions at the central level in Beijing argued for the CAFTA initiative before the CAFTA decision was made in 2001. The Ministry of Foreign Affairs (MFA), the Ministry of Foreign Trade and Economic Cooperation (MOFTEC) and the latter body of Ministry of

---

[59] Interview with an senior official of the China-ASEAN Business and Investment Summit Secretariat, Nanning, Guangxi, 19 August, 2010

Commerce (MOC), the Ministry of Agriculture (MOA), the State-owned Assets Supervision and Administration Commission (SASAC) and the National Development and Reforms Commission (NDRC) joined the hot argument for the CAFTA initiative. Among them, the MFA, MOFTEC and MOC were more liberal and the MOA, SASAC and NDRC were more conservative (Jiang Y. , 2010, pp. 241-250). In particular, the MOFTEC and the MOA were the most related stakeholder for this FTA initiative. The former asserted Beijing would benefit economically from the CAFTA initiative in a long term while the latter were concerned that China's agriculture sector would suffer from the cooperation between China and ASEAN in consideration of the comparative disadvantage of China's agricultural products. 'Both the MOA and local governments were concerned, but they were told by Premier Zhu to look at the big picture of China's national interests and by MOFCOM to calculate the total balance sheet of imports and exports (Jiang Y. , 2010, p. 243)'. Then they got to an agreement for the CAFTA initiative and they decided to intensify economic relations with ASEAN in spite of the potentially negative implications on China's agricultural sector.

Therefore, it is not certain that the benefits the enhanced agricultural cooperation between China and ASEAN provided are able to offset the negative influence China's commitments within the WTO framework brought about. It is risky to make such a judgment in terms of the relatively small market scale of the ASEAN members in comparison with that in the developed countries of the western world. However, the agricultural cooperation between China and ASEAN, to some extent, ideally balanced and partly diminished the negative influences China's accession to the WTO brought about by finding a new trading market and a new investment destination for China's agricultural products and its agriculture-related companies, let alone the better economic relations between China and ASEAN through agricultural cooperation. To summarize, China's agricultural cooperation with ASEAN is not only the inevitable need for the sustainable development of Chinese agriculture and the development of agricultural enterprises, but also the need for foreign policy (Chen & Lv, 2009, p. 46).

7.4   Conclusion

As analysed above, China initiated regional economic cooperation in that it adopted regional diplomacy and the limitation of the world market within the framework of the WTO. China's entry into the WTO remarked the new stage of China's opening up. The disparity between West China and East China and the gap of income and development between urban and rural areas were given first priority in Beijing's agenda of domestic reforms.

The economic cooperation between China and ASEAN and the completion of the CAFTA built up China's issue-initiating capability and tested the capability through the practice of CAFTA over ten years. China created a domino effect in East Asia by initiating economic cooperation in the form of FTAs. Japan and Korea launched negotiations with ASEAN to set up bilateral FTAs shortly after China's proposal of the CAFTA. China made a great economic concession in negotiating with ASEAN for the CAFTA by fully opening the agricultural market and designating agriculture as one of the five cooperative pillars between China and ASEAN. This stood in marked contrast to Japan and Korea, who were not willing to open their agricultural markets to ASEAN. That is a major reason why the quality of ASEAN-Japan Comprehensive Economic Partnership Agreement (AJCEP) and Korea-ASEAN Comprehensive Cooperation Partner Agreement (KACPA) were criticized. Despite this, the economic cooperation among East Asian countries helped increase members' overall economic strength, built up their capability of making a larger voice in the world and created the eventual tripod era in the world, together with Western Europe and North America.

In addition, China was well placed as the third leader for East Asian regionalism since the Second War ended, after a decade of economic cooperation in East Asia in 2000s. China, following Japan in the 1960s and 1970s with the flying-geese programme and America in the 1980s and 1990s with APEC, proved to be the one who was capable of leading economic cooperation to make great achievements in economic development in East Asia. Bilateral economic cooperation between China and ASEAN, as the substance of the regional economic integration in East Asia, reflected four features of East Asian regional integration drew a gradual future for it and led to the third way to come. Economic cooperation within the ASEAN+1 and ASEAN+3, as represented in the bilateral cooperation between China and ASEAN, suggested a slow, if not at a stagnant, future for the East Asian region. ASEAN was in a dilemma between the East Asian Free Trade Area (EAFTA) initiated by China and the Comprehensive Economic Partnership in East Asia (CEPEA) initiated by Japan. This forced the third way to come. The three Northeast Asian countries would enter into economic cooperation without ASEAN before the ASEAN Community was founded.

8 East Asian Economic Integration: Features and Future

In the late 1990s, East Asian economic integration evolved in a swift and intensified manner driven by the strong momentum provided by the 1997-8 AFC. East Asia grew from a region where there was no PTA before the AFC to be a vibrant region with over forty PTA/FTA agreements between/among various members after the crisis. The 1997-8 AFC not only provided the impetus for regional economic integration in East Asia, but also acted as the watershed for it. This was embodied through the changes of the geographical scope within which economic integration burgeoned, the workable framework within which regional cooperation took place, the role of the engine and the role of the leader. Before the crisis, the geographical scope of regional integration was trans-oceanic/ Asia-Pacific. Thereafter, geographically it retracted into East Asia. The APEC, which used to act as a cooperative platform before the crisis, was marginalized and replaced by the ASEAN+3 mechanism after the crisis. ASEAN, which was overshadowed by the APEC before the crisis, played the role of engine for the economic integration in East Asia after the crisis. Japan and the United States used to play the leading role by originally initiating and managing to launch the cooperative proposals in the 1970s, 1980s and 1990s, while China rose to lead the economic integration in East Asia after the crisis. In a word, China led the East Asian economic integration within the framework of ASEAN+3 after the crisis, with ASEAN as the engine.

On the way to economic integration in East Asia, there emerged four features in contrast with the economic integration in West Europe and North America. Firstly, there was the absence of an unqualified leader in East Asian economic integration; moreover, there was no powerful engine for regional economic integration in East Asia; in addition, regionalism driven by nation-states accounted for more of the progress in economic integration, although regionalization also burgeoned; and finally, East Asian countries preferred bilateralism rather than multilateralism as the main substructure of economic integration, although the latter also started.

With regard to the first feature, China played a leading role in the integration process, based on its significance in regional trade and investment cooperation and the great economic concessions it made to ASEAN. However, China was not an unqualified leader. First of all, China was motivated by a series of domestic problems and the consequent inward-looking policy when initiating regional cooperative proposals in the East Asian region. As a result of the reform and opening up implemented in the late 1970s, China encountered severe disparities not only between East and West China but also between the urban and the rural at home. In order to mitigate the disparities, China chose to establish the CAFTA in a more liberal manner. The establishment of the CAFTA marked a new stage of China's opening up, however it was implemented with a view to solving the domestic problems caused by the intensified reforms. With such inward-looking motives, China was not able to take the responsibility of an unqualified leader with a regional mission. In addition, there were many other external factors which constrained China from a full endeavour as a leader. The cliché of the 'China threat' was one of them. China, taking great efforts to avoid the resurgence of the 'China threat', kept a low profile in the region. In the meanwhile, the United States and Japan were competing with China for the leadership in East Asia. China's role as the leader in East Asian economic integration, based on the inward-looking motives and constrained by external factors, was important determinant of the incremental approach to integration in East Asia.

With respect to the second feature, the France-Germany axis acted as the engine of the integration process in Western Europe after they reconciled in the wake of the Second World War. However, in East Asia, since it was unlikely that China and Japan would overcome their painful history, rebuild political confidence and cooperate on economic issues soon, ASEAN had to play the role of the engine. However it adopted an incremental way to promote regional economic integration in East Asia, as it did in Southeast Asia. First of all, ASEAN members are usually divided into two groups: ASEAN-6 (including the six original members of ASEAN) and CLMV (four new members of ASEAN) according to their development stages. Thus the CLMV group could enjoy flexibility in the timetable for completing the FTA. Moreover, all traded products were divided into different classifications to follow different timetable for phase-out of tariffs. In order to bridge the development gap between the original members and the new members, it made sense for ASEAN to do this. However, its direct result was that the whole process of East Asian economic integration could only evolve in an incremental way.

Regarding to the third feature, the integration process developed quickly in West Europe because regionalization moved faster than regionalism. Those MNCs provided critical impetus to promote the integration process, and many elites who insisted on a fast integration process also derived from MNCs. In East Asia, inadequate participation of non-government actors was the third feature in regional economic integration.

As to the fourth feature, due to lacking experience in multilateral interactions, East Asian countries were reluctant to launch multilateral negotiations and cooperation. They would rather negotiate and sign bilateral agreements one by one than launch multilateral negotiations and endorse multilateral agreements.

This chapter has five sections. The first section investigates the first feature related to China's role. It offers an analysis of China's role as the leader in East Asian economic integration. Although China's role in bilateral trade and investment cooperation with ASEAN has been analysed in two previous chapters, it is further defined as the leader of the region-wide integration at the regional level in East Asia. Then evidence is supplied to support the argument that China is not an unqualified leader that could achieve the regional mission because of its inward-looking motives, its diplomatic profile of 'never claim leadership' and some other external constraints. The second section refers to the second feature related to ASEAN's role. ASEAN's role was investigated in the previous chapter related to ASEAN's economic policy after it diverted from an inward-looking policy to an outward-looking one, which provided a powerful driving force for economic integration not only in Southeast Asia but also in East Asia. Here, ASEAN is further defined as less-than-powerful-engine given ASEAN's incremental way of implementing regional cooperation and integration. The third section presents clear proofs for the third feature that the regionalism accounts for more than the regionalization in East Asian integration. The fourth section discusses the features of bilateralism and multilateralism in East Asian economic integration. Both of them are sub structures in East Asian integration, and the former is preferred to the latter by East Asian countries. The last section concludes the chapter with some discussion about the future of regional economic integration in East Asia. Three issues are considered: Will the US be included or excluded from economic integration in East Asia? Will ASEAN+3 or the East Asia Summit (EAS) be the key framework for economic integration in East Asia? And which proposal will be chosen by ASEAN as the main cooperative programme when promoting economic integration in East Asia- the China-initiated EAFTA or the Japan-initiated Comprehensive Economic Partnership in East Asia (CEPEA)?

8.1   China: Not an Unqualified Leader

A plethora of academic works sought to clearly define China's role in East Asian economic integration. Most scholars agreed that China held a special status in East Asian cooperation mechanisms and economic integration; however, they were very cautious not to make the conclusion that China was a universally acknowledged leader. For example, it was argued by some scholars that China played 'a constructive role in regional economic and political affairs (Vatikiotis, 2003, p. 68).' Moreover, it was claimed by some scholars that China 'plays an important and constructive role (Luo, 2001, p. 24)' in regional cooperation as well. In addition, 'China is supposed to play the centric role in East Asia (Pang, 2001, p. 29)'. In other words, China's role was 'critical in promoting East Asian regional cooperation. As a regional great power in general and an influential great power in particular, China was the backbone to promote regional cooperation and development (Zhang, 2001, p. 24)'. Some staff from the Research Institute of Economy, Trade and Industry (REITI), sited in Japan, contended that 'China, which hopes to form at some point a counter power comparable to the U.S. and Europe by uniting Asian countries, has become an advocate of East Asia-wide integration (Naoko, 2002, p. 11).' In contrast, some scholars make a more precise identification for China's role by concluding that 'China, perhaps, can assume the lead role in the future (Harvie & Lee, 2002, p. 22)'. After nearly a decade's development of East Asian integration, based on the facts during the past decade, we have more reasons to argue that China played a *de facto* leading role in regional economic integration in East Asia.

8.1.1   China: a de *facto* leading role

First of all, China impressed all neighbouring countries with its huge economic capacity and dynamic, stable and long-term economic development at a rapid pace. After the reform and opening-up policy was implemented in the late 1970s, China went through fast economic growth for more than three decades. The average annual GDP growth for 1978-2009 period was over 9%. China was the engine of the economic miracle in East Asian and beyond. Now, China is the second biggest economy in the world, and will definitely be among the most important economies in East Asian economic integration. In addition, China has the biggest population, which constitutes one of the biggest markets in the world, and attracts more and more partner countries to trade/invest in China.

Furthermore, China held a significant position in trade and investment cooperation in East Asia. According to data from the Bureau of Statistics of China in 2010, China is the third biggest trading partner of ASEAN. According to the trade statistics from the Ministry of Finance, Japan in 2006, and China was the first biggest trading partner of Japan. According to trade statistics from South Korea Trade-Investment Promotion Agency (KOTRA) in 2008, China was the biggest trading partner of South Korea. Based on the statistics from 'the Ministry of Economic Affairs, ROC', Taiwan in 2004, mainland China was the biggest trading partner of Taiwan. Based on the trade statistics from the Trade and Industry Department, the Government of the Hong Kong Special Administrative Region (Hong Kong SAR), mainland China had been the biggest trading partner of Hong Kong since 1985. In the meanwhile, China continued to be one of the main investment sources for ASEAN, Hong Kong and Taiwan. Generally speaking, China was one of the most important trading and investing partners for most East Asian countries. This laid a solid foundation for China's leading role in East Asian economic integration.

Thirdly, China cultivated the capability to initiate cooperative proposals of economic integration in East Asia. It originally proposed to set up the first FTA in East Asia in 2000 and virtually completed it in 2010. China's move on FTA in the region caused a 'domino effect'. Shortly after China's proposal, both South Korea and Japan took similar initiatives with ASEAN as well, and they finally concluded negotiations respectively in 2005 and 2008. In addition to the proposal of CAFTA, China also took the initiative in conducting a joint research on the feasibility of a free trade area among the three great powers in Northeast Asia at the 5th Leaders Summit of China, Japan and South Korea in 2003. China's striking move, reflecting its proposal-initiating capability, was its suggestion of considering the feasibility of the East Asia Free Trade Area (EAFTA) at the 6th ASEAN+3 Summit among leaders of ASEAN, China, Japan and South Korea in 2002. In the next few years, at every ASEAN+3 Summit, China's leaders always underlined the far-reaching implications of the EAFTA for East Asian economic integration and the necessity of conducting research on its feasibility, moreover, China urged that any efforts necessary to be made make it happen (Wen, 2003) (Wen, 2004) (Wen, 2005) (Wen, 2007). In this regard, the East Asian Vision Group (EAVG) and East Asian Studies Group (EASG) were assigned as task force to investigate the feasibility of such a FTA. Ultimately, the EASG's report supporting the establishment of such an FTA was rejected by the EAVG because 'Tokyo saw such a FTA in a mid- to long-term perspective (Naoko, 2002, p. 12)'. Then the EAFTA was brought to a standstill temporarily. However, this cannot stop the EAFTA from being completed in the future. The 4th and 5th EAS in 2009 and 2010 made it clear that the EAFTA proposal would be examined and considered again[60]. This not only exemplified China's capability of proposal-initiating but also vividly illustrated China's unremitting efforts to make the proposal into reality.

Finally, China contributed significantly to bridging the development gap among East Asian countries by making great economic concessions to those relatively underdeveloped countries. Singapore was accused of 'offering almost nothing to the poorer states (Ravenhill, 1995, p. 864)', which undermined its status as an unqualified leader in ASEAN integration. China's concessions when negotiating the CAFTA with ASEAN members stood in stark contrast to Singapore. First of all, China promised to give the MFN treatment to those ASEAN countries who are not WTO members. Moreover, ASEAN-4 members have another five years to finally complete their free trade area with China in 2015. In addition, ASEAN-4 were allowed to set out their exclusion list of products which would be exempted by China in the EHP programme, and ASEAN-6 were permitted to list their specific products which should not be excluded from the EHP by China. In fact, China made unilateral economic concessions not only to the relatively underdeveloped ASEAN-4 members but also to the other relatively developed ASEAN-6 members. 'China's attention to ASEAN as a group is a welcome boost, in that it has helped to renew the third-party interest in ASEAN, and because it signals China's recognition of ASEAN's value as a collective entity (Ba, 2003, p. 642)'. Finally, apart from the economic concession to ASEAN, China provided more aid to ASEAN after the 2008 global financial crisis broke out. In April 2009, China earmarked funds of 10 billion US dollars and declared the foundation of the China-ASEAN Investment Fund, with a view to supporting the development of local resources, energy, transportation, communication, water conservancy, electric power, aerospace, modern agriculture and so forth in ASEAN. Besides, China also supplied 15 billion dollars of credit loans to ASEAN and another 207 million RMB of special assistance to less developed ASEAN members in a bid to show China's sincere determination and courage to fight against the global crisis together with ASEAN.

8.1.2   China: Not a Unqualified Leader

The aforementioned four reasons provided evidence for the argument that China was the *de facto* leader in East Asian economic integration. However, when we analysed its role within a theoretical framework of Complex interdependence, we found that it was not an unqualified leader because of a number of internal and external factors. One of the internal factors referred to China's inward-looking motives behind its regional proposals. As analysed in the Chapter Six, four key factors prompted China to shift its attitude towards East Asian economic integration. First and foremost, China shifted its grand strategy. Beijing put forth a New Concept of Security, claiming that periphery stability was a *sine qua non* of China's economic security. Not seeing the possibility of economic cooperation among three Northeast Asian nations, China engaged ASEAN in Southeast Asia. Moreover, the establishment of the CAFTA was anticipated to develop Southwest China, part of West China, where many minorities lived and the local economy lagged far behind that of East China. Thirdly, in order to offset the negative influence of China's entry into the WTO

---

[60] See Chairman's Statement of the 4th East Asia Summit, Cha-am Hua Hin, Thailand, 25 October, 2009 and Chairman's Statement of the 5th East Asia Summit (EAS), Ha Noi, Vietnam, 30 October, 2010.

on domestic agriculture, agriculture was designated as the first priority area in the economic cooperation between China and ASEAN. The mutual complementarity in the agriculture sector between two sides was conducive to agricultural development and to narrowing the urban-rural disparity at home in China. Finally, Beijing anticipated as an indirect result of the CAFTA, Taiwan's status would be further dwarfed and paved the way for eventual resolution of Taiwan issue. In sum, Beijing's motives for shifting its attitudes toward East Asian economic cooperation were rooted deeply in its eagerness to resolve domestic problems rather than to focus on the regional mission of East Asian economic integration. On the contrary, regional integration was expected to serve China by maintaining regional economic prosperity and political stability.

The other internal factor was related to China's grand strategy of 'peaceful rising' and the diplomatic guideline put forward by Deng Xiaoping, the core of the second generation of leaders of China. The 'peaceful rising' was in details in Chapter of Literature Review; so it was not iterated here. This guideline, which became known as the '28 Character' strategy, denoted to 'observe calmly, stand firmly, respond carefully, hide the light, be good at maintaining a low profile, never claim leadership and make some contributions' (冷静观察、稳住阵脚、沉着应付、绝不当头、韬光养晦、善于守拙、有所作为). The strategy, which was put forth after the Tiananmen Square Incident took place in 1989 and the world/region underwent radical changes, guided China's diplomatic and security policy during the next decades. Although certain aspects of this strategy have been debated in recent years, -namely the relative emphasis placed upon 'never claim leadership' or 'make some contributions', taken as a whole, the strategy suggested both a short-term desire to downplay China's ambitions and a long-term strategy to build up China's power to maximize options for the future. Therefore, at the moment, China has no desire to take on the responsibility as the leader in East Asian economic integration because to claim the leadership would absolutely go against its diplomatic guideline and the 'peaceful rising' strategy. In addition, China made great efforts to convince its neighbours that China was a responsible great power after the 1997-8 AFC. China did not want to claim the leadership in East Asia to avoid the probable resurgence of 'China threat' fears. If it was the case that East Asian economic integration depended on 'China's desire to act the role of a regional great power (Kim, 2004)', then the whole process would be gradual and incremental, because China did not think the time was ripe for it to claim such a leadership. Last but not lease, China's brand 'FTA Strategy' (Hu, 2007) considered it necessary to establish FTA with economic partners not only in East Asia but beyond. China had no intention to put all the eggs (FTA) in the same basket (East Asia). Besides the CAFTA, China took efforts to establish FTA with economic partners in Europe and Africa. In East Asia, China was accustomed to acting as a supporter of ASEAN. China supported ASEAN to play a positive (Jiang, 1997)/important (Zhu, 2000)/main (Wen, 2003)/central (Wen, 2010) and even the dominant role (Wen, 2004) (Wen, 2005) in regional cooperative mechanism and regional cooperation process. In the meanwhile, China promised not to seek for any special status and never to claim hegemony (Zhu, 1999). China's support for ASEAN to take the dominant role, on the one hand, saved China the embarrassment of claiming the leadership, and on the other hand, excluded the possibility of anyone else's claiming the leadership.

The United States and Japan were competing with China for the leadership in East Asian economic integration. This constituted the external factor why China could not take full leading responsibility in economic cooperation in East Asia. More precisely, the US was an extra-regional great power beyond East Asia. However, this did not hinder the US from playing a critical role in East Asia. In the security field, the US-led bilateral security alliance system remained dominant till present and the US was the key to stability of Asia (Kreft, 2004, p. 50). Although the US's role in economic cooperation was not as important as it was in the security field, its role in the economic field still cannot be overlooked. During the Clinton administration (1993-2001), the US made an attempt to utilize APEC as the main instrument to push trade liberalization in Asia Pacific. This made the APEC maximize its role in trade liberalization in Asia-Pacific region during the Clinton administration. Nevertheless, the APEC did not perform a role as active as expected when the 1997-8 AFC broke out. At the APEC Summit in Vancouver Canada in 1997 shortly after the crisis began, the US led Summit leaders to focus on the EVSL programme instead of working out any arrangement to prevent the AFC from quickly spreading. East Asian countries and ASEAN in particular were extremely disappointed at the US and the APEC's apathetic response to the 1997-8 AFC. What made them despair more was the US-led IMF's securing a package for South Korea, Indonesia and Thailand. The IMF's prescription required reducing the governmental budget, implementing high interest rates, and restricting imports of certain industrial products etc., which caused region-wide 'resentment' (Richard, 1998, p. 333) in East Asia. Hence, the US's and APEC's influence in East Asia dropped and the US's diminished because it was excluded from the newly emerging ASEAN+3 cooperative mechanism.

However, as the biggest economy in the world, the US's role in East Asia cannot be overlooked. According to data from China Customs, the Unites States is the second biggest trade partner of China in 2010. According to the trade statistics from the Association for the Promotion of International Trade, Japan (JAPIT), the US was the second biggest trade partner of Japan, only next to China in 2010. According to the statistics from the Trade-Investment Promotion Agency (KOTRA) sited in South Korea in 2008, the US was the second biggest trade partner of South Korea, again only next to China. Meanwhile, the US was the biggest single export destination and the biggest single source country of foreign investment for China and ASEAN beyond East Asian region. In terms of the role in trade and investment exchange with its East Asian partners, the US played a no less important role than China did. Moreover, after Barack Obama became president in 2009, the US showed an obvious intention to come back to East Asia by sending an ambassador to ASEAN (this was delayed indefinitely during Bush Administration), signing the TAC with ASEAN in 2009 (this was declined by the US during the Bush Administration as well) and sending representatives to attend the EAS (for the first time in history) in 2010. When attending the 14th ASEAN Summit in Thailand in 2009, Hillary Clinton, the US Secretary of State, made it clear that she strongly believed 'the US (would) become more involved in things in the region (East Asia)' and she declared 'the United States is back! (Burns, 22 July, 2009)'. It was imagined that China would be further constrained from having the leading role in regional economic integration in East Asia when the US's diminished involvement in East Asia integration was revived. The US, however, preferred trade liberalization in the scope of Asia Pacific within APEC to regional integration in the scope of East Asia within the framework of ASEAN plus Three/One. At the APEC conference in November 2009, the US declared its joining the TPP agreement, which the US used as an instrument to cope with the East Asian cooperation process (Shen, 2010). 'It is too early to presume the effectiveness of the TPP and that what is the US's next plan to contest the leadership of economic cooperation in Asia-Pacific region. However, it is sure that the US will not be mute at the restructuring of the economic order in East Asia/Asia-Pacific. Its first move was to join the TPP agreement, further became the dominant force in it with a view to making it the rudiment of an Asia-Pacific FTA led by the US'[61]. This will further constrain China's fully taking the leading responsibility in economic integration in East Asia.

Japan is another alternative for leader in economic integration in East Asia. 'Japanese government could not afford to let China gain an uncontested leadership position in the (East Asian) region (Stubbs, 2002, p. 443)'. As a matter of fact, Japan desired the status of leader for decades. During the 1960s and 1970s, Japan led the East Asia march on the way to economic integration with the 'flying goose' programme. During the 1997-8 AFC, 'Japan did demonstrate instances of leadership... Most significant was Japan's

---

[61] Interview with an official of Institute of the American Studies, CICIR, Beijing, 12 July, 2010

AMF (Asian Monetary Fund) proposal, with an anticipated $100 billion in funding, which gained wide support from key Asian countries (Ba, 2003, p. 636).' However, the proposal was aborted because of the strong objection from the US and China. In this regard, the US would have liked to handle the East Asian financial crisis within the securing package of the IMF instead of the East Asia's own survival plan. As to China, it was trying to avoid Japan's leadership in dealing with the crisis and the Japanese Yen's domination in East Asia.

To some extent, the 1997-8 AFC was the turning point for the exchange of the old leadership of Japan and the new leadership of China. When Japan's proposal was rejected by the US and China during the crisis, China accumulated capacity and capability to act as the leader. During the crisis, China convinced its Southeast Asian neighbours of its 'responsible great power' image by promising not to devalue the Chinese RMB and providing financial support to crisis-hit countries-Indonesia and Malaysia. China's initiative in proposing the CAFTA made Japan feel that it lagged behind China. Soon, Japan put forth a similar proposal to ASEAN in the hope of setting up a free trade area between Japan and ASEAN. Nevertheless, the bilateral negotiations between Japan and ASEAN at one point came to a stalemate because of the differences over how to proceed with the talks. 'Japan hoped to prioritize signing bilateral free trade accords with the advanced ASEAN economies and to combine them later into a single FTA with the regional entity, without impairing the bilateral pacts. But ASEAN felt such negotiation tactics could split them and reduce their bargaining power (S.a., April 10, 2006).' Most importantly ASEAN thought Japan's negotiation tactics ran counter to ASEAN's objective of bridging the development gap between the advanced economies and the relatively underdeveloped economies in ASEAN. The ASEAN-Japan Comprehensive Economic Partnership Agreement (AJCEP) was finally endorsed in April 2008 after the negations resumed in 2006. However, the quality of the AJCEP was generally criticized because Japan refused to open its agricultural and fishery market. In the Framework Agreement between China and ASEAN, five priority cooperative sectors were designated, with the first priority given to the agriculture, which was initiated by ASEAN. In contrast, in the AJCEP between Japan and ASEAN, the sector of agriculture, fisheries and forestry ranks tenth among the total thirteen priority areas in which Japan and ASEAN would give priority to undertake economic cooperation activities. This reflected Japan's 'continued reluctance to liberalize agriculture' (Lincoln, 2010, p. 166) (Ba, 2003, p. 636) and unwillingness to open its agricultural market to its ASEAN partners. As a matter of fact, Japan has never opened its agricultural, fishery or forestry markets to any economic partners. When the US initiated the EVSL within the framework of APEC in the late 1990s, Japan refused because it included the sectoral liberalization of fisheries and forestry. Similarly, Japan seemed unlikely to make any concessions on agricultural, fishery or forestry cooperation with ASEAN this time. Given the fact that most ASEAN members are agricultural countries and great importance was attached to agricultural cooperation by ASEAN, the AJCEP was easily accused of poor quality. Therefore, the AJCEP could not play such an important role as the Framework Agreement between China and ASEAN did in promoting East Asian economic integration. Based on a similar reason, Japan seemed powerless in leading the economic integration in East Asia. However, the last thing Japan would like to see is China seized the leadership. Therefore, Japan would try every means to stop this happening, which constituted another external factor constraining China from taking responsibility for leadership in economic integration in East Asia.

In summary, although China had a leading influence on East Asian economic integration after the 1997-8 AFC, there was still no unqualified leader in East Asia (Zhu N. , 2004, p. 35), owing to some internal and external factors. The internal factors included China's inward-looking motives to mitigate the domestic problems by regional economic cooperation and its strategic guide-line of 'never claim leadership'. The external factors referred to the US's reconciliation to being marginalized in the process of economic

167

integration in East Asia and Japan's competition for the leadership. Those factors constrained China from taking the full responsibility and playing an unqualified role as the leader. Hence, there was an incremental economic integration in East Asia

8.2   ASEAN: A Weak Engine

As analysed in Chapter Three, ASEAN acted as the engine for East Asian economic integration because it shifted its inward-looking economic policy into an outward-looking one. It focused on the economic integration process not only in Southeast Asia but also in East Asia after the 1997-8 AFC, and provided a strong momentum for East Asian economic integration. Before the 1997-8 AFC, ASEAN focused more on intra-ASEAN economic integration in Southeast Asia. The financial crisis made ASEAN aware of the urgent need to cooperate with its neighbours in Northeast Asia to fight against the shocks of liberalization and globalization in the future. Therefore, during the crisis, ASEAN developed cooperation with China, Japan and South Korea, starting from the financial cooperation within the framework of the ASEAN+3. The framework of ASEAN+3, with ASEAN as the basis and the centre, became one of the cooperation mechanisms in East Asia. In return, through the cooperation within the frameworks based on and centric at ASEAN, ASEAN reaffirmed its role as the engine of regional economic integration in East Asia.

Above all, ASEAN has wealthy experience in (sub) regional economic integration when trying to establish AFTA. Through decades of integration from the 1960s onward, ASEAN accumulated experience in regional economic integration, which happened to be what the other three great powers in Northeast Asia lacked. This laid a solid foundation for ASEAN integration to exert a model influence on a wider economic integration in East Asia. During the negotiations, ASEAN provided the AFTA agreement as the text template for bilateral agreement between China and ASEAN, because China did not have any agreement template. For example, both China and ASEAN agreed to use the Framework Agreement on ASEAN Investment Area (FA-AIA) as a template for the negotiated investment agreement at the China-ASEAN Trade Negotiations Committee Working Group on Investment (TNC-WGI). In contrast with ASEAN, who was more sophisticated in multilateral negotiations in trade and investment cooperation, 'China lacks both experienced and textual basis to serve as reference (Chen, 2006, p. 6)'. Given that the CAFTA was the first free trade area between China and its economic partner, this was not hard to understand. As a result of following ASEAN's experience in economic integration, 'the CAFTA architecture and many of the provisions contained therein are largely inherited from the ASEAN Free Trade Area (AFTA) (INAMA, 2005, p. 559)'. And obviously, the CAFTA architecture was the model for the Japan-ASEAN Comprehensive Economic Partnership (JACEP) and South Korea-ASEAN FTA (KAFTA) architectures. During the negotiations between ASEAN and the other two partners-Japan and South Korea, it was obvious that the Framework Agreement on Comprehensive Economic Cooperation between China and ASEAN (CA-FACEC) acted as the text template for them. The JACEP and the Framework Agreement on Comprehensive Economic Cooperation between South Korea and ASEAN (KA-FACEC) also followed CA-FACEP although they also made some complementation, adjustment and deletion to it case by case. For example, 'the different stages of economic development among ASEAN Member States and the need for flexibility' was recognized and underlined in all CA-FACEC, KA-FACEC and JACEP.[62] As to the objectives of these agreements, one of them in the CA-FACEC was to 'facilitate the more effective

---

[62] See the Preamble of Article One in The Framework Agreement on Comprehensive Economic Cooperation between ASEAN and China, Phnom Penh, Cambodia, 4 November, 2002; The Framework Agreement on Comprehensive Economic Cooperation between South Korea and ASEAN, Kuala Lumpur, Malaysia, 13 December, 2005; and the Article Two in The Agreement on Comprehensive Economic Partnership Among Japan and ASEAN, Tokyo, Japan, April 2008

economic integration of the newer ASEAN Member States and bridge the development gap among Parties'[63]. There was an exactly similar description in the KA-FACEC, that one of the objectives was to 'facilitate the more effective economic integration of the new ASEAN Member countries and bridge the development gap between the Parties'[64] The JACEP also had the same regulations, stating that one of its objectives was 'supporting ASEAN economic integration, bridging the development gap among ASEAN Member states'.[65] By emphasizing the intra-ASEAN imbalance in economic development and setting similar objectives to take care of ASEAN's imbalance in three agreements respectively with China, Japan and South Korea of FTA, ASEAN made itself the 'FTA hub' (Bui, 2008, p. 29) of the agreements and 'the integration hub in East Asia' (Kwon, Winter 2004, p. 93) (Kawai & Wignaraja, 2009, p. 3).

However, ASEAN did not focus solely on East Asia economic integration. When ASEAN chose economic partners to establish free trade areas in East Asia, it also took into consideration the possible free trade areas with India, Australia and New Zealand in the wider Asia-Pacific region. After negotiations, ASEAN endorsed the FTA agreement with Australia and New Zealand together. As a result, with ASEAN as the centre, there emerged two concentric circles of FTA. In the first was the East Asia FTA circle, where there were three bilateral FTA agreements between ASEAN and China/Japan/South Korea. In the second was the Asia-Pacific FTA circle, where there were the agreement between ASEAN and India and the agreement among ASEAN, Australia and New Zealand. This suggested that ASEAN's FTA policy included, but was not limited to East Asia; it transcended the geographical scope of East Asia and reached Asia-Pacific. Thus, ASEAN's focus on regional economic integration in East Asia was distracted by the wider integration process in the wider Asia Pacific, let alone its incremental way of promoting integration in East Asia. Particularly when it came to the second decade of the 21st century, ASEAN readjusted the geographical scope of its focus. Susilo Bambang Yudhoyono, the President of Indonesia and the current Chairman of ASEAN pointed out in early 2011 that 'ASEAN can help shape and evolve the larger regional architecture in the Asia-Pacific' (Susilo, Feb 24, 2011), which presaged there was a great possibility that ASEAN would shift its geographical focus to Asia-Pacific region from East Asian region.

Although it acted as the engine, ASEAN adopted an incremental way, as it did with ASEAN integration in Southeast Asia, to promote the integration process in East Asia. When establishing the AFTA, ASEAN divided its ten members into two groups of ASEAN-6 and CLMV based on the difference in economic development stage among members. The two groups of members followed different timetables to complete the FTA; the ASEAN-6 was planned to complete the establishment of the AFTA by 2003 while the CLMV was planned by 2008, giving the relatively underdeveloped members additional five years for adoption of the agreement. This approach was also transplanted in regional economic integration in East Asia. When negotiating to establish the CAFTA, the ten ASEAN members were divided into two groups as well. The group of ASEAN-6 was planned to set up the FTA with China in 2010, while the CLMV was planned to by 2015. When establishing the KAFTA between South Korea and ASEAN, the ten ASEAN members were divided into three groups. The ASEAN-6 would complete the FTA with South Korea by 2012, Vietnam by 2018 and the remaining three relatively underdeveloped countries by 2020. The JAFTA adopted the similar groupings, ASEAN-6 to establish the FTA with Japan within 10 years after the JACEP agreement took effect, Vietnam within 15 years and the remaining three members within 18 years. These grouping were

---

[63] See Article One in The Framework Agreement on Comprehensive Economic Cooperation between ASEAN and China, Phnom Penh, Cambodia, 4 November, 2002
[64] See Article One in The Framework Agreement on Comprehensive Economic Cooperation between South Korea and ASEAN, Kuala Lumpur, Malaysia, 13 December, 2005
[65] See Article Three in The Agreement on Comprehensive Economic Partnership Among Japan and ASEAN, Tokyo, Japan, April, 2008

based on the various economic development stages of members. ASEAN'S adoption of an incremental approach to regional economic integration aimed to narrow the development gap between the ASEAN-6 and newer CLMV members.

The classifications of traded goods, whose tariffs were supposed to be reduced, are another illustration of ASEAN's incremental approach. When negotiating to establish AFTA, ASEAN classified traded goods into three kinds: protected ones, temporarily protected ones and sensitive ones, according to their possible response to the importation of foreign goods after the FTA was established. Different classifications follow different tariff-reduction plans. During negotiation of the CAFTA between China and ASEAN, they classified the traded goods into Normal Track and Sensitive Products. The former was further divided into Track One products and Track Two products, which had the common objective of reducing the tariff to zero, but Track Two products enjoyed more flexibility in timing of tariff reduction. The latter was further divided into two groups as well: the generally sensitive products and highly sensitive products. Both of them followed different tariff-reduction timetables in ASEAN-6 members and CLMV members. In the EHP, ASEAN members were allowed to have their Exclusive list, of products on which tariffs were not anticipated to reduce to a great extent.[66] Besides with the CAFTA, the incremental promotion of regional economic integration was adopted with the KAFTA and JAFTA. In light of the base tariffs and the tariff-reduction speed, traded goods are classified into categories indicated with 'A' 'B' 'C' 'R' 'X'. Take the schedule of tariff reduction for various categories in Cambodia as an example. The tariff of goods indicated with 'A' shall be eliminated as from the date of entry into force of the JACEP agreement; the tariffs on 'B' shall be eliminated in accordance with a specific schedule agreed by Cambodia and Japan; tariffs on 'C' shall apply at the base rates as from the date of entry into force of the JACEP agreement, the tariffs on 'R' shall be reduced in accordance with the terms and conditions set out in the note agreed by both sides, and goods labelled with 'X' shall be excluded from any tariff commitment.[67] The KAFTA also followed a similar goods classification to the CAFTA case. Goods are classified into two categories of Normal Track and Sensitive areas, which followed different tariff-reduction plans.[68]

In summary, in order to narrow the development gap between the original six members and the four new members, ASEAN adopted an incremental way to promote regional economic integration in Southeast Asia and East Asia by dividing members into groups to follow different timetables for FTA establishment. In order to protect the weak sectors/products in ASEAN members, ASEAN classified traded goods with China, Japan and South Korea into different categories to make sure the weak products enjoy longer term protection. Such an incremental approach, to some extent, facilitated narrowing the development gap and the catching-up of the underdeveloped members. However, as a result, it extended the period of FTA establishment in East Asia. When the priority was given to bridging the development gap between the original members and new members, the objective of regional economic integration in East Asia receded. This led to an incremental process of regional economic integration in East Asia. In contrast with the cases in Western Europe and North America, East Asia started later, and made slower progress, which made East

---

[66] For more detailed information, refer to the Appendix 3 of the Framework Agreement on Comprehensive Economic Cooperation between ASEAN and China, Phnom Penh, 4 November, 2002. Available at: http://gjs.mofcom.gov.cn/aarticle/Nocategory/200212/20021200056693.html?3235458188=4166435054 (Accessed on 25 January, 2011)
[67] For more detailed information, refer to the Annex 1 Schedules for the Elimination on Reduction of Customs Duties of the Agreement on Comprehensive Economic Partnership among Japan and Member States of ASEAN, Tokyo, April 2008. Available at: http://www.mofa.go.jp/policy/economy/fta/asean/annex1.html (Accessed on 25 January, 2011)
[68] For more detailed information, refer to the Framework Agreement on Comprehensive Economic Cooperation among South Korea and ASEAN members. Available at: http://www.fta.go.kr/pds/fta_korea/asean/2.pdf (Accessed on 26 January, 2011)

Asia an insufficiently powerful force as to form a tripod world.

8.3   Regionalism versus Regionalization in East Asia

Regionalism and regionalization are two paths in parallel leading toward regional integration. They are distinguished from each other by the different derivations of the driving force and the contrary evolving directions. 'Regionalism 'connotes those state-led projects of cooperation that emerged as a result of inter-government dialogues and treaties' (Breslin & Higgot, 2000, p. 344); it is a region-building process driven by formal state-led initiatives (Nair, 2009, p. 111); and it is a top-down process (Dent, 2008, p. 7). Regionalization 'refers to those processes of integration which, albeit '…seldom unaffected by state policies', derive their driving force 'from markets, from private trade and investment flows, and from the policies and decisions of companies' (Hurrell, Regionalism in Theoretical Perspective, 1995, p. 39), rather than the predetermined plans of national or local governments' (Breslin & Higgot, 2000, p. 344), and it is a more informal 'bottom up' process (Katada, 2007, p. 128). However, regionalism and regionalization also share something in common. They have the common objective of enhancing regional economic cooperation and promoting regional integration in economy, politics and society.

In East Asia, regionalization emerged in the 1960s in the form of the 'flying geese' paradigm initiated by Japan after the Second World War. Japan was the head goose. Japanese corporations transferred mature technology and even the whole mature sectors to the NIEs such as Hong Kong, South Korea, Singapore and Taiwan. When the technology or the sectors got mature in the NIEs countries, they were transferred to the relatively underdeveloped countries such as other ASEAN members and China. In the meanwhile, the industrial structure of Japan and NEIs was upgraded to a more advanced level. This form of regionalization was so successful that it led to the economic miracle in East Asia in the 1990s. Governments also actively participated in the process; however, their role was much eclipsed by the market, investment flows and Japan's MNCs. When the 1997-8 AFC broke out, East Asian countries became aware of the necessity of the government participation in sustainable economic growth and the imperativeness of governmental governance for macro-economic stability. Then, regionalism became the central path of regional integration in East Asia. As the catalyst, the 1997-8 AFC directly led to the birth of the inter-state cooperation framework of ASEA+3, which attached emphasis to inter-governmental cooperation and paid relatively little attention to cooperation at the enterprise level.

Take the economic cooperation between China and ASEAN as an example. The inter-governmental negotiations and treaties dominated the whole economic cooperation process, and there was hardly anything for the enterprises to do but to take part in the process passively. Among the five great dialogue institutions between China and ASEAN, the CABC was the only one which was mainly made up of Chambers of Commerce and well-known enterprises from China and ASEAN. It conducted some surveys in the wake of the endorsement of the Framework Agreement between China and ASEAN in 2002 and at the very eve of the completion of the CAFTA in 2009. According to a senior official from the Chinese Secretariat of the CABC, 'about 80% of Chinese enterprises neither know much about the CAFTA, nor do they have any idea about the timetables that China and ASEAN members will follow to open their markets to each other. Many traded goods fail to obtain the preferential tariff reduction because they are not attached with their certificate of Origins.'[69] In December, 2009, with only one month to go before the final completion of the CAFTA, , '90% of Chinese enterprises did not read ATG, the ATS, the IA of the Framework Agreement between China and ASEAN (Xiao, Hu, & Chen, 31 December, 2009)', based on

---

[69] Interview with a senior official from CABC, Beijing, 13 July, 2010

the survey made by the CABC in China. Therefore, the CABC decided to hold some enterprise symposiums to train the leaders of more than 20 state-owned enterprises and private companies from machinery, steel, equipment manufacturing and other industries. Even after the CAFTA was completed in 2011, it was said the utilization rate of the free trade agreement between China and ASEAN was at only 10% (Zhao, 24 January, 2011). A similar phenomenon took place in ASEAN members and in particular in the four newer members. This demonstrated that both Chinese and ASEAN enterprises did not actively participate in the economic cooperation process between China and ASEAN. That cooperation at enterprise level was ignored to some extent and that enterprises had to passively join the economic cooperation process made the East Asian integration mainly dominated by and reflected on regionalism rather than regionalization.

However, the participation of enterprises and regionalization were seen as the pragmatic direction of the integration and East Asian countries made great efforts to help enterprises participate in regional economic cooperation. Take the CAExpo and the CABIS as examples. At these two venues, 'the participation of enterprises is increasing intensively, more and more enterprise participants participated, and the organizers of the two events, are trying to lead the meetings in a pragmatic way.'[70] In 2004, when the first CAExpo was held, 1505 enterprises from China, ASEAN and other economies attended the meeting. Total trade value amounted to 1.1 billion US dollars. In 2010, when the seventh summit was held, 5360 enterprises attended and total trade value reached 1.7 billion dollars. 'The CAExpo was an effort that the governments of China and ASEAN took in order to promote regionalization. And the reality showed evidence that it was a success.'[71] Although the total trade value did not see a rapid growth, the number of enterprise participants did. This illustrated that the degree to which enterprises participate in economic cooperation was rising and that regionalization driven by enterprises, market and investment flows was burgeoning as well.

In the meanwhile, some government and enterprise elites also advocated that the enterprises, and particularly private enterprises and small-and-medium enterprises (SMEs) to participate in economic cooperation between China and ASEAN. As Myanmar Prime Minister Soe Win said at the third CABIS in 2006, 'I hope we pay attention to the cooperation and development of small-and-medium enterprises (SMEs). It is well known that the SMEs play a significant role in economic growth.' Furthermore, 'private enterprises play a critical role in strengthening sectoral cooperation and enhancing comprehensive cooperation...Without the cooperation between the public and private enterprises, deepening sectoral cooperation will be a bubble (Soe, 2006).' When Chairman Sati of ASEAN Federation of Commerce and Industry (ASEAN-CCI) spoke at the third CABIS in 2006, he asked members to 'put the focus of the business and trade on supporting and promoting SMEs (Sati, 2006)'. Although the encouragement of the elites did not have direct implications for Sino-ASEAN economic cooperation at the enterprise level, they did enlighten South Korea and Japan, who signed FTA agreements with ASEAN later than China. In their FTA agreements with ASEAN, they both listed economic cooperation among SMEs between the two sides as priority cooperation area.

Although inter-governmental negotiations and treaties dominated economic cooperation between South Korea and ASEAN and that between Japan and ASEAN, other factors, e.g. economic cooperation at the enterprise level were also stressed. Unlike the CA-FACEC, where the economic cooperation of SMEs was excluded from the priority cooperation areas, SMEs cooperation was clearly listed in the priority cooperation areas in the KA-FACEC and JACEP. Not only did the KA-FACEC and JACEP categorize the economic cooperation of SMEs as one of their priority cooperation areas, but they also gave it a relatively

---

[70] Interview with a senior official of the CABIS, Nanning, Guangxi, 19 August, 2009
[71] Interview with a senior official of Institute of South, Southeast Asia and Pacific Studies, CICIR, Beijing, 10 July, 2010

high priority. In the KA-FACEC, economic cooperation of SMEs ranked third among the total nineteen priority areas. In the JACEP, it ranked seventh among the totally thirteen priority cooperation areas. There is no evidence of justifying the benefits of enterprise participation in economic cooperation made for regional integration, as it is not long time since the KA-FACEC and JACEP entered into force. However, it is undeniable that regionalization will contribute greatly to regional integration, as illustrated by the case of Western European integration.

Moving on to investigate the reasons for regionalism's precedence over the regionalization in East Asia, two aspects are relevant. On the one hand, the market economy in East Asia in general and in China and ASEAN members in particular was so underdeveloped that the market, private enterprises and SMEs could not play a pivotal role in promoting economic integration. China is an economy in transition, where the status of market economy is not recognized by advanced economies within the WTO. The four new ASEAN members and some original members are also developing countries, where the market economies are not quite developed. The undeveloped market economies in East Asia stopped industrial elites from emerging to take the responsibility to promote regional economic integration. Therefore, the existing economic systems and underdeveloped market economies, to a great extent, limit the general progress of regional economic growth. Furthermore, the great economic gap between the developed economies in East Asia (e.g. Japan, South Korea, Hong Kong and Taiwan, Singapore etc.) and the developing economies (e.g. China, CLMV, Indonesia, the Philippines etc.) added to the difficulty of enhancing regional economic cooperation and promoting a rapid regional economic integration. On the other hand, the 1997-8 AFC reminded East Asian countries of the weakness of liberalization and globalization. They valued, more than before, the role of governments in maintaining economic stability and accomplishing economic growth at the national level as well as in managing regional macro-economy and promoting economic integration at the regional level. The greater attention paid to the role of government than to the market decided that regionalism took precedence over regionalization as the central path leading to regional integration in East Asia.

8.4   Bilateralism versus Multilateralism in East Asia

Bilateralism and multilateralism are two kinds of sub-structure of regional order, and two forms of inter-state interaction. Here, bilateralism means the interaction form is the one where two and only two nation-state actors in a given region launch bilateral economic negotiations, reach bilateral agreements in order to promote the regional economic integration and reconstruct the regional economic order. Multilateralism refers to the sub-structure and the interaction form among three or more than three parties. In the case of regional economic integration in Western Europe and North America, multilateralism acts as the main and dominant sub-structure and form of inter-state interaction. In Western Europe, the original integration institution- the European Coal and Steel Community (ECSC) was founded in 1951 through multilateral negotiations and agreement among six parties: France, Germany, Italy, Belgium, Netherland and Luxemburg. This laid a solid basis for subsequent multilateral endeavours to promote integration farther. After multilateral negotiations, the European Atomic Energy Community (EURATOM) and European Economic Community (EEC) were set up in the late 1950s. Thus, Western Europe constructed a multilateral regional order in economic integration. In North America's case, although economic integration was originally based on the bilateral FTA agreement between Canada and US, its critical step- the endorsement of the 'North American Free Trade Agreement' (NAFTA) in 1994-was completed through tripartite negotiations among Canada, Mexico and US. Thereafter a multilateral regional order in economic integration was established in North America. Overall, both Western European and North American integration were cases of multilateral negotiations, multilateral agreements and multilateral regional order. Their members took part in the multilateral negotiations and reached multilateral agreements with a view to promoting regional economic integration. East Asia's case is distinguished from its counterparts in Western Europe and North America because of the 'lack of multilateral economic arrangements in Asia (Hellmann, 2007, pp. 841-842)' and bilateralism constituted the original and dominant sub-structure and form of inter-state interaction. In East Asia, the main underlying cooperative framework was bilateral and most of the cooperation agreements were bilateral. Bilateralism was preferred to multilateralism by East Asian countries when the initial economic cooperation between governments began. Multilateralism stumbled in the late 2000s, particularly in a few cases among China and the ten ASEAN members as well as among Japan and the ten ASEAN members. Nevertheless, East Asian economic integration was still characterized by bilateralism because ASEAN was seen as a collective entity. In addition, bilateral agreements were not limited to any two countries in East Asia; sometimes, one party of bilateralism went beyond the region of East Asia.

In East Asia, there are so many cooperative institutions of economic integration at various levels that some scholars call it 'Spaghetti noodles'. At the multilateral level, there are APEC (including most of East Asian countries), EAS (an ASEAN-centric institution with members of China, Japan, South Korea and Australia, New Zealand, India), ASEAN+3 (another ASEAN-centric institution with members of China, Japan and South Korea) and so on. At the bilateral level, there are three ASEAN+1 (ASEAN plus China; ASEAN plus Japan and ASEAN plus South Korea) cooperative mechanisms in parallel. Among these cooperative frameworks on economic integration, much reliance was placed on the multilateral ASEAN+3 and the bilateral ASEAN+1 by East Asian countries. Many constructive and far-reaching proposals, initiatives and statements were put forth or released through the ASEAN+3 and the ASEAN+1 mechanisms. For instance, the first FTA proposal in East Asia-the CAFTA, was proposed at the fourth China-ASEAN Summit within the framework of ASEAN+1 (ASEAN plus China) in Singapore in 2000. Study of the feasibility of establishing the East Asian FTA was initiated at the seventh Leaders Summit of ASEAN, China, Japan and South Korea within the framework of ASEAN+3 in Indonesia in 2003. In late 2003, ASEAN and Japan held a special summit within the framework of ASEAN+1 (ASEAN plus Japan) and released the Tokyo Declaration. It identified the establishment of the EAC as the long-term objective of East Asian cooperation. It can be said that most of the decisive steps and objectives of East Asia integration were agreed and implemented through the ASEAN+3 and ASEAN+1 frameworks, whereas the latter was the constituent basis for the former. As Cai concluded, 'while APT (ASEAN+3) provides a forum of consultation and cooperation for ASEAN and three Northeast Asian countries, specific dialogues for substantial cooperation are conducted largely though three parallel mechanisms of APO (ASEAN+1) forums (Cai, 2003, p. 395)'. Therefore, bilateralism, reflected by the ASEAN+1 framework, was the mainstream of the sub-structure of East Asian economic integration. As to multilateralism, there was not an 'absence of a multilateral mechanism for regional cooperation (Yu, 2003, p. 268)' in East Asian economic cooperation; APEC, the ASEAN+3 and EAS are good cases in point. Nevertheless, apart from the ASEAN+3, most of the multilateral mechanisms became 'talk shops' finally.

In East Asia, 'such bilateralism is being utilized by many East Asian countries and members of ASEAN+3' (Bui, 2008, p. 29). At present, there were three bilateral free trade areas going in parallel in East Asia, which were respectively between China and ASEAN (CAFTA), Japan and ASEAN (JACEP), and South Korea and ASEAN (KAFTA). Take the CAFTA as an example. The CAFTA agreement included five components: the CA-FACEC, ATG, ADSM, ATS, and the IA. The previous four agreements were endorsed after China negotiated with every single member of ASEAN. Therefore, the bilateral interaction between China and every single ASEAN member dominated the economic cooperation process between China and

ASEAN. The Framework Agreement between China and ASEAN was only a gathering of ten bilateral agreements between China and each individual ASEAN member. However, when it came to the IA negotiations, things changed. After barely a decade's negotiations between China and individual ASEAN members and endorsement of the four previous bilateral agreements, both China and ASEAN accumulated somewhat negotiating experience and they made an attempt to launch multilateral negotiations. In the end, the IA was agreed in 2009 after multilateral negotiations among China and the ten ASEAN members. In the case of the CAFTA, previous bilateral negotiations laid a good foundation for the subsequent multilateral negotiations of IA. It can be said that bilateralism was preferred when the initial inter-state interactions of economic cooperation began, while multilateralism was flourishing on the basis of bilateralism.

The JAFTA suggested another case of bilateralism and multilateralism in East Asia. Before the final free trade agreement with ASEAN as a whole was endorsed in 2008, Japan had various bilateral trade agreements with seven of ten ASEAN members, excluding three less developed economies of Cambodia, Lao and Myanmar. When negotiations of FTA began, Japan hoped to prioritize existing bilateral free trade accords with the advanced ASEAN economies where it had already had some kind of trade agreements and then to bring in those relatively underdeveloped economies. However, ASEAN did not like to be disaggregated, as they thought it would weaken their collective negotiating power. Thus, ASEAN insisted on launching a new round of multilateral negotiations so as to reach an agreement on FTA between Japan and ASEAN as a whole. In the end the JACEP was agreed in the form of multilateral cooperation and was endorsed after multilateral negotiations among Japan and the ten ASEAN members. The JAFTA agreement was signed half a decade later than the CAFTA agreement, while the former was being mainly multilateral and the latter basically bilateral. Apart from the difference between China and Japan, ASEAN's insistence on multilateral negotiations with Japan by taking ASEAN as a whole played a critical part in the multilateral outcome. This illustrates that 'multilateralism was the evolving trend of inter-state interaction in East Asia. On the basis of three ASEAN+1 cooperation frameworks, regional cooperation among a few actors will be one of the structural forms in East Asia.'[72]

Of special note is that East Asian countries tended to extend bilateralism beyond East Asia. Three great powers in East Asian and ASEAN in Southeast Asia all chose to conclude FTA agreements with some extra-regional countries. As displayed by Table 8.1, China concluded five bilateral agreement with intra-regional economies and six with extra-regional economies. All its bilateral FTA agreements under negotiation/consideration were with extra-regional economies, except the one with South Korea. In contrast with China, Japan made many more bilateral FTA agreements with intra-regional economies, including ASEAN as a whole and ASEAN members individually. South Korea's case was more like China's, making more bilateral agreements with extra-regional economies than with intra-regional economies. All its bilateral agreements under negotiations/considerations are with extra-regional economies, except the two respectively with China and South Korea. In the meanwhile, China, Japan and South Korea were all considering establishing a multilateral FTA with each other. As to ASEAN, it concludes bilateral agreements with both intra-regional economies such as China, Japan and South Korea and extra-regional economies such as India. Economies in East Asia did not focus only on intra-regional bilateralism, but also focus on extra-regional bilateralism. As to the reasons, 'they are attributed to the outward-orientation of economies in East Asia. Much of trade and investment of East Asian economies are exchanged with extra-regional economies, which decides that they cannot focus only on intra-regional

---

[72] Interview with the director of the EGEC, Beijing, 9 July, 2010

partners. They must be attracted by extra-regional markets. This is another factor for an incremental economic integration in East Asia'.[73] When we return our attention to the bilateralism and multilateralism, we can see that Table 8.1 supplies hard evidence that bilateral agreements far outnumber their multilateral counterparts. This shows that bilateralism was the favourite form of interaction for countries in East Asia because of the lower cost of bilateral negotiations and agreements compared to multilateral ones.

Other than the lower cost, three factors constituted the underlying reasons for the popularity of bilateralism. First, East Asian countries lacked successful experience of multilateral cooperation. 'The successful cultivation of multilateral institutions that encompass economic as well as political cooperation has a very short history-essentially post World War Two. Moreover, the nations of East Asia have had no real experience in this matter' (Hellmann, 2007, p. 842). Apart from ASEAN, which had some multilateral integration experience, no party in East Asia was accustomed to participating in regional multilateral economic cooperation. Most of them felt safer holding bilateral negotiations. Another factor relates to ASEAN. ASEAN made great efforts to obtain international acceptance as a collective entity since it came into birth in 1960s. Nevertheless, it lacked a centripetal force to coordinate all members' different interests and then to form an overall strength as a whole. Therefore, all members had to negotiate individually with other parties. As a result, only bilateral agreements could be concluded and bilateral cooperation dominated the economic integration process in East Asia. The final factor is the deep political mistrust between China and Japan, which dimmed the prospect for multilateral cooperation among China, Japan and other parties in the near future. This constituted the structural factor shaping the future of an incremental economic integration in East Asia.

---

[73] Interview with a director of the China Southeast Asian Studies Association (CSASA), Nanjing, 18 June, 2009

Table 8.1 Bilateral/Multilateral FTA Agreements in East Asia and beyond

Bilateral and Multilateral FTA Agreements of China, Japan, Korea and ASEAN in East Asia and beyond				
		Bilateral FTA Agreements in Effect	Bilateral FTA Agreements under Negotiations	Bilateral FTA Agreements under Consideration
China	Intra-region	ASEAN, Singapore, Hong Kong, Macau and Taiwan	N/A	Korea
	Extra-region	Pakistan, Chile, New Zealand, Peru and Costa Rica	GCC, Australia, Iceland, Norway and SACU	India, Japan-Korea and Switzerland
Japan	Intra-region	ASEAN, Brunei, Indonesia, Malaysia, Philippines, Singapore, Thailand, Viet Nam	Korea	China-Korea
	Extra-region	Chile, Mexico and Swizterland	Australia and India	-
Korea	Intra-region	Singapore and ASEAN	N/A	Japan, China, Japan-China
	Extra-region	Chile, EFTA, India, US, EU and Peru	Canada, Mexico, GCC, Australia, New Zealand, Colombia and Turkey	MERCOSUR, Russia, Israel, ASCU and Central America
ASEAN	Intra-region	China, Japan and Korea	-	-
	Extra-region	Australia-New Zealand, India	EU	-

Notes: 1. Region refers to East Asia
2. GCC: Gulf Cooperation Council, SACU: Southeran Africa Customs Union, EFTA: the European Free Trade Association,
   EU: European Union
3. Although the Closer Economic Partnership Agreements between mainland, China and Hong Kong/Macau/ Taiwan are not bilateral
   agreements concluded by two national governments, they show bilateral characteristics.
4. '-' means: the data is not available

Source: Minister of Commerce, China, available at: http://www.mofcom.gov.cn
Minister of Foreign Affairs and Trade, Korea, available at: http://www.mofat.go.kr
Minister of Foreign Affairs, Japan, available at: http://www.mofa.go.jp
ASEAN Secretariat, available at: http://www.aseansec.org

8.5   Future of Regional Economic Integration in East Asia

As previously analysed, four features characterized the regional economic integration process in East Asia. There was no unqualified leader ruling the path towards regional integration, choosing the dominant structure of the economic integration and identifying the long-term objectives of regional integration in East Asia. Furthermore, there was no powerful engine supplying instructive experience of economic integration, exerting a normative influence on the process and acting as a powerful driving force for economic integration in East Asia. In addition, East Asian economic integration derived from the regional fight against the shock of globalization and liberalization in the late 1990s. In contrast with the precedent cases of regional economic integration in Western Europe and North America, East Asian countries placed overarching value on their national governmental authority and sovereignty, for which they saw the pivotal role in stopping the regional financial crisis spreading unexpectedly fast, maintaining regional economic stability at the regional level and obtaining tremendous economic growth at the national level. Therefore, they preferred regionalism driven by inter-governmental arrangements to regionalization driven by market, private trade and investment flows, and companies, as the main path towards the regional economic integration. Finally, due to the lack of experience of and wish of multilateral cooperation among three great powers in Northeast Asia and ASEAN in Southeast Asia in general, bilateralism became the key form of inter-state interaction and the dominant sub-structure of regional economic integration in East Asia.

All these four features contributed to the incremental future of regional economic integration in East Asia. Owing to lack of an unqualified leader, they hesitated whether to include the US in the regional economic integration or not. In the meanwhile, all participants swung between China and Japan and it was not decided whether to choose a general regional FTA agreement initiated by China or by Japan. Due to lack of a powerful engine, there was no driving force in the near future, which was capable of providing the catalyst for regional cooperation as the 1997-8AFC did in the late 1990s. Given that they felt safer with bilateralism than multilateralism and yet realized the significance of multilateralism as an efficient and effective regional structure, they were uncertain whether to rely more on bilateralism than on multilateralism or *vice versa*. As a direct result, they were not sure of the pros and cons of the EAS and ASEAN+3[74]. Therefore, whether the US would be included in the regional economic integration process, and whether the EAS or the ASEAN+1 is the key forum for the participants, to a large extent, will decide the future of the regional economic integration in East Asia.

8.5.1   Inclusive or Exclusive of the US?

At the moment of China's economic ascendancy and political rising in East Asia, will the US walk away, stand by, or take an active part in East Asia? This is not only an issue of concern to the US, but also an issue of concern to East Asian countries. It was asserted that 'the United States is a prerequisite for the fruition of the regional project (in East Asia)' (Nair, 2009, p. 114), while it was argued that 'it is impossible for the US to participate (into the East Asian regional economic integration) as a member because the US is not an East Asian country' (Feng, 2002, p. 8). Then how will East Asia as a whole coordinate with the US? It depends on the US's interest, objectives and its role in East Asia.

Admittedly, the US shares common interest with East Asia in both security and economy areas. To maintain East Asia stability in security and to strive for economic prosperity also conform to the US's

---

[74] In consideration of the little possibility for China and Japan to cooperate with view to promoting a workable multilateral cooperative mechanism in the near future in East Asia before China's status of full market economy is recognized, the ASEAN+3 was essentially based on three bilateral mechanisms of AESAN+1.

interest in East Asia. Therefore, the last thing the US wants is to be excluded from the restructure of order in East Asia. However, the US seemed somehow clumsy when properly incorporating itself to the current process of East Asian economic integration. Above all, the US preferred an Asia-Pacific cooperation framework rather than an East Asian cooperation framework from which it was excluded. In retrospect of what the US did in the 1990s within the framework of the APEC in regard to regional cooperation, the US would like to play an important role within the wider geographical scope of Asia-Pacific. Thus, the EAS, which constituted not only East Asian members of ASEAN, China, Japan and South Korea, but also of Asia Pacific members of Australia, India and New Zealand, was the US's favoured stage. After Obama became president, Washington sent an ambassador to ASEAN and signed the TAC so that it met all the conditions to formally attend the EAS as a member. At the 2010 EAS, the US and Russia were invited to send representatives to attend it. At present, the EAS was discussing whether to include the US and Russia. Should this become a reality, there would be a danger that the EAS would turn into an abattoir where the worldwide great powers played games over there. Moreover, in retrospect of the EVSL programme initiated by the US within the APEC in the late 1990s, the US's focus of economic cooperation in Asia-Pacific was economic liberalization (instead of economic integration), so that the US could have an access to a more liberalized market in Asia-Pacific. This differentiated from what East Asian countries favoured. East Asia preferred regional integration as the approach and the establishment of the EAC as the ultimate objective. In this regard, the US and East Asia had nothing in common. In other words, should the US continue to insist on economic liberalization instead of economic integration in East Asia, it would be hardly popular to join the economic integration process in East Asia. Finally, learning from the lessons of the 1997-8 AFC, East Asian countries knew that it was unrealistic to expect the US to play a securing role (as it did during the Mexican financial crisis in 1994) in any crisis in East Asia. Therefore, the East Asian states needed to have their own leader and regional structure for their own, of their own and on their own. If another financial crisis happened, their own leader and cooperation mechanisms would be what they could rely on. Certainly, this does not exclude the possibility of the US's playing a positive role. In light of the close trade and investment exchange between the US and East Asian countries, East Asia may keep an open attitude towards the U.S. Given their common interest in East Asia, they have great opportunities to coordinate and cooperate well. For example, close cooperation between the future East Asian FTA and the wider Asian-Pacific FTA led by the U.S. is a very interesting possibility.

8.5.2   EAS or ASEAN+3 to build the regional community?

Among so many cooperation mechanisms at various levels, which one will dominate the regional economic integration process and efforts of community building in East Asia remains a pending issue for participants. In 2005, when the first EAS meeting was held, the chairman statement asserted on 14 December 'that the EAS together with the ASEAN+3 and the ASEAN+1 processes could play a *significant* (italic by the author) role in community building in the region'. At the second EAS meeting in January 2007, the EAS's status in community building in East Asia seemed more uncertain when it was asserted in Chairman Statement that 'EAS *complements* (italic by the author) other existing regional mechanisms, including the ASEAN dialogue process, the ASEAN + 3 process, the ASEAN Regional Forum (ARF), and APEC in community building efforts'. At the third EAS meeting in November 2009, the participants focused strongly on EAS's role and diminished the uncertainty shown at the second summit by stating in Chairman Statement that 'EAS should continue to *help* (italic by the author) build a united and prosperous East Asia' and the EAS 'would *help* (italic by the author) build an East Asian community'. The EAS's gradually decreasing status illustrated its ineffectiveness in community building in East Asia. On the contrary, the ASEAN+3's active role obtained governmental appreciation in East Asia. At the meeting on the occasion of the 10th Anniversary of the ASEASN+3 cooperation in 2007 in Singapore, heads of the governments of the ASEAN, China, Japan and South Korea released the 'Second Joint Statement on East Asian Cooperation'. There, it was clearly reaffirmed that 'the ASEAN plus Three would remain as the *main* (italic by the author) vehicle towards the long-term goal of building an East Asian Community' and East Asia cooperation was 'building on the foundations of ASEAN plus Three cooperation'. Thereafter, the originally unstable status of the EAS was undermined while that of the ASEAN+3 was more consolidated. It is foreseen that the EAS will be further marginalized in playing some part in building the EAC if it accepts the US and Russia as members. It will probably turn into another talk shop as post-EVSL APEC.

It makes sense for the EAS to be diluted given that not much common interest exists among Asia-Pacific countries. In history, when the 1997-8 AFC severely hit most of the Asian countries, the Pacific countries stood by. The APEC disappointed all the crisis-hit countries by initiating the EVSL proposal at the very outset of the crisis. Not sharing much common interest, EAS participants did not have a sound basis for economic cooperation for crisis survival. They could only find some functional areas to cooperate. The EAS designated five priority cooperation areas, which were finance, education, energy, disaster management and avian flu prevention. This stood out in marked contrast to the four priority cooperation areas of the ASEAN+3, which were political and security cooperation, economic and financial cooperation, energy, environment, climate change and sustainable development cooperation as well as social and development cooperation. Comparison between the two sides illustrated that the ASEAN+3 was a more powerful alternative, which was bound to play its role in regional economic integration and community building in East Asia.

In addition, the competition between the ASEAN+3 and the EAS is also the competition of leadership between China and Japan. China preferred the former while Japan preferred the latter. Most of China's significant proposals were initiated within the framework of the ASEAN+3. As to Japan, who was deeply disturbed by China's rise and very worried about its precarious status in East Asia, it suggested enlarging the membership of the EAS to include Australia, India and New Zealand in order to have more allies to balance China. Then Japan put forth the proposal of the Comprehensive Economic Partnership in East Asia (CEPEA) of East Asian economic integration based on the EAS framework. The Japanese version of East Asian economic integration competed with the Chinese version of the proposal for the EAFTA based on the ASEAN+3 framework. This was another small detail illustrating the competition between China and Japan for the leadership of regional economic integration in East Asia.

8.5.3   CEPEA or EAFTA?

In 2010, both China and Japan put forth their own proposals for East Asian regional economic integration (EAFTA and CEPEA) to the ASEAN plus Working Groups, where their studies would be investigated. As a preliminary assessment, the concept paper of 'Roadmap on Trade Facilitation among ASEAN Plus Three' drafted by Beijing and the other of 'Initial Steps towards Regional Economic Integration in East Asia: A Gradual Approach' drafted by Tokyo were submitted to the ASEAN Plus Working Groups for consideration. At present, not much information is available on details of the two concept papers or the proposals of CEPEA and EAFTA. However, based on the available sources and reasonable conjectures, there are some clues.

First and foremost, within the five year plans of the two concept papers, both Beijing and Tokyo expressed their respect for 'ASEAN as the central role' (Ministry of Economy, Trade and Industry, Japan, 2010) (Wen, 2010) in East Asian regional economic integration. In addition, both Beijing and Tokyo were supportive to the 'ASEAN Connectivity Master Plan' and Tokyo even suggested expanding the 'ASEAN Connectivity Master Plan' to become an 'East Asian Connectivity Master Plan'. Whether they respected

ASEAN as the central role or they supported the 'ASEAN Connectivity Master Plan', China and Japan exposed a similar intention to gain ASEAN's approval of their own proposals for East Asian regional economic integration. ASEAN, taking advantage of the opportunity afforded by the competition between Beijing and Tokyo, was striving to gain all the benefits as it could. The financial sponsorship from Beijing and Tokyo that ASEAN received for physical infrastructure development was only a minimal example.

There was another obvious difference between China's and Japan's concept papers. China was firm in insisting on the ASEAN+3's key role in promoting regional economic integration in East Asia, while Japan placed more reliance on EAS. China claimed that to promote the East Asian Free Trade Area with the ASEAN+3 as the main channel, while Japan supported economic integration among ASEAN +6 members. Therefore, Japan's version of the concept paper focused geographically on Asia-Pacific instead of East Asia, as it asserted in the title of the concept paper. That China and Japan preferred different cooperation frameworks to promote regional economic integration in East Asia created a difficulty for ASEAN to account on.

Another difficulty derived from the different focuses of China and Japan in the concept papers. Beijing focused only on trade facilitation, while Tokyo covered many more items. In the Japanese concept paper, Tokyo suggested commencing discussion on seven items of cooperation as 'initial steps' of East Asian regional economic integration. The main items of cooperation areas covered trade in goods, trade facilitation, economic cooperation, physical infrastructure and enhancement of connectivity, investment and trade in service and so on. In contrast, as for the main contents of the paper, China placed its attention only on the *trade facilitation* but kept an open attitude to the *trade and investment liberalization,* while Japan aimed at realizing full benefits of *trade and investment liberalization and facilitation*. At the risk of oversimplification, Japan's concept paper was not gradual at all, although it was titled 'a gradual approach'. Japan was ambitious to liberalize trade and investment, which probably ran against ASEAN's incremental approach to promoting the regional economic integration in East Asia step by step. As to China, due to the underdeveloped market economy at home, Beijing also preferred regional economic integration in an incremental way, which might conform to ASEAN's preferred approach.

Although it proposed to rush in to promote regional economic integration in East Asia, Japan was presumed not to open its agricultural market to its East Asian economic partners in light of its rejection of EVSL within the APEC and its reluctant consideration of agricultural cooperation with ASEAN in the JACEP agreement. At present, there were neither regional nor domestic changes so radical as to change Japan's conservative and protective attitude towards its own agricultural market. Therefore, there was little chance for Japan to make any concession to open its agricultural market to partners in East Asia within the proposal of CEPEA. This was not attractive enough for ASEAN to support the CEPEA. As to China, in the CAFTA agreement, Beijing made numerous economic concessions in exchange for ASEAN's consent to the establishment of the CAFTA. However, the focus on trade facilitation in the concept paper obviously showed that China meant to promote regional economic integration in an incremental, if not slow, way. In addition, there did not include an article of accession in the CAFTA agreement, which might not change in the proposal of EAFTA. Thus, ASEAN faced the problem of making a choice between China and Japan. This was not a simple choice for the approach, the main framework and the proposals; in essence, this was the choice for the leadership of regional economic integration in East Asia. The lack of substantial cooperation between China and Japan placed a chance for ASEAN. This could lead to a dark future for regional economic integration in East Asia. Admittedly, three Northeast countries began to negotiate to establish a Northeast Asian Free Trade Area (NAFTA) was for sure an exciting progress. However, that the expected investment agreement among three Northeast countries did not come into reality at the 4th China, Japan and South Korea Leaders Summit further eclipsed the future of East Asian economic integration.

In the next few years, there is not much possibility of China and Japan cooperating in regional economic integration in East Asia before 2015. 'There is no doubt that the historic painful memory and contemporary political distrust were also part of the reason for a dim economic cooperation among Northeast Asian countries. However, it was not powerful enough to reverse the overall trend of East Asian integration. Historical factor did not work much in reality.'[75] *Inter alia*, Japan's waiting for the world's acceptance of China's status as a full market economy is another part of the reason. As is well-known, China's status as a full market economy was not recognized by most of the trading partners in the world and Japan was no exception. Japan's hesitation to cooperate with China derived from its 'wait and see' attitude towards China's fulfilment of economic transition. As stated clearly by Japan, its economic policy towards China was limited 'to support the transition to a market economy and assistance toward WTO agreement compliance' (Ministry of Economy, Trade and Industry, Japan, 2006). If Japan decided to establish a FTA with China only after checking China's completion of economic transition and China's reorganization as a market economy by the WTO, then there was not a great chance for Japan and China to cooperate in efforts of regional economic integration in East Asia shortly. Assuming that only after 15 years since China's accession into the WTO in 2001, will the WTO consider recognizing China's full status as a market economy and Japan follows, thus there is not much possibility for Sino-Japan cooperation on regional economic integration in East Asia in the remaining few years before 2015.

The remaining part of the reason relates to China. 'China is probably not confident enough to cooperate with much more advanced economies (like Japan) (Feng, 2002, p. 4)'. 'China is a country, where it is not long since its opening up, it lacks experience on opening up, and the anti-risk capability is not strong. Swift and extensive liberalization and particularly the investment liberalization are bound to have a deep implication on China's economy and as a result, the opening-up will be forced to accelerate. China's process of opening-up is, therefore, disrupted. This will pose a distress and challenge to China (Wang & Liu, 2003, p. 10).' China, therefore, took a very incremental, conservative and cautious approach to promoting economic integration of East Asia as a whole. This was because Japan, a very competitive developed economy, joined the club of East Asian economic integration. Unless Japan would change its idea or China could gain acceptance as a full market economy in advance before 2015, there will not be much possibility for Sino-Japanese cooperation and similarly no breakthrough for an all-encompassing regional economic integration in East Asia.

---

[75] Interview with a junior official from Institute of South and Southeast Asian Studies, CICIR, Beijing, 7 July, 2010

9 Conclusion

The book is in the mainstream of the second wave of regionalism studies after the 1997-8 AFC, with post-crisis East Asia as the focus of scholars' attention. This book was written over a decade after the second wave started. During the decade, China emerged impressively as a global player; it also played an increasingly significant role in economic integration in East Asia. The research project found that there were few studies on the implications for China's domestic policy of regional integration during the second wave of regionalism studies. To fill this gap in scholarship, the book aimed to interpret China's economic policy on regionalism before and after 2001 by analysing its economic policy towards ASEAN. The bilateral economic relationship between China and ASEAN was the most important bilateral relationship in East Asia, in contrast with that between Japan and ASEAN as well as that between South Korea and ASEAN. During the past 2001 period, China's attitude towards economic cooperation with ASEAN shifted, which also marked a change in its attitude towards regional economic integration.

9.1 Objectives Achieved

With respect to Research Question 1 (see Introduction), the book investigated the inward-looking motives that prompted China to shift its attitude towards economic cooperation with ASEAN by describing China's economic policy towards ASEAN before and after 2001 and analysing the bilateral economic relations on trade and investment between China and ASEAN. Finally it addressed whether China and ASEAN were competitive or mutually complementary in trade in the third markets and whether China crowded out ASEAN's FDI flows from developed economies after its accession to the WTO in 2001. In addition, the author intends to discuss China's motive for initiating the FTA with ASEAN. Three explanations were offered: diplomatic goodwill towards neighbouring countries, the economic development of China's West/Southwest, and the development of China's agriculture.

In regard to Research Question 2 (see Introduction), the book explored the impact of the national domestic economic policy of China on the East Asian regionalism. The book identified China and ASEAN's roles in economic integration in East Asia, and detected the subtlety between regionalism/regionalization and bilateralism/multilateralism in East Asia. These features were summarized on the basis of bilateral economic cooperation between China and ASEAN, which was considered the substance of economic integration in East Asia. Besides, the book also projected the outlook for East Asian economic integration based on further identifications of China and ASEAN's roles and the two features of regionalism and bilateralism in East Asia.

9.2 Research Findings

The book presented empirical studies of China's policy on trade cooperation with ASEAN before and after 2001, analysed Sino-ASEAN trade relations in the 1990s and 2000s and addressed the issue whether China and ASEAN was competitive or mutually complementary in trade in the third markets. Regarding China's trade policy before and after 2001, it was found that Beijing diverted its focus onto regional trade agreements after it entered the WTO. Although neither China's 'peaceful rising' strategy nor its FTA strategy was confined geographically to East Asian region, the CAFTA was the first free trade area in East Asia; China made great efforts to establish it during the past decade. The focus of China's trade policy diverted from the international level to the regional level in East Asia, which promoted the emergence of the first FTA in East Asia. With the CAFTA, China and ASEAN's status as increasingly important trade partners for each other was strengthened. By 2010, China and ASEAN became each other's third biggest trade partner. The book applied the RCA index to measure the trade competitiveness of China and ASEAN in the third market of the United States. The RCA index of S1-6 Manufactured Goods among China and ASEAN-5 in the American market indicated that the competition in S1-6 was in favour of China and Indonesia instead of Malaysia, the Philippines, Singapore and Thailand during both the 1990s and the 2000s; the RCA index of S1-7 Machinery and Transport Equipment suggested that the competition in S1-7 was in favour of Malaysia and Singapore in the 1990s; China and the Philippines also caught up in the 2000s and meanwhile Malaysian and Singapore's advantage further expanded. The RCA index of S1-0 Food and Live Animals among China and ASEAN-5 in the American market disclosed that China had no advantage in competition in S1-0 with ASEAN-5 during the past two decades and in contrast, Indonesia, the Philippines and Thailand had relatively great advantage in S1-0. The book concluded that China had comparative advantage in S1-6, but had disadvantages in S1-7 and S1-0 in contrast with ASEAN-5 countries in the American market, which meant that China was not a trade competitor of ASEAN.

The book also considered China's policy on investment cooperation with ASEAN before and after 2001, analysed Sino-ASEAN investment relations in the 1990s and 2000s and discussed the issue whether China crowded out ASEAN's FDI flows from developed economies after its accession to the WTO. It was found that Beijing concentrated on attracting inward investment from partners in the 1990s by implementing the 'bringing-in' policy; it encouraged Chinese enterprises to invest outwards and took ASEAN as the first investment destination in the 2000s by implementing the 'going-out' policy. Sino-ASEAN investment relations changed as a result. China turned from a net FDI recipient of ASEAN in the 1990s to be the key FDI source for ASEAN in the 2000s. With respect to the 'FDI crowd-out' issue, the book found that in the Japanese case, ASEAN's share in total Japanese outward FDI in Asia (excluding Near and Middle East and OECD) in 2002 reduced by 16% than that in 2001. These share diverted to China, Taiwan who joined the WTO on 11 November 2001 and on 1 January 2002 respectively, and India, who was one of the BRICs with great attraction of world-wide FDI. In the meanwhile, ASEAN did not pay adequate attention to attracting FDI from extra-ASEAN partners in 2002 because members were busy in the final push to complete the AFTA. This also resulted in much less Japanese FDI flows in 2002. Except for 2002, China and ASEAN showed high interdependence in attracting FDI flows. Finally, the book adopted the UNCTAD Inward FDI Performance Index to measure whether China, ASEAN-5 or BCLMV had good capability of attracting inward FDI flows after 2001. The outcome indicated that both China and ASEAN-5's performance after 2001 obviously dropped to a great extent; on the contrary, BCLMV performed increasingly well. Thus, in the long term, China and ASEAN performed worse in attracting FDI, yet BCLMV performed better in it. Therefore, the book concluded that China did not divert ASEAN's FDI from developed countries after its accession to the WTO except in 2002 in the Japanese case.

To explore the motives for China's shifting attitude towards economic cooperation with ASEAN and towards regional economic integration in East Asia, the book examined China's domestic politics and economy at the national level. In the political area, China carried out 'regional diplomacy', which underlined the significance of the surrounding countries on China's stability and development in general and ASEAN's significance for China in particular. China saw the stability and prosperity of East Asian region as one of China's development goals. In the economic area, China joined the WTO in 2001, within which, however, most of its members did not recognize China as a full market economy; and they would not take it into consideration until after fifteen years. Thus, China could not have full access to the markets of WTO members particularly in the West, who were the key export destinations for Chinese products. In response to the fifteen years' limitation, China turned its sight to the regional markets in East Asia. China's political and economic grand strategy was the radical factor in shifting China's attitude towards economic cooperation with ASEAN and that towards economic integration in East Asia.

Besides, China faced two serious domestic economic problems caused by radical economic reforms. One was the growing gap between East and West China; the latter was, in some degree, ignored during the early phases of opening up. The other was the increasing disparity between urban and rural areas, which was a result of domestic economic reforms. Beijing believed that enhancing economic cooperation with ASEAN would help solve these two domestic problems. As far as the first problem was concerned, Southwest China, which was located adjacent to ASEAN, benefited significantly from enhanced economic cooperation between China and ASEAN by expanding trade and investment exchanges with ASEAN, facilitating resources reallocation and optimal industrial restructuring in Southwest China and increasing local residents' income in Southwest China. As far as the second problem was concerned, China's commitments to the agricultural sector within the framework of the WTO posed serious challenges to China's agriculture, peasants and rural areas. In order to offset the negative implications of China's WTO-accession to the agricultural sector, peasants and rural area, Beijing gave agricultural cooperation the first priority when enhancing economic cooperation with ASEAN. It proved to be a good idea especially in consideration of mutual complementarity in the agricultural sector between China and ASEAN. As a result, China benefited from the bilateral agricultural cooperation in a strategic sense. On the one hand, China found another big market for Chinese agricultural products, apart from those in the western developed countries and found a potential investment destination for Chinese agriculture-related companies. On the other hand, China's agricultural exports accounted for increasing shares in ASEAN's total agricultural trade. This strengthened ASEAN members' reliance on Chinese agricultural markets and the cost of destroying the reliance increased to an unsustainable extent with the expanding and deepening of bilateral agricultural cooperation. Given the relatively small agricultural market, the benefits from enhanced agricultural cooperation between China and ASEAN were hardly able to totally offset the negative impacts of China's commitments within the WTO framework. However, the agricultural cooperation between China and ASEAN, to some extent, balanced and partly diminished the negative impacts.

It makes sense to argue that the establishment and completion of the CAFTA aimed to help solve China's domestic problems caused by intensified economic reforms at home although it marked a new stage of China's opening up. China's domestic grand strategy to maintain regional stability and prosperity in East Asian region and to explore regional markets was the crucial factor that prompted China to shift its attitude towards economic cooperation with ASEAN. That China intended to solve domestic development problems of the Southwest region and agriculture was the key motive for China's shifting attitude towards economic cooperation with ASEAN and towards regional economic integration in East Asia.

The book also presented an analysis of East Asian regionalism at a regional level based on bilateral relations between China and ASEAN. It further identified China's role as the leader in economic integration in East Asia due to its great power status, significant position in trade and investment cooperation in East Asia, its proposal-initiating capability and the great economic concessions it made to ASEAN. It argued that China was not an unqualified leader because to be a leader went against its 'peaceful rising' strategy; moreover, China's FTA strategy was not confined to the East Asia region. With the United States and Japan struggling to be the leader, China kept a low profile and its real intention was covered. ASEAN's role was further identified as the engine of East Asian regionalism owing to its wealth of experience in (sub) regional economic integration and the driving force it provided by diverting its inward-looking economic policy to an outward-looking one after the 1997-8 AFC. However, ASEAN did not focus solely on East Asian economic integration; it looked beyond Southeast Asia and reached not only East Asia, but also Asia-Pacific. Besides, ASEAN chose to promote East Asian economic integration in an incremental way and prioritized Southeast Asian integration over that of East Asia, which undermined the basis for it to be a powerful engine.

The book summarized two features of economic integration in East Asia, on the basis of studies of bilateral economic cooperation between China and ASEAN, supplemented by another two sets of bilateral economic cooperation, between Japan and ASEAN and between South Korea and ASEAN. The book found that in East Asia, regionalization emerged in the 1960s in form of the 'flying goose' paradigm, while regionalism emerged after the 1997-8 AFC in the form of the cooperative mechanism of ASEAN+3. Thereafter, regionalism became the central path of regional integration in East Asia because of the immature market economy in countries in East Asia and great economic gap among them. Also the book found that bilateralism was the main form of inter-state interaction and sub-structure of regional order in East Asia, although multilateralism also grew in importance.

With regard to the future of East Asian economic integration, a somewhat pessimistic attitude was adopted for three reasons. First, the United States acted as an external constraint for it; moreover, Japan's stance was just to wait and see the fulfilment of China's domestic economic transition; and finally ASEAN prioritized Southeast Asian integration over that in the wider East Asia and it was hovering between East Asia and Asia-Pacific. Depending solely on Beijing, it would be difficult for East Asian economic integration to make a breakthrough before China's full market status is reconsidered in 2015.

9.3   Further Research Directions

Due to time and funding constraints, the book could not address a number of related issues. However, these will become the subject of the author's future research. Firstly, it was noticed that ASEAN was very worried about two issues after China's accession to the WTO. On the one hand, they were worried that China would compete with ASEAN for western markets after its WTO-accession; on the other hand, they were afraid that China would crowd out ASEAN's FDI from developed economies after its WTO-accession. Quantitative analysis was conducted on these two issues. However, it was not possible to conduct in-depth elite interviews in ASEAN countries and as a result there was no adequate qualitative data on the two issues. Therefore, it is planned in future to go to Southeast Asia to conduct some elite interviews and collect further qualitative data on these two issues.

Secondly, the research revealed that bilateral economic cooperation between China and ASEAN accelerated Taiwan's decline in East Asia and further marginalized it after Taiwan was excluded from the ASEAN+3 cooperative mechanism in the wake of the 1997-8 AFC. The endorsement of the Economic Cooperation Framework Agreement (ECFA) was believed to deepen Taiwan's reliance on mainland China, which paved the way for a possible final political resolution of the Taiwan issue for Beijing. However, no in-depth analysis was conducted on this. In light of the great sensitivity of this issue, perhaps it would have been wise to do elite interviews in mainland China; in addition to the significant benefit from interviewing some Taiwanese elites. Therefore, to further collect primary and secondary sources on this matter and to do elite interviews in Taiwan, if possible, will help improve the research findings on this issue.

Finally, the book paid attention to the governance of economic cooperation with ASEAN from the central level. However the provincial/local level and provincial governments seemed to have some authority governance in establishing economic cooperation with ASEAN. The book did not elaborate on this in detail. To analyse China's economic policy from both the central level and the provincial/local level would help improve the research findings. Thus, these three aforementioned issues will become the basis of the author's future research. This will add depth and breadth to the research project.

9.4   Research Contributions

This book contributed to East Asian regionalism studies in four ways. One contribution came from the research content. The book presented detailed research on domestic motives for China's shifting attitude towards East Asian regionalism from an inward-looking perspective. Existing literature tended to seek for the motives from an outward-looking perspective. This literature concluded that China aimed to build up its rule-making capability within the world and regional trade frameworks, to enhance China's role in East Asia and the wider Asia-Pacific, and to defuse American influence in East Asia and to prompt multi-polarity in the world. However, the book argued that outward-oriented motives did not show the full picture. The book analysed inward-oriented motives for China's shifting attitude. It found that the establishment of the CAFTA and promotion of economic integration in East Asia was a new stage of China's opening up. However, the policy was supposed to diminish domestic problems of disparity between East and West China as well as between urban and rural areas, caused by intensified economic reforms at home. In a word, China intended to address the domestic problems caused by the intensified economic reforms and the imbalanced regional opening up. These inward-looking motives for China's shifting attitude towards regional economic integration in East China are new in academia and they have not been found in existing literature. The book contributed to the second study wave of new regionalism by elaborating its features in the East Asian case, based on studies of bilateral economic cooperation between China and ASEAN, supplemented by the other two sets of bilateral economic cooperation between Japan and ASEAN, and between South Korea and ASEAN.

Another contribution lies in creatively applying the theoretical framework of complex interdependence theory to explaining the economic cooperation between China and ASEAN. Both of the two actors were non-Western actors; moreover, China and some members of ASEAN are underdeveloped economies. Although complex interdependence theorists argued that their theory were more suitable for democratic/developed economies in the West and less for communist/underdeveloped actors, the empirical research by applying the theory to studies of economic cooperation between China and ASEAN proves to be successful after remedying its weaknesses. Firstly, the author applied the theory to investigating the relative gains/losses in economic cooperation between China and ASEAN by addressing the problem whether China was competitive in trade with ASEAN in the American market and the issue whether China crowded out ASEAN's FDI from developed economies. The answer that China was an increasingly complementary partner of ASEAN and China showed high interdependence in attracting external FDI with ASEAN in the 2000s in turn proves the assumption of relative gains/losses of complex interdependence to be accurate and effective. In addition, by comparing China's domestic economic policy towards ASEAN in the 1990s and 2000s, the book successfully remedied the weakness of applying the complex interdependence theory (which was focusing on the regime changes at the international level) to the studies at the regional and national levels. Finally, by treating the United States and Japan as external factors of China-led economic integration in East Asia, the book also confirmed the assumption of the severity of the external constraints of complex interdependence theory.

Another contribution is derived from the research method of elite interview. The research projects interviewed elites at the regional level from the EGEC, EPG, CAExpo and CABIS, who focused on inter-governmental economic cooperation; and from the ACBC and CAC, who concentrated on economic cooperation of enterprises and commercial chambers. Moreover, the research also interviewed those elites at the national level in MFA and MOC, China. Elites at the provincial/local level in Guangxi Region from Guangxi Provincial Department of Commerce were interviewed. In addition, the interviews included not only elite researchers on China-ASEAN economic cooperation from Guangxi Academy of Social Science,

Guangxi University and Nanjing University, but also elite practitioners of China-ASEAN economic cooperation from NCCE. Finally, the research interviewed those elites on China-ASEAN economic cooperation from the biggest official think tank of CICIR in Beijing. The quotations of the interviewees in the book are relatively unusual for academic work on China and have not been found in the literature so far.

The last contribution came from the application of original Chinese-language literature to English-language scholarship. The book incorporated a great deal of Chinese-language literature into the studies of an English-language book and has brought interpretations from Chinese scholarship to Western academia. Approximately half of the literature referred in the book was originally written in Chinese and the author's research was informed by it. Moreover, it was appropriately incorporated into the English-language book. This is a significant contribution of the book with respect to research literature sources. Thus, the specific focus of the book, research method of elite interviews and the research sources of Chinese-language literature are the main contributions of this book.

Bibliography

English-language Bibliography

Achary, A. (2004, Spring). How Ideas Spread: Whose Norms Matter? Norm Localization and Institutional Change in Asian Regionalism. *International Organization*, Vol. 58, p. 239.

Achaya, A. (2003). Will Asia's Past Be Its Future? *International Security*, Vol. 28, No. 3, p. 152.

(2008). *Agreement on Comprehensive Economic Partnership among Japan and Member States of ASEAN.* available at: www.aseansec.org/agreements/AJCEP/Agreement.pdf (Accessed on 23 January 2011).

Andrew, W.-W. (1995). Regionalism,Globalization and World Economic Order. In L. Fawcett, & A. Hurell, *Regionalism in World Politics: Regional Organization and International Order* (pp. 92-97). Oxford: Oxford University Press.

ASEAN Secretariat. (1980-1981). *ASEAN Annual Report.* available at: http://www.aseansec.org/9894.htm (Accessed on 5 November, 2009).

ASEAN Secretariat. (1982-1983). *ASEAN Annual Report.* available at: http://www.aseansec.org/9890.htm (Accessed on 5 November, 2009).

ASEAN Secretariat. (1983-1984). *ASEAN Annual Report.* available at: http://www.aseansec.org/9888.htm (Accessed on 5 November, 2009).

ASEAN Secretariat. (1984-1985). *ASEAN Annual Report.* available at: http://www.aseansec.org/9097.htm (Accessed on 5 November, 2009).

ASEAN Secretariat. (1985-1986). *ASEAN Annual Report.* available at: http://www.aseansec.org/8974.htm (Accessed on 5 November, 2009).

ASEAN Secretariat. (1987-1988). *ASEAN Annual Report.* available at: http://www.aseansec.org/9664.htm (Accessed on 5 November, 2009).

ASEAN Secretariat. (1988-1989). *ASEAN Annual Report.* available at: http://www.aseansec.org/9614.htm (Accessed on 5 November, 2009).

ASEAN Secretariat. (1989-1990). *ASEAN Annual Report.* available at: http://www.aseansec.org/9553.htm (Accessed on 5 November, 2009).

ASEAN Secretariat. (1991-1992). *ASEAN Annual Report.* available at: http://www.aseansec.org/9096.htm (Accessed on 7 November, 2009).

ASEAN Secretariat. (1992-1993). *ASEAN Annual Report.* available at: http://www.aseansec.org/8972.htm (Accessed on 7 November, 2009).

ASEAN Secretariat. (1995-1996). *ASEAN Annual Report.* available at: http://www.aseansec.org/9292.htm (Accessed on 7 November, 2009).

ASEAN Secretariat. (1997-1998). *ASEAN Annual Report.* available at: http://www.aseansec.org/9121.htm (Accessed on 7 November, 2009).

ASEAN Secretariat. (1998-1999). *ASEAN Annual Report.* available at: http://www.aseansec.org/9085.htm (Accessed on 7 November, 2009).

ASEAN Secretariat. (1999-2000). *ASEAN Annual Report.* available at: http://www.aseansec.org/8947.htm (Accessed on 7 November, 2009).

ASEAN Secretariat. (2002-2003). *ASEAN Annual Report.* available at: http://www.aseansec.org/ar03.htm (Accessed on 8 November, 2009).

ASEAN Secretariat. (2004-2005). *ASEAN Annual Report.* available at: www.aseansec.org/AR05/TOC.pdf (Accessed on 8 November, 2009).

ASEAN Secretariat. (2006-2007). *ASEAN Annual Report.* available at: http://www.aseansec.org/ar07.pdf (Accessed on 10 November, 2009).

ASEAN Secretariat. (2007-2008). *ASEAN Annual Report.* available at: http://www.aseansec.org/AR-08.pdf (Accessed on10 November, 2009).

Atkinson, P., & Amanda, C. (1997). Analysing Documentary Realities. In D. Silverman (Ed.), *Qualitative Research: Theory, Method and Practice* (p. 47). London: SAGE Publications.

Ba, A. D. (2008/2009, Winter). Book Review on ASEAN-China Economic Relations. *Pacific Affairs , Vol. 81, No. 4*, p. 663.

Ba, A. D. (2003, July/August). China and ASEAN: Renavigating Relations for a 21st –Century Asia. *Asian Survey , Vol. XLIII, No. 4*, p. 624 .

Ba, A. D. (2003). Renavigating Relations for a 21st-Century Asia. *Asian Survey , Vol.43, No. 4*, p. 642.

Berg, B. L. (1989). *Qualitative Research Methods for the Social Science.* Boston, Mass: Allyn and Bacon.

Berkofsky, A. (2005, Jul/Aug). China's Asian Ambitions. *Far Eastern Economic Review , Vol. 168, No. 7*, p. 20.

Blondel, J. (2006). Citizens' Value in East and Southeast Asia. In I. Marsh (Ed.), *Democratisation, Governance and Regionalism in East and Southeast Asia* (p. 223). Abingdon: Routledge.

Breslin, S. (2006). China's Rise to Leadership in Asia- Strategies, Obstacles and Achievements. Papers presented at the conference on Regional Powers in Asia, Africa, Latin America, the Near and Middle East, German Institute of Global and Area Studies, Hamburg, December 2006.

Breslin, S., & Higgot, R. (2000). Studying Regions: Learning from the Old, Constructing the New. *New Political Economy , Vol. 5, No. 3*, p. 345.

Buckley, P. J., Clegg, J., Cross, A. R., & Tan, H. (Spring 2005). China's Inward Foreign Direct Investment Success: Southeast Asia in the Shadow of the Dragon. *Multinational Business Review , Vol. 13, No. 1*, pp. 7-8.

Bui, G. T. (2008). Intra-regional Trade of ASEAN Plus Three: Trends and Implications for East Asian Economic Integration. *CNAEC Research Series 08-04* , p. 29.

Burns, R. (22 July, 2009). Hillary Clinton declares the U.S. 'is back' in Asia. *The China Post* .

Cai, K. G. (2003). The ASEAN-China Free Trade Agreement and East Asian Regional Grouping. *Contemporary Southeast Asia , Vol. 25, No. 3*, pp. 388-399.

Cai, K. G. (2005). The China-ASEAN Free Trade Agreement and Taiwan. *Journal of Contemporary China , Vol. 45, No. 4*, p. 591.

Candra, A. C. (2005). Indonesia and Bilateral Trade Agreements (BTAs). *Pacific Affairs , No. 4*.

Candra, A. C. (2009). *Indonesia and the ASEAN Free Trade Agreement: Nationalists and Regional Integration Strategy.* Lanham, MD: Lexington Books.

Candra, A. C., & Lontoh, L. A. (2011). Indonesia-China Trade Relations: The Deepening of Economic Integration amid Uncertainty? . *Trade Knowledge Network Working Paper* , p. 7.

Chen, H. (January 2006). China-ASEAN Free Trade Area: The Hurdles of Investment Negotiations. *EAI Background Brief* , *No. 271*, p. 9.

Cheng, J. Y. (2003). Regional Impact of China's WTO Membership. *Asian Affairs: An American Review* , *Vol. 29, No. 4*, p. 218.

Cheng, J. Y.-s. (2004). The ASEAN-China Free Trade Area: Genesis and Implications. *Australian Journal of International Affairs* , *Vol. 58, No. 2*, p. 257.

Christoffersen, G. (2007). Book Review on China's Rise and the Balance of Influence in Asia. *Pacific Affairs* , *Vol. 80, No. 3*, p. 501.

Das, D. K. (2007). Foreign Direct Investment in China: Its Impact on the Neighboring Asian Economies. *Asian Business and Management* , *No. 6*, pp. 285-301.

Dent, C. M. (2008). *East Asian Regionalism* . New York: Routledge.

Dosch, J. (2007). Managing Security in ASEAN-China Relations: Liberal Peace of Hegemonic Stability. *Asian Perspective* , *Vol. 31, No. 1*, p. 213.

Feng, X. (2002). China and ASEAN Can Share the Prosperity Together-Interview with Zhang Yunling, Director, Institute of Asia-Pacific Studies, CASS. *China and World Economy* , *No. 1*, p. 8.

Finch, J. (1999). It's Great to Have Someone to Talk to: The Ethics and Politics of Interviewing Women. In A. Bryman, & R. G. Burgess (Eds.), *Qualitative Research: Volume II* (p. 70). London: SAGE Publication.

(2002). *Framework Agreement on Comprehensive Economic Cooperation between ASEAN and China.* available at: http://www.aseansec.org/13196.htm (Accessed on 23 January 2011).

(2005). *Framework Agreement on Comprehensive Economic Cooperation between Korea and ASEAN.* available at: http://www.fta.go.kr/pds/fta_korea/asean/2.pdf (Accessed on 23 January 2011).

Frost, E. L. (2008). *Asia's New Regionalism.* Boulder: Lynne Rienner Publishers.

Fung, K. C., Iizaka, H., & Tong, S. (June 2002). Foreign Direct Investment in China: Policy, Trend and Impact. (pp. 1-14). Paper prepared for an international conference on 'China's Economy in the 21st Century', held on 24-25 June 2002, Hong Kong.

Greenwald, A. (2006). The ASEAN-China Free Trade Area (ACFTA): A Legal Response to China's Economic Rise? *Duke Journal of Comparative and International Law* , *Vol. 193, No. 16*, p. 197.

Haas, E. B. (1970). The Study of Regional Integration: Reflections on the Joy and Anguish of Pretheorizing. *International Organization* , *No. 4*, p. 622.

Hamilton-Hart, N. (2003, May). Asia's New Regionalism: Government Capacity and Cooperation in the Western Pacific. *Review of International Political Economy* , *Vol. 10, No. 2*, pp. 222-245.

Harvie, C., & Lee, H.-H. (2002). New Regionalism in East Asia: How Does It Relate to the East Asian Economic Development Model? *Working Paper Series 2002, Department of Economics, University of Wollongong, WP 02-10* , p. 22.

Hellmann, D. C. (2007, November/December). A Decade after the Asian Financial Crisis-Regionalism and International Architecture in a Globalized World. *Asian Survey*, *Vol. XLVII, No. 6*, pp. 841-842.

Hemmer, C., & Katzenstein, P. J. (2002, Summer). Why is There No NATO in Asia? Collective Identity, Regionalism, and the Origins of Multilateralism. *International Organization*, *Vol. 56, No. 3*, p. 575.

Hettne, B., & Söderbaum, F. (2000). Theorising the Rise of Regionness. *New Political Economy*, *Vol. 5, No. 3*, pp. 463-468.

Hew, D. (May 2006). Economic Integration in East Asia: An ASEAN Perspective. *UNISCI Discussion Papers*, *11*, p. 54.

Hira, A. (2007). *The East Asian Model for Latin American Success: The New Path*. Aldershot: Ashgate.

Hoffmann, S., & Keohane, R. O. (1990). Conclusion: Community Politics and Institutional Change. In W. Wallace (Ed.), *The Dynamics of European Integration* (p. 281). London: Pinter Publisher.

Hurrell, A. (1995, October). Explaining the Resurgence of Regionalism in World Politics. *Review of International Studies*, *Vol. 21*, p. 334.

Hurrell, A. (1995). Regionalism in Theoretical Perspective. In L. Fawcett, & A. Hurrell (Eds.), *Regionalism in World Politics: Regional Organization and International Order* (pp. 38-39). Oxford: Oxford University Press.

Hurrell, A. (1995). Regionalism in Theoretical Perspective. In L. Fawcett, & A. Hurrell (Eds.), *Regionalism in World Politics: Regional Organization and International Order* (pp. 39-45). Oxford: Oxford University Press.

INAMA, S. (2005). The Association of South East Asian Nations- People's Republic of China Free Trade Area: Negotiating Beyond Eternity with Little Trade Liberalization. *Journal of World Trade*, *Vol. 39, No. 3*, p. 559.

Jones, M. E. (2004). Forging an ASEAN Identity: The Challenge to Construct a Shared Destiny. *Contemporary Southeast Asia*, *Vol. 26, No. 1*, p. 140.

Katada, S. N. (2007). Book Review of 'Peter J. Katzenstein and Takashi Shiraishi (eds.), Beyond Japan: The Dynamics of East Asian Regionalism (Ithaca: Cornell University Press 2006). *International Studies Review*, *Vol. 9, Issue 1*, p. 128.

Katzenstein, P. J., Hamilton-Hart, N., Kato, K., & Yue, M. (2000). *Asian Regionalism*. New York: Cornell University Press.

Kawai, M., & Wignaraja, G. (2009, April). The Asian 'Noodle Bowl', Is It Serious for Business? *ADBI Working Paper Series*, *No. 136*, p. 3.

Kazmin, A. L., McNulty, S., & William, H. (13 October, 2003). Foreign Investors Desert Southeast Asia for China: Still Reeling from the Financial Crisis of Three Years Ago, ASEAN Feels Eclipsed by its Northern Rival. *Financial Times* .

Keohane, R. O., & Hoffmann, S. (1996). Conclusion: Community Politics and Institutional Change. In M. O' Neill, *The Politics of European Integration* (pp. 288-289). London: Routledge.

Keohane, R. O., & Nye, J. S. (1989). *Power and Interdependence.* the US: Harper Collins Publishers.

Khoo, N., R., M. L., & Shambaugh, D. (2005). Correspondence-China Engages Asia? Caveat Lector. *International Security*, *Vol. 30, No. 1*, p. 210.

Kim, S. S. (2004). Regionalization and Regionalism in East Asia. *Journal of East Asian Studies , Vol.Jan-April.*

Ko, S.-l. (5 August, 2010). ECFA Not a Country-to-Country Agreement, Ma Says. *Taipei Times .*

Ko, S.-l. (2 August, 2010). Roughed-up Chinese Official Comes Back. *Taipei Times .*

Kreft, H. (2004). he United States-Is it the key to the Stability of Asia. *International Economics and Politics , No. 12*, p. 50.

Kuik, C.-c. (2005). Multilateralism in China's ASEAN Policy: Its Evolution, Characteristics, and Aspiration. *Contemporary Southeast Asia , Vol. 27, No. 1*, p. 118.

Kwon, Y. (Winter 2004). Toward a Comprehensive Partnership: ASEAN-South Korea Economic Cooperation. *East Asian Review , Vol. 16, No. 4*, p. 93.

Lincoln, E. J. (2010, January). Asian Regionalism. *Asia Policy , No. 9*, p. 166.

Lincoln, E. J. (2004). *East Asian Economic Regionalism.* Washington: Brookings Institution Press.

Liou, T.-H. (2007, Spring/Summer). Asia's Response to China's FTA Strategy: Implications for Asian Economic Integration. *The Journal of East Asian Affairs , Vol.21*, pp. 197-199.

Liu, F.-K., & Régnier, P. (2003). *Regionalism in East Asia: Paradigm Shifting?* London: Routledge.

Lloyd, P. J. (2002). New Regionalism and New Bilateralism in Asia-Pacific. *ISEAS Document, Visiting Researchers Series, No. 3*, p. 2.

Lloyd, P. J. (2002). New Regionalism and New Bilateralism in the Asia-Pacific. *ISEAS Document, Visiting Researchers Series , No. 3*, pp. 1-22.

Maanen, J. V., SØrensen, J. B., & Mitchell, T. R. (2007). The Interplay between Theory and Method. *Academy of Management Review , Vol. 32, No. 4*, p. 1145.

Mansfield, E. D., & Milner, H. V. (1999). The New Wave of Regionalism. *International Organization , Vol. 53, No. 3*, pp. 596-599.

McKibbin, W. J., & Woo, W. T. (2004). Quantifying the International Economic Impact of China's WTO Membership. *China and World Economy , Vol. 12, No. 2*, p. 9.

McKibbin, W. J., & Woo, W. T. (2003). The Consequences of China's WTO Accession on its Neighbors. *Working Papers in International Economics of the Lowy Institute for International Policy (Sydney, Australia), No. 6*, pp. 12-15.

Medeiros, E. S., & Fravel, M. T. (2003, November/December). China's New Diplomacy. *Foreign Affairs , Vol. 82, No. 6*, p. 28.

Ministry of Economy, Trade and Industry, Japan. (2006, April). Global Economic Strategy.

Ministry of Economy, Trade and Industry, Japan. (2010, August 26). Initial Steps towards Regional Economic Integration in East Asia: A Gradual Approach.

Morck, R., Yeung, B., & Zhao, M. (2008). Perspectives on China's Outward Foreign Direct Investment. *Journal of International Business Studies , Vol. 39*, p. 337.

Nair, D. (2009, April). Regionalism in the Asia-Pacific/East Asia: A Frustrated Regionalism? *Contemporary Southeast Asia: A Journal of International and Strategic Affairs , Vol. 31, No. 1*, p. 111.

Naoko, M. (2002, Nov. 29). Talking Regional, Acting Bilateral - Reality of "FTA Race" in East Asia. *Jiji*

Top Confidentia , p. 11.

Narine, S. (2002). *Explaining ASEAN: Regionalism in Southeast Asia.* Boulder: Lynne Rienner.

Novak, N. (5 August, 2010). A Downturn Would Strip the ECAFA's Thin Façade. *Taipei Times* .

Novak, N. (5 August, 2010). The Political Reality of 'Buy Taiwan. *Taipei Times,* .

Odendahl, T., & Shaw, A. M. (2002). Interviewing Elites. In J. F. Gubrium, & J. A. Holsterin (Eds.), *Handbook of Interview Research: Context and Method* (p. 312). Thousand Oaks: Sage Publications.

Oxford Analytical. (2010, January, 14). ASEAN/China: Trade Agreement has Built-in Tensions.

Oxford Analytical. (19 January, 2005). East Asia: ASEAN Carves Niche in Regional FDI Patterns. *Oxford Analytical Daily Brief Service* , p. 1.

Oxford Analytical. (08 January, 2001). South-east Asia: China's WTO Entry Challenges Region. *Oxford Analytical Daily Brief Service* , p. 1.

Pitsuwan, S. (2010). The Completion of CAFTA will benefit both sides and realize win-win. In S. Punch, K. F. (1998). *Introduction to Social Research: Quantitative and Qualitative Approaches.* London: SAGE Publication.

Plummer, G. M. (2006, July). The ASEAN Economic Community and the European Experience. *ADB Working Paper Series on Regional Economic Integration* , p. 1.

Pushpanathan, S. (2010). *The ASEAN-China Relationship.* available at: http://www.amchamchina.org/article/index/6294 (Accessed on 6 July 2010).

Rajan, R. S. (2005). Trade Liberalization and the New Regionalism in the Asia-Pacific. *International Relations of the Asia-Pacific* , *Vol. 5*, pp. 217-133.

Ravenhill, J. (1995, September). Economic Cooperation in Southeast Asia: Changing Incentive. *Asian Survey* , *Vol. 35, No. 9*, p. 864.

Ravenhill, J. (2010, February). The New East Asian Regionalism: A Political Domino Effect. *Review of International Political Economy* , *Vol. 18, No. 1*, pp. 11-12.

Ravenhill, J. (2010, May). The New East Asian Regionalism: A Political Domino Effect. *Review of International Political Economy* , *Vol. 17, No. 2*, pp. 185-186.

Restall, H. (June 2007). Book Review of 'China: Fragile Superpower: How China's Internal Politics could Derail its Peaceful Rise?'. *Far Eastern Economic Review* , *Vol. 170, No. 5*, p. 72.

Richard, H. (1998). The Asian Financial Crisis: A Case Study in the Politics of Resentment. *New Political Economy* , *No. 3*, pp. 333-356.

S. a. (2005-2006). The Fourth ASEAN-China Business Council (ACBC) Meeting. In *Report of Activities for Malaysia-China Business Council.* Available at: www.asli.com.my/documents/mcbc2005-2.pdf (Accessed on 19 March, 2011).

S.a. (13 August, 2010). Agricultural Sector should not be Overlooked. *Taipei Times* .

S.a. (April 10, 2006). Japan, ASEAN Resumes FTA Talks, Aim for Deal by Next March. *East Economic News* .

Schwalbe, M. L., & Wolkomir, M. (2002). Interviewing Men. In J. F. Gubrium, & J. A. Holsteri (Eds.), *Handbook of Interview Research: Context and Method* (p. 312). Thousand Oaks: Sage Publications.

Schwarz, A., & Villinger, R. (2004). Integrating Southeast Asia's Economies. *The Mckinsey Quarterly* , *1*, p. 43.

Shambaugh, D. (2004/2005, Winter). China Engages Asia: Reshaping the Regional Order. *International Security* , *Vol. 29, No., 3*, p. 99.

Shaun, B. (2003). Reforming China's Embedded Socialist Compromise: China and the WTO. *Global Change, Peace and Security* , *Vol. 15, No. 3*, p. 229 .

Shen, M. (2010). Trans-Pacific Partnership: The United State's Response to East Asian Cooperation.

Sheng, L. (2003). China-ASEAN Free Trade Area: Origins, Development and Strategic Motives. *ISEA Working Papers, International Politics and Security Issues* , *Series No. 1*, p. 6.

Sheng, L. (2003). China-ASEAN Free Trade Area: Origins, Developments and Strategic Motivations. *ISEAS Working Paper, International Politics and Security Issues Series, No. 1*, p. 4 .

Shih, H.-c., & Chao, V. Y. (18 August, 2010). ECFA Recieves Legislative Approval. *Taipei Times* .

Shiraishi, T. (2006). The Third Wave: Southeast Asia and Middle- Class Formation in the Making of a Region. In P. J. Katzenstein, & T. Shitaishi (Eds.), *Beyond Japan: The Dynamics of East Asian Regionalism* (p. 241). London: Cornell University Press .

Spencer, L., Ritchie, J., & O'Connor, W. (2003). Analysis: Practices, Principles and Processes. In J. Ritchie, & J. Lewis (Eds.), *Qualitative Research Practice: A Guide for Social Science Students and Researchers* (p. 200). London: SAGE Publications.

Stephens, N. (2007). Collecting Data from Elites and Ultra Elites: Telephone and Face-to-Face Interviews with Macroeconomists. *Qualitative Research* , *Vol. 7, No. 2*, p. 207.

Stubbs, R. (2002). ASEAN Plus Three: Emerging East Asian Regionalism? *Asian Survey* , *Vol. 42, No. 3*, pp. 441, 449.

Susilo, B. Y. (Feb 24, 2011). Repositioning ASEAN in New World Order. *The Straits Times (Singapore)* .

Terada, T. (2003). Constructing an 'East Asian' Concept and Growing Regional Identity: from EAEC to ASEAN+3. *The Pacific Review* , *Vol. 16, No. 2*, p. 253.

The EGEC. (2001). *Forging Closer ASEAN-China Economic Relations in the Twenty-first Century.* A report submitted by the ASEAN-China Expert Group on Economic Cooperation, October 2001.

UNCTAD. (2002). *World Investment Report.*

Vatikiotis, M. R. (2003, April). Catching the Dragon's Tail: China and Southeast Asia in the 21st Century. *Contemporary Southeast Asia* , *Vol. 25, No. 1*, p. 68.

Väyrynen, R. (2003). Regionalism: Old and New. *International Studies Review* , *Vol. 5, No. 1*, p. 27.

Wanadi, J. (2004). China and Asia-Pacific Regionalism. In K. Ryosei, & J. Wang (Eds.), *The Rise and a Changing East Asian Order* (pp. 37-48). Tokyo: Japan Center for International Exchange.

Wong, J., & Chan, S. (2003). China's Outward Direct Investment: Expanding Worldwide. *China: An International Journal* , *Vol. 1, No. 2*, p. 278.

Wong, J., & Chan, S. (May/June 2003). China-ASEAN Free Trade Agreement-Shaping Future Economic Relations. *Asian Survey* , *Vol. XLIII, No. 3*, p. 507.

Wong, J., Zou, K., & Zeng, H. (2000). New Dimensions in China-ASEAN Relations. In J. Wong, K. Zou,

& H. Zeng (Eds.), *China- ASEAN Relation: Economic and Legal Dimensions* (p. 9). Singapore: World Scientific Publishing Company.

Wong, J., Zou, K., & Zeng, H. (2006). New Dimensions in China-ASEAN Relations. In J. Wong, K. Zou, & H. Zeng (Eds.), *China-ASEAN Relations* (p. 9). Singapore: World Scientific Publishing Company.

Wu, F. (1994, January 20). The 5th Column: China Capitalises on ASEAN. *Far Eastern Economic Review , Vol. 57, No. 3*, p. 17.

Wu, F., Siaw, P. T., Sia, Y. H., & Keong, P. K. (2002). Foreign Direct Investment to China and Southeast Asia: Has ASEAN Benn Losing Out? *Economic Survey of Singapore, Feature Article/ Foreign Direct Investments, Third Quarter* , p. 110.

Wu, J. (1 August, 2010). Wake up to the ECFA before It Is a Nightmare. *Taipei Times* .

Wu, J., & Wang, S. (13 August, 2010). Taiwan is Building a Bridge too far to China. *Taipei Times* .

Yang, T., & Chen, K. (11 August, 2010). Economist Plays Down Potential ECFA Benefits. *Taipei Times* .

Yu, H.-S. (2003). Explaining the Emergence of New East Asian Regionalism: Beyond Power and Interest- Based Approaches. *Asian Perspective , Vol. 27, No. 1*, p. 268 .

Chinese-language Bibliography

CABIS. (2009, April 23). *CABIS*. Retrieved March 19, 2011, from http://www.cabisummit.org/html/article/YJGcontent_176.html

CAExpo. (2006, August 17). Retrieved March 19, 2011, from CAExpo: http://eng.caexpo.org/ab_caexpo/t20060817_73326.html

Cai, P. (2004). Change of International Organization and China's Peaceful Emergence. *Word Economy Studies* , No. 10, pp. 33-38.

Cao, Y. (2007). Review of ASEAN. *Southeast Asian Studies* , No. 4, p. 15.

Chen, B. (2007). China's FDI from Southeast Asian countries: Status quo and Prospect. *Market Froum* , No. 1, p. 41.

Chen, H. (2008). Analysis of the Main Reasons for FDI's Diversion from China to ASEAN. *Review of Economic Research* , No. 24, p. 36.

Chen, H. (2006, January 19). China-ASEAN Free Trade Area: the Hurdles of Investment Negotiations. *EAI Background Brief* , No. 127, p. 6.

Chen, Q., & Lv, Z. (2009). The Current Situation and Prospect of Agricultural Cooperation between China and ASEAN. *Southeast Asian Studies* , No. 4, p. 46.

Chen, S., & Wang, B. (2001). Deng Xiaoping's 'The National Interest' in Chinese Diplomatic Relations with Neighbors. *Journal of China University of Mining and Technology* , No. 1, p. 20.

Chen, W. (2003). Analysis of the bilateral trade relations between China and ASEAN. *Contemporary Asia-Pacific Studies* , No.8, p. 43.

Chen, W. (2006). The Impact of China-ASEAN Free Trade Area n Taiwan Province's Economy. *Journal of International Trade* , No.8, p. 54.

Cheng, M. (2006). The Spill-over Effects and Implications of ASEAN Integration. *Inquiry into Economic Issues* , No. 65, p. 137.

Deng, X. (1993). *Selected Works of Deng Xiaoping (Volume Three)*. Beijing: People's Publishing House.

Fu, X. (2004). New Regionalism: A New Approach to the East Asian Development Model. *World Economics and Politics* , No. 3, p. 68.

Gao, H. (2010). China-ASEAN Free Trade Area is a Cooperative Platform to Fight Against the Financial Crisis. In S. Liu (Ed.), *China-ASEAN Free Trade Area Series (Interpretation of CAFTA Agreements)* (p. 21). Nanning: Guangxi Normal University Press.

Geng, X. (2003). *New Regionalism and the Change of Asia-Pacific Regional Structures*. Beijing: Beijing Univesity Press.

Geng, X. (2001). Study of the New Regionalism-Analysis from a Different Angle. *World Economics and Politics* , No. 1, p.22.

Geng, Y. (2009). The Performance and Competitiveness of ASEAN Agricultural Products in Chinese Market. *Journal of International Trade* , No. 5, p. 59.

Guo, H. (2006). Direct Investment between China and ASEAN: Trend and Development. *Around*

197

Southeast Asia , *No. 8*, p. 20.

Guo, H. (2007). Economic Security, Domestic Politics and ASEAN Regional Economic Cooperation. *World Economy and Politics* , *No. 6*, p. 62.

Guo, X., & Wu, G. (2007). Analysis on Drive Mechanism of China-ASEAN Free Trade Area. *World Economy Study* , *No. 1, Vol. 155*, pp. 68-73.

Hu, A., & Men, H. (2005). The Significance to Study China's Strategy on the East Asia 【n】 Integration. *International Review* , *No. 3*, p. 26.

Hu, J. (2007). *Hold High the Great Banner of Socialism with Chinese Characteristics and Strive for New Victories in Building a Moderately Prosperous Societ.* Report at the Seventeenth CPC National Congress on 15 October, 2007.

Hu, J. (2007). *Hold High the Great Banner of Socialism with Chinese Characteristics and Strive for New Victories in Building a Moderately Prosperous Society in All Respects.* Report to the Seventeenth National Congress of the Communist Party of China on 15 October, 2007.Available at: http://cpc.people.com.cn/GB/104019/104099/6429414.html (Accessed on 25 May, 2010).

Hu, J. (2009). *Join Hands to Promote Peaceful Development of Cross-strait Relations; Strive with Unity of Purpose for the Great Rejuvenation of the Chinese Nation.* Beijing: People's Publishing House.

Hu, S. (2001). ASEAN: Present and Prospect. *China International Studies* , *No. 1*, p. 51.

Hu, Z., & Wang, W. (2002). East Asia Cultural Ring: Transmission, Fragmentation and Reconstruction -- Comments on the International Symposium on 'Relations between East Asia Han Cultural Ring and China. *International Review* , *No. 2*, p. 74 .

Huang, C. (2009). China and ASEAN: The Trend and Strategy of Investment Liberalization. *Guangxi Economy* , *No. 10*, p. 21.

Jia, D. (2002). How Does China's Agriculture Face Clashes and Challenges after China's Entry into WTO? *Science and Technology Review* , *No. 10*, pp. 3-4.

Jia, J., & Li, X. (1997). Complementarity and Competitiveness on Trade between China and ASEAN. *World Economics Papers* , *No. 5*, pp. 21-26.

Jiang, Y. (2010). China's Pursuit of Free Trade Agreement: Is China Exceptional? *Review of International Political Economy* , *Vol. 17, No. 2*, p. 251.

Jiang, Z. (2002). *Build a Well-fare Society in an All-Round Way and Create a New Situation in Building Socialism with Chinese Characteristics.* Report Delivered at the Sixteenth National Congress of the Communist Party of China on 8 November, 2002.

Jiang, Z. (1997). *Hold High the Great Banner of Deng Xiaoping Theory for an All-round Advancement of the Cause of Building Socialism With Chinese Characteristics Into the 21st Century.* Report Delivered at the Fifteenth National Congress of the Communist Party of China on 12 September, 1997.

Jiang, Z. (1997). *To Forge A Good-neighbourly Partnership of Mutual Trust toward 21st Century.* Speech at the China-ASEAN Leaders Informal Summit on 16 December, 1997, available at: http://my.china-embassy.org/chn/zt/dyhzzywj/dmxlfh1997/t299298.htm (Accessed on 8 August 2009).

Li, C. (1999). On Economic Regionalization. *Pacific Journal* , *No. 2*, p. 11.

Li, H., & Kang, P. (2002). The Greater West Development and the China-ASEAN Free Trade Area.

Western Forum, No. 7, p. 24.

Li, J., & Huang, J. (2005). Analyzing the Complementarity on Trade Structure between China and ASEAN. *Special Zone Economy*, No. 7, p. 11.

Li, L. (1999). Discussion on the Market Fostering and Prospect in the trans-national area in Southwest China and the neighboring counties. *Guangxi Market and Price*, No. 9, p. 6.

Li, X., & Wang, X. (2005). ASEAN's Role and Influence in Asia-Pacific Region. *International Politics*, No. 11, p. 112.

Liao, X., & Xia, L. (2008). Survey Report on Agricultural Imports from ASEAN. *The New Orient*, Vol. 155, No. 11, p. 5.

Lin, T., & Lin, C. (2004). Changing Trend of Economic and Trade Relations between Taiwan and ASEAN. *Taiwan Research Quarterly*, Vol. 85, No. 3, p. 40.

Liu (Ed.), *China-ASEAN Free Trade Area Series (Interpretation of CAFTA Agreements)* (p. 15). Nanning: Guangxi Normal University Press.

Liu, J. (2006). Peaceful Rise is China's Strategic Choice. *World Economics and Politics*, No. 2, pp. 36-40.

Liu, S. (2008). The Role and Impact of Building the CAFTA-An Analysis Based on International Political Economics Theory. *International Survey*, No. 1, pp. 65-69.

Liu, X. (2004). Regional Identity and Regionalism in East Asia. *Contemporary International Relations*, No. 5, p. 18.

Liu, Y. (2007). Economic and Trade Coperation between China and ASEAN: Status Quo and Prospect. *Forum of World Economy and Politics*, No. 6, p. 59.

Liu, Z., Huang, S., & Wang, L. (2006). A Research Summary on the Trade Structure of Export in Agricuture Products from China to ASEAN. *Around Southeast Asia*, No. 4, pp. 35-38.

Long, Y. (26 April, 2002). The Establishment of China-ASEAN Free Trade Area is of Great Significance. *People's Daily*.

Lu, B. (2009). The Southeast Asian Factors for China's Rising. *New Economy*, No. 6, p. 58.

Lu, G. (2005). To Question the New Regionalism. *International Politics*, No. 12, p. 25.

Luo, J. (2001). East Asia: Facing the New Century Together- Interview with Mr. Wang Yi, the Assistant Foreign Minister on issues of East Asian regional cooperation. *World Affairs*, No. 1, p. 24.

Ma, X., & Sun, X. (20002, August). Thoughts on Present Agricultural Development in the Western Part of China after Joining the WTO. *Journal of Tianshui Normal University*, Vol. 22, No. 4, p. 50.

Mang, L. (June 2003). Set-up of Sino-ASEAN Free Trade Zone [China-ASEAN Free Trade Area] and the Great Development of West China. *Journal of Guangxi Commercial College*, No. 2, Vol. 20, p. 7.

Men, H. (2003). China's Development of National Strategic Interest. *Strategy and Management*, No. 2, p. 83.

Men, H. (2003). Mutual enlightening and incorporations among theoretical paradigms of international relations. *World Economics and Politics*, Vol. 5, p. 43.

Men, H. (2003). Mutual enlightening and incorporations among theoretical paradigms of international relations. *World Economics and Politics*, Vol. 5, p. 43.

Niu, H. (2005). Regionalism in East Asia: A Constructivist Explanation. *Contemporary International Relations*, *No. 12*, p. 1.

Pang, Z. (2001). ASEAN and East Asia: Subtle East Asian Regionalism. *Pacific Journal*, *No. 2*, p. 29.

Pang, Z. (2001). China's Asia Strategy: Flexible Multilateralism. *World Economics and Politics*, *No. 10*, p. 32.

Pang, Z. (2004). To Ascertain Peaceful Nature of China's Rise-On the Theoretical Issues Concerning 'Peaceful Rise'. *International Review*, *No. 3*, pp. 1-8.

Peng, S. (2006). The Internal Restricting Factor for Economic Integration in East Asia. *International Forum*, *Vol.8, No. 4*, p. 47.

Qin, D. (February-March 2007). Full Record for China-ASEAN Bilateral Cooperation: On Investment. *South China Review*, p. 6.

Qin, S., & Chen, W. (2006). On the Recent Cooperation and Development in ASEAN. *International Politics*, *No. 12*, p. 122.

Qin, Y., & Wang, Y. (2004). Building the Community the East Asian Way. *Journal of China Foreign Affairs University*, *No. 12*, p. 8.

Qiu, D. (2005). China-ASEAN FTA: Pondering over China's peaceful Rising from a Geo-economic Perspective. *Contemporary Asia-Pacific*, *No. 1*, p. 10.

Qiu, D. (2004). The Formation and Significance of China-ASEAN Free Trade Area. *China International Studies*, *No. 2*, p. 19.

Qiu, H., Yang, J., & Huang, J. (2007). The Impact of the China-ASEAN Free Trade Area on China's Agricultural International Trade and its Regional Development in Agricuture. *Management World*, *No. 9*, p. 57.

Ren, D. (2005). Nationalism and Regionalism: The Dilemma in the Concept Building of Northeast Asian Security in the post Cold War Time. *International Politics*, *No. 12*, p. 124.

Rong, J., & Yang, C. (2006). An Empirical Analysis of Agricultural Products: Competitiveness and Complementarity between China and ASEAN Countries. *Journal of International Trade*, *No. 8*, pp. 45-49.

S.a. (14 October, 2010). Exploring the Establishment of Military Mutual Trust Mechanism is Conducive to Stability across the Taiwan Strait. *People's Daily Oversea Edition*.

Sati. (2006). *Speech at the third China-ASEAN Business and Investment Summit, Nanning, Guangxi on 31 October, 2006*.

Shi, J. (August 2006). Analysis of the Position Choice of FDI in Our Country. *Journal of Jinzhong University*, *Vol. 23, No. 4*, p. 33.

Shi, Z. (2003). Export Similarity and Trade Competition: A Comparative Study on China and ASEAN Countries. *Finance and Trade Economics*, *No. 9*, p. 53.

Soe, W. (2006, October 31). Speech at the third China-ASEAN Business and Investment Summit, Nanning, Guangxi on 31 October, 2006.

Song, D., & Li, G. (2002). Economic Coopeartion in East Asia Regional Enhanced to Promote Economic Development in China. *International Economic Cooperation*, *No. 5*, p. 31.

Song, J. (2005). On Competition and Complementarity on Trade between China and ASEAN. *Journal of Innet Mongolia Finance and Economics College* , *No. 3*, pp. 87-91.

Song, Y., & Yao, J. (2005). A Review on Rise of the Burgeoning Big Powers and the Existing Big Powers' Strategies. *Studies of International Politics* , *No. 2*, pp. 3-7.

Su, C. (2006). Zhoubian Institutions and Zhoubianism: China's Approach to Governance in East Asia. *World Economics and Politics* , *No. 1*, p. 10.

Tang, S. (2008). Strategic Selection in Agricultural Cooperation between China and ASEAN. *World Agriculture* , *Vol. 356, No. 12*, p. 5.

Tang, Y. (2002). China's Status and Prospect in Asian Complementary Investment. *Collected Essays on Finance and Economics* , *Vol. 99, No. 6*, p. 54.

The Ministry of Commerce of People's Republic of China, National Bureau of Statistics of PRC, and State Administration of Foreign Exchange. (2003). *2003 Statistical Bulletin of China's Outward Foreign Direct Investment*. Beijing: China Statistical Publishing House.

The Ministry of Finance, State Administration of Taxation, and General Administration of Customs of PRC. (2001). *The Preferential Tax Policies on the Western Development Issues*. Beijing.

The State Council of PRC. (2000). *The State Council on the Implementation of a number of Western Development Policies and Measures Notice (Guo Fa [2000] 33)*. Beijing.

Wang, C. (2009). The Complementary Analysis of China-ASEAN Agricultural Products Trade. *Future and Development*, , *No. 4, Vol. 30*, p. 36.

Wang, H., & Liu, L. (2003, September). From Invisible to Visible: A Discussion of the Change of the Motives Force of China's Regional Economic Cooperation. *Northeast Asia Forum* , *No. 5*, p. 10.

Wang, J. (2004). On Mutual Economic Complementarity between China and ASEAN. *Journal of Guangxi University (Philosophy and Social Science)* , *No.1, Vol. 26*, p. 63.

Wang, J. (2005). The Legal and Policy Considerations of China-ASEAN FTA: The Impact on the Multilateral Trading Systems. In H. K. Leong, & S. C. Ku (Eds.), *China and Southeast Asia: Global Changes and Regional Challenges* (p. 43). Singapore: Seng Lee Press Pte Ltd.

Wang, J., & Zeng, P. (2008). On Mutual Complementarity of Trade between China and ASEAN. *Economic Perspective* , *No. 9*, p. 23.

Wang, Q. (2005). Asian Regional Economic Integration and China. *International Studies* , *No. 4*, p. 56.

Wang, Q. (2006). Development of ASEAN Regional Integration and Bilateral Relations of its Members. *Contemporary Asia-Pacific* , *No. 6*, p. 13.

Wang, Q. (2004). Economic Complementarity and Competition between China and ASEAN and its Evolving Tendency. *Southeast Asian Studies* , *No. 2*, p. 10.

Wang, T. (2003). New Regionalism in East Asia. *Contemporary Asia-Pacific* , *No. 1*, p. 52.

Wang, Y. (2003). New Development of China-ASEAN Free Trade Area Building. *Contemporary Asia-Pacific Studies* , *No. 1*, p. 59.

Wei, B. (2007). Identity Delemma of China in Transition. *Contemporary International Relations* , *No. 7*, p. 37.

Wei, H. (2005). China-ASEAN Cooperation and East Asian Integration. *Contemporary International Relations*, *No. 9*, p. 21.

Wei, M. (2002). The Conceptualization of China-ASEAN Free Trade Area and Its Prospect. *International Studies*, *Vo. 4*, pp. 53-54.

Wen, J. (2007). *Build a Peaceful, Prosperous and Harmonious East Asia*. Speech at the 10th ASEAN+3 Summit in 2007.

Wen, J. (2003). *China's Development and Asia's Rejuvenation*. Speech delivered at the ASEAN Business and Investment Summit on 7 October 2003, available at: http://www.fmprc.gov.cn/eng/topics/zgcydyhz/dqc/t27711.htm (Accessed on 21 October 2010).

Wen, J. (2003). *Compose A New Chapter of East Asian Cooperation*. Speech at the 7th ASEAN+3 Summit in 2003.

Wen, J. (2005). *Consolidate and Deepen Cooperation for a Better Future*. Speech at the 9th ASEAN+3 Summit in 2005.

Wen, J. (2003). *Promoting Peace and Prosperity By Deepening Cooperation in All-round Way*. Speech at the 7th China-ASEAN Leaders Summit on 8 October, 2003, available at: http://my.china-embassy.org/chn/zt/dyhzzywj/dmxlfh2003/t300017.htm (Accessed on 8 August 2009).

Wen, J. (2010). *speech at the 13th China-ASEAN Leaders Summit on 29 October, 2010*. Available at: http://www.gov.cn/ldhd/2010-10/30/content_1733739.htm (Accessed on 12 January, 2011).

Wen, J. (2004). *Speech at the 8th China-ASEAN Leaders Summit on 29 November, 2004*. available at: http://my.china-embassy.org/chn/zt/dyhzzywj/dmxlfh2004/t300063.htm (Accessed on 8 August 2009).

Wen, J. (2005). *Speech at the Nineth China-ASEAN Leaders Summit on 12 December, 2005*. Available at: http://my.china-embassy.org/chn/zt/dyhzzywj/dmxlfh2005/t300077.htm (Accessed on 8 August 2009).

Wen, J. (2010). Speech at the thirteenth ASEAN +3 Summit, Hanoi, Vietnam, 29 October, 2010.

Wen, J. (2004). *Strengthen Cooperation, Mutually Beneficial and Win-win*. Speech at the 8th ASEAN+3 Summit in 2004.

WenJiabao,. (2003). China's Development and Asia's Rejuvenation. Speech delivered at the China-ASEAN Business & Investment Summit, 7 October, 2003. Available online at: http://www.fmprc.gov.cn/eng/topics/zgcydyhz/dqc/t27711.htm (Accessed on 13 April, 2009).

Writing Group of Guangxi Academy of Social Science. (2006). The Retrospect of China-ASEAN Dialogue Relationship within Fifteen Years. *Around Southeast Asia*, *No. 6*, p. 1.

Wu, C. (2006). Analysis of China's investments in ASEAN Countries. *Southeast Asian Affairs*, *Vol. 125, No. 1*, p. 41.

Wu, Z., & Li, M. (2003). The Characteristics and Cause of Asian Regionalism. *International Forum*, *No. 6*, p. 14.

Xia, L. (2005). New East Asian Regionalism: Development and Influence. *Contemporary Asia-Pacific Studie*, *No. 6*, p. 22.

Xiao, H., & Hu, T. (2006). The Factors and Prospects of the Agricultural Products Trade between China and ASEAN. *The World of Survey and Research*, *No. 7*, p. 20.

Xiao, X., Hu, Q., & Chen, X. (31 December, 2009). 90% of Chinese Enterprises do know the timetable for

China and ASEAN to Open Markets for Each Other. *Guangzhou Daily* .

Xing, Y., & Wan, G. (2006). Exchanges Rates and Competition for FDI in Asia. *The World Economy* , *Vol. 29, Issue. 4*, pp. 420-421.

Xing, Y., & Zhan, Y. (2006). New Status, Interest and Vision: A Constructivist Analysis on China's Current Diplomacy. *Contemporary International Relations* , *No. 11*, p. 18.

Xu, S. (2007). The Development of China-ASEAN Relations in the Past 40 Years and Its Inspiration: from a Perspectivre of 'Common Interests'. *Southeast Asian Studies* , *No. 3*, p. 56.

Xue, F. (March 2007). On Mutual Trade Complementarity between China and ASEAN. *Market Modernization* , *No.3, Vol. 498*, p. 29.

Yan, X. (2004). Peaceful Rise and Peace Building. *International Studies* , *No. 3*, pp. 12-16.

Yao, M. (2003). Discussion of Government Supportive Policy on Agriculture after China's Accession to the WTO. *Future and Development* , *Vol. 24, No. 3*, p. 14.

Ye, Y. (2007). Analysis on Monetary Cooperation in East Asia and the Role of China. *Southeast Asian Studies* , *No. 4*, p. 65.

Yin, X. (2004). The Impact of the China-ASEAN Free Trade Agreement on Regional Trade. *The Journal of East Asian Affairs* , *Vol. 18, No. 2*, p. 322.

Yu, L., & Wang, J. (2004). Regional Cooperation and Investment: Studies on the Developing Mode of China's Free Trade Area. *Review of Economic Research* , *No. 49*, p. 12.

Zeng, T. (1996). Comprehensive Analysis on the Status and Trend of the Taiwan-ASAN Relations. *Southeast Asian Studies* , *No.2*, p. 39.

Zhang, B. (2004). The Economics Relations between China and East Asia and its Prospect. *Studies of International Politics* , *Vo.4*, p. 55.

Zhang, H. (July 2009). Complementarity and Competition on Sino-ASEAN Economic and Trade Relationship. *Social Scientist* , *No.7, Vol. 147*, pp. 116-118,125.

Zhang, J. (2006). China's Motives for Enhancing East Asian Cooperation in Post- Cold War Period. *Contemporary Asia- Pacific Studies* , *No. 4*, p. 17.

Zhang, X. (2003). Current Situation and Prospects of ASEAN Countries' Direct Investment in China. *International Economic Cooperation* , *No. 12*, p. 38.

Zhang, Y. (2004). A Probe into East Asian Regionalism. *Contemporary Asia-Pacific* , *No. 12*, p. 3.

Zhang, Y. (2009). *China and Asian Regionalism.* Singapore: World Scientific Publishing.

Zhang, Y. (2006). China's Economic Integration with East Asia. *Contemporary Asia-Pacific* , *No.1*, p. 6.

Zhang, Y. (2005). How to Understand the Development of East Asian Regional Cooperation? *Contemporary Asia-Pacific* , *No. 8*, p. 3.

Zhang, Y. (2001). On the Evolving Prospect of East Asian Cooperation. *International Economic Review* , *No. 3-4*, p. 24.

Zhang, Y., & Xu, P. (November 2003). An Empirical Research on Trade Competitive Power and Trade Comparability between China and ASEAN. *The Theory and Practice of Finance and Economics* , *Vol. 24, No. 126*, p. 85.

Zhang, Y., & Zhang, J. (2008). Nature of Monetary and Options for RMB in Future. *Journal of Contemporary Asia-Pacific Studies (Bimonthly)* , No. 2, p. 43.

Zhang, Z. (2002). The Significance and Prospect: Building China-ASEAN Free Trade Area. *Forum for World Economics and Politics* , No. 1, p. 23.

Zhao, R. (2002). Establishment of China-ASEAN Free Trade Area: Constrains and Prospects. *World Economics and Politics Forum* , No. 3, p. 28.

Zhao, R. (2002). Establishment of China-ASEAN Free Trade Area: Constraints and Prospects. *Forum of International Economics and Politics* , Vol. 3, pp. 28-30.

Zhao, S. (24 January, 2011). The Utilization Rate of the CAFTA was only 10%. How to Address it? *People's Daily Overseas Edition* .

Zhao, Z. (1987). *Along the Path of Socialism with Chinese Characteristics*. Beijing: People's Publishing House.

Zhou, X. (2007). China-ASEAN Agricultural Cooperation Progress and Impact Analysis. *Agricultural Economy* , No. 1, p. 28.

Zhou, Y. (July 2003). Industrial Relationship between China and ASEAN: Competitive or complementary? *Business Economics and Administration* , No. 7, Vol. 141, pp. 56-59.

Zhu, N. (2004). Economic Regionalism in East Asia: Lack and Reconstruction of the Axis. *Contemporary Asia-Pacific* , Vol. 11, p. 35.

Zhu, R. (2001). *Join Hands in Creating a New Situation of China-ASEAN Cooperation*. available at: http://www.mfa.gov.cn/chn/pds/wjb/zzjg/yzs/dqzz/dnygjlm/zyjh/t25643.htm (Accessed on 24 June, 2009).

Zhu, R. (2000). *speech at the 4th China-ASEAN Leaders Summit on 25 November, 2000*. available at: http://my.china-embassy.org/chn/zt/dyhzzywj/dmxlfh2000/t299347.htm (Accessed on 8 August 2009).

Zhu, R. (1999). *Speech at the China-ASEAN Leaders Informal Summit on 28 November, 1999*. Available at: http://my.china-embassy.org/chn/zt/dyhzzywj/dmxlfh1999/t299339.htm (Accessed on 8 August 2009).

Zhu, R. (2000). *Speech delivered at the 4th ASEAN-China Leaders Summit in Singapore*. available at: http://www.mfa.gov.cn/chn/pds/wjb/zzjg/yzs/dqzz/dnygjlm/zyjh/t25644.htm (Accessed on 24 June, 2009).

Zhu, Y. (2005). China's Regional Advantage and Regional Impact of Attracting FDI Flows. *Journal of Liaoning Economic Vocational Technical College* , No. 1, p. 7.

Interviewee List

1. Anonymous1, an official of Institute of the American Studies, CICIR, Beijing, on 12 July, 2010
2. Anonymous2, a senior official of Institute of South and East Asian Studies, CICIR, Beijing, on 10 July, 2010
3. Anonymous3, an associate professor of Institute of South and East Asian Studies, CICIR, Beijing, on 6 July, 2010
4. Anonymous4, a junior official of Institute of South and East Asian Studies, CICIR, Beijing, on 7 July, 2010
5. Anonymous5, an official of Institute of the American Studies, CICIR, Beijing, on 15 July, 2010
6. Deng Shijun, the director of the International Conference, CABIS, Nanning, 19 August, 2010
7. Gao Ge, professor of the Business School, University of Guangxi, Nanning, 23 August, 2010
8. Gong Qijun, the vice director of the Bureau of CAExpo, Nanning, 20 August, 2010
9. Gu Xiaosong, the vice director of Guangxi Academy of Social Science, Nanning, 16 August, 2010
10. Lu Minghua, professor of international relations theory in the School of International Studies, Nanjing University, Nanjing, 12 August 2011
11. Huang Fei, the general secretary of the CACAC, Nanning, 20 August, 2010
12. Ma Jixian, the former official of the MOC, China, Nanning, 19 August, 2010
13. Qi Wei, an official of MFA, China, Beijing, 24 July, 2010
14. Qin Yaqing, the special assistant of Qian Qianchen (the former Premier and Chinese member of the EPG), Nanjing, 23 April, 2010
15. Shu Yang, the president of NCCE, Nanning, 17 August, 2010
16. Sun Jianqiu, the deputy director of Guangxi Provincial Department of Commerce, Nanning, 18 August, 2010
17. Zhang Yunling, the director of the EGEC, Beijing, 9 July, 2010
18. Zheng Junjian, the director of the Bureau of CAExpo, Nanning, 20 August, 2010
19. Zheng Xianwu, the director of CASAS, Nanjing, 18 June, 2010

This book is the result of a co-publication agreement between Social Sciences
Academic Press (China) and Paths International Ltd.

East Asian Economic Integration: A China-ASEAN Perspective
Author: Wang Liqin
ISBN: 978-1-84464-362-2

Paths International Ltd
www.pathsinternational.com

Published in United Kingdom

CPSIA information can be obtained at www.ICGtesting.com
Printed in the USA
BVOW09*1053010516

446304BV00005B/12/P